Algrove Publishing Limited
1090 Morrison Drive
Ottawa, Ontario
Canada K2H 1C2

Canadian Cataloguing in Publication Data

Main entry under title:

   The international cyclopedia of monograms : alphabets, initials, cyphers, types, crests, coats-of-arms, emblems, badges, shields, decorations

(Classic reprint series)
Reprint of the ed. published: Chicago : G.P. Engelhard, 1910.
ISBN 0-921335-86-5

   1. Monograms. 2. Heraldry. 3. Decoration and ornament. I. Series: Classic reprint series (Ottawa, Ont.)

CR13.I58 1999   745.6   C99-900865-X

Printed in Canada
#10999

Publisher's Note

*T*here was a certain fascination with monograms in the late Victorian era. It was as if all those without a title or coat of arms had decided that they should at least have an elaborate monogram. Designing monograms became a popular activity. In the equivalent of the "letters" columns of woodworking journals of the day, it was common to see requests for monogram designs and the requested monogram appear in a later issue. It was probably from such sources that this book of monograms was compiled. Typical of the day, the publishers decided that it was also worthwhile to include a potpourri of other information, much of it without introduction or explanation. But then, possibly you know what an ullum and goog are (see page 332).

Leonard G. Lee, Publisher
Ottawa
September, 1999

THE INTERNATIONAL

CYCLOPEDIA OF MONOGRAMS

ALPHABETS, INITIALS, CYPHERS, TYPES, CRESTS, COATS-OF-ARMS, EMBLEMS, BADGES, SHIELDS, DECORATIONS.

A COLLECTION FROM THE WORLD'S MASTERPIECES FOR THE USE OF ENGRAVERS, STATIONERS, JEWELERS, DRUGGISTS, DESIGNERS, ARTISTS AND ALL OTHERS ENGAGED IN OR RELATED TO THE GRAPHIC ARTS.

CHICAGO:
G. P. ENGELHARD & COMPANY
1910

INTRODUCTORY

It is believed that this volume comprises altogether the most extensive collection of Types, Monograms, Coats-of-Arms, Crests and other designs ever issued for the use of silversmiths, jewelers, engravers, stationers, printers, druggists and others engaged in or related to the graphic arts.

The modern development of the type industry furnishes an opportunity for fine letter-press printing comparing favorably for many uses with the more expensive engraved work. Not that it will ever displace the latter where elegance and refinement in highest degree is desired and where the item of cost is wholly subordinate, but for all semi-formal social functions, for popular announcements and for fine circular and card work the modern type faces answer most purposes admirably.

The Monogram Section embraces the masterpieces of many of the noted artists of the world. The reproductions are from the following works to which we acknowledge our indebtedness:

"Dictionaire du Chiffre—Monogramme et des Couronnes Nobiliaires Universelles," by C. Demengeot.

"Chiffres & Monogrammes, et Suite de Compositiones Decoratives," by Gustave Boussenot.

"Gewerbe Monogramm," by Martin Gerlach.

"Chiffres et Monogrammes," by H. Renoir.

"Monograms," by J. Gordon Smith.

"Ornamental Alphabets, Ancient and Mediæval," by F. Delamotte.

"Zir Schripten," by Karl Klimsch.

"Monograms and Cyphers," by A. A. Turbayne and other members of the Carlton Studio.

The publishers would have preferred to present the Monograms in groups according to their authorship in order that credit in every instance might be given, but this method would have seriously impaired the value of the volume as a work of reference in that it would impose the necessity of consulting every group in order to find all the various forms of any single monogram.

The present arrangement will be found to be strictly alphabetical so far as conditions would permit. To find the forms of any desired monogram, as, for instance, BN, it is only necessary to turn the pages to the letter B and follow them alphabetically to N. The same is true if the design be for three or more letters or any desired name.

An innovation to be found, we believe, in no other similar work, has been to number the figures serially on each page in order to facilitate their ready designation in orders or correspondence.

For the part devoted to Crests and Coats-of-Arms we are largely indebted to the "Encyclopedia Heraldica," by William Berry, for many years registering clerk to the College of Arms, London. This magnificent old work, now become exceedingly rare, merits recognition as a classic in its field and we deem its restoration for use in popular form a public service.

Believing that the volume in its comprehensiveness and adaptability for ready reference is incomparably more valuable than any other accessible to American artists and artisans it is confidently tendered them in the hope that its mission will have full justification in the satisfaction of its users and the promotion of the best in its field of art.   THE PUBLISHERS.

Index to Contents

PART I.

Illustrating and Engraving

=Initials=

Alphabets, Old and Modern, German, Greek, Hebrew Letters

KING EDWARD CYPHER

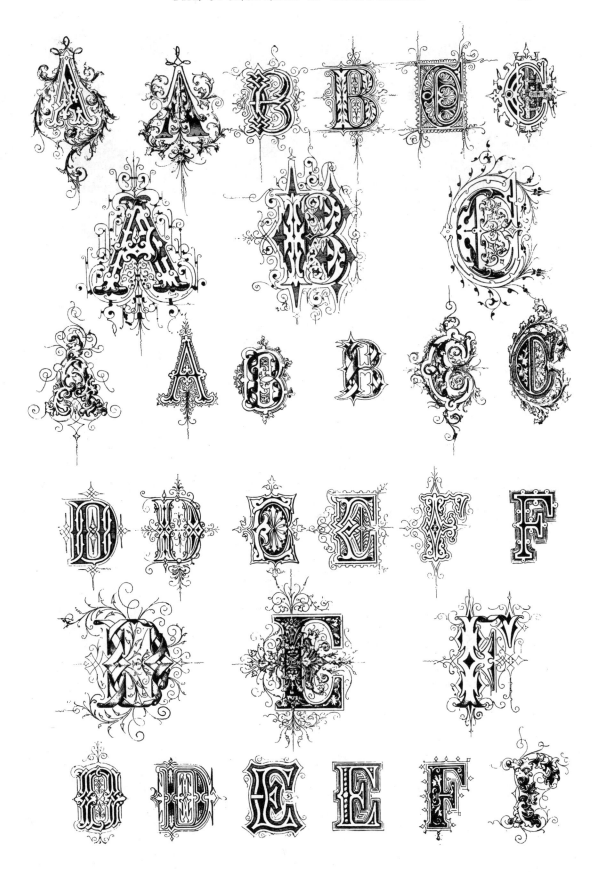

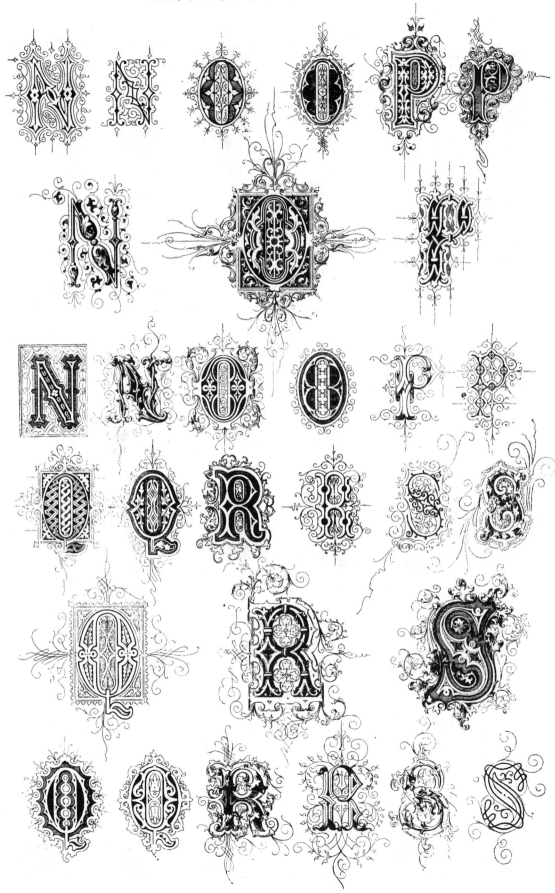

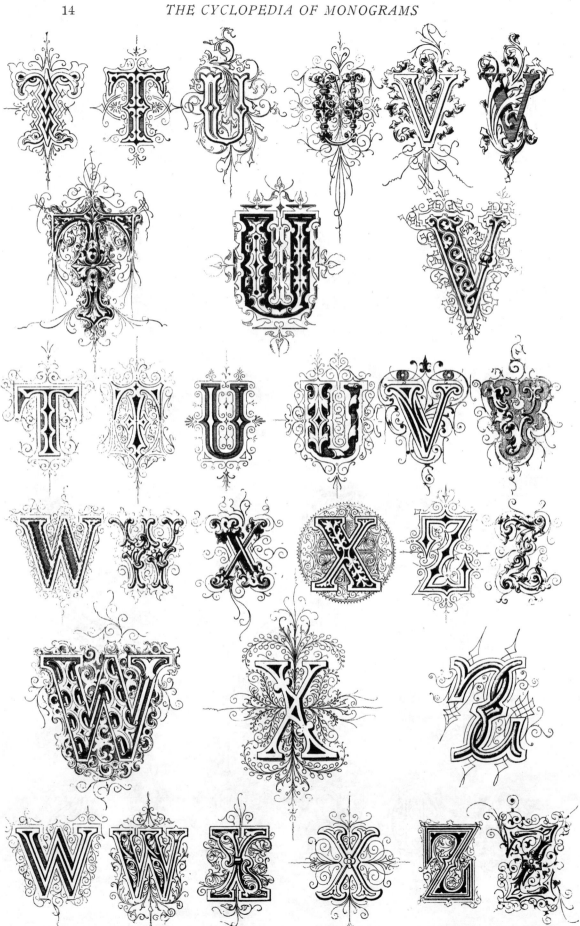

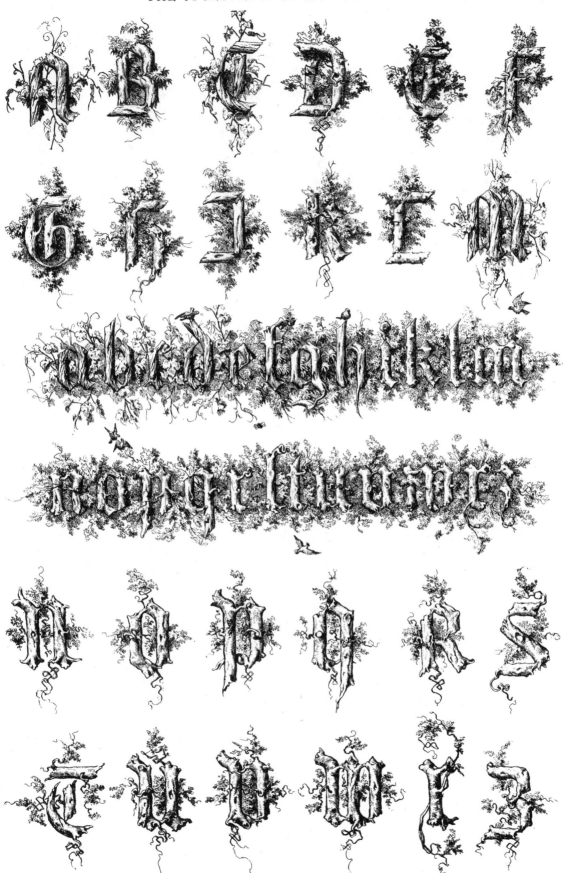

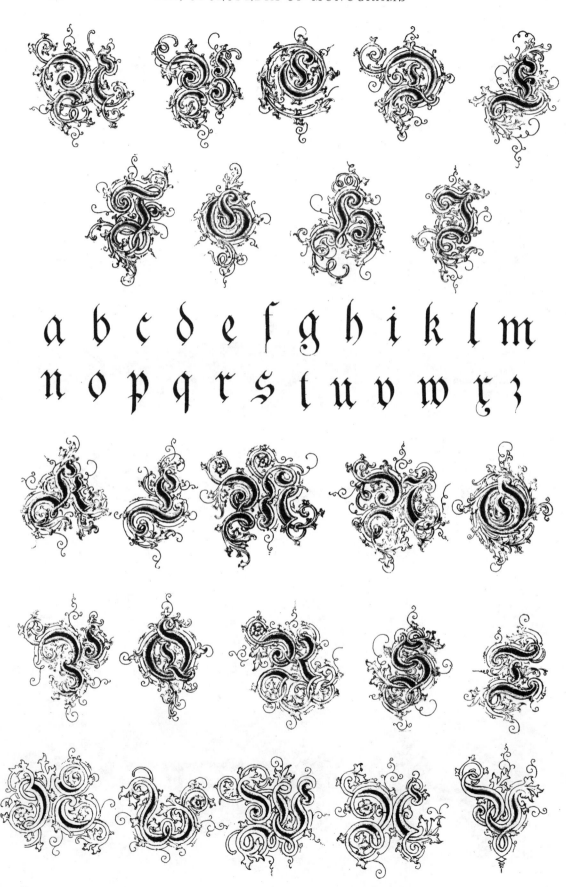

a b c d e f g h i k l m
n o p q r s t u v w x z

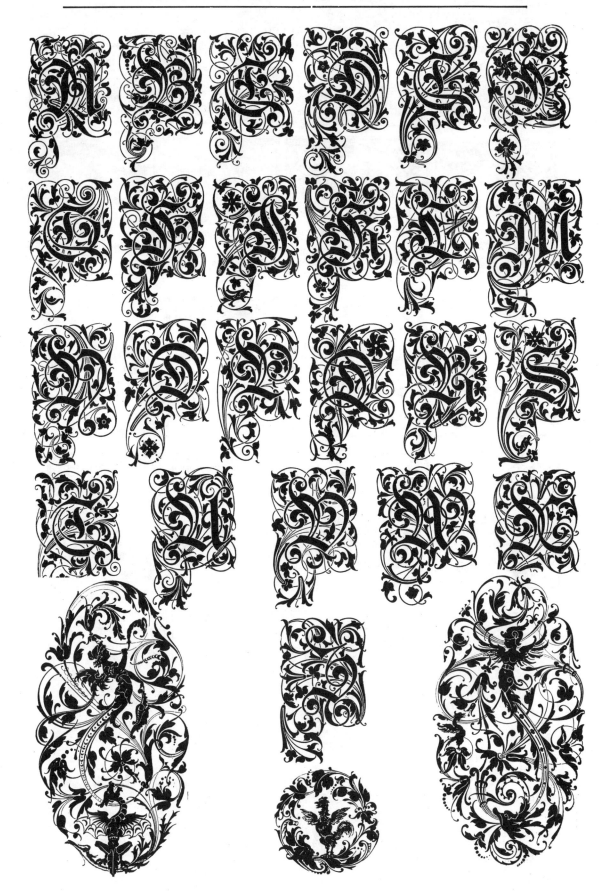

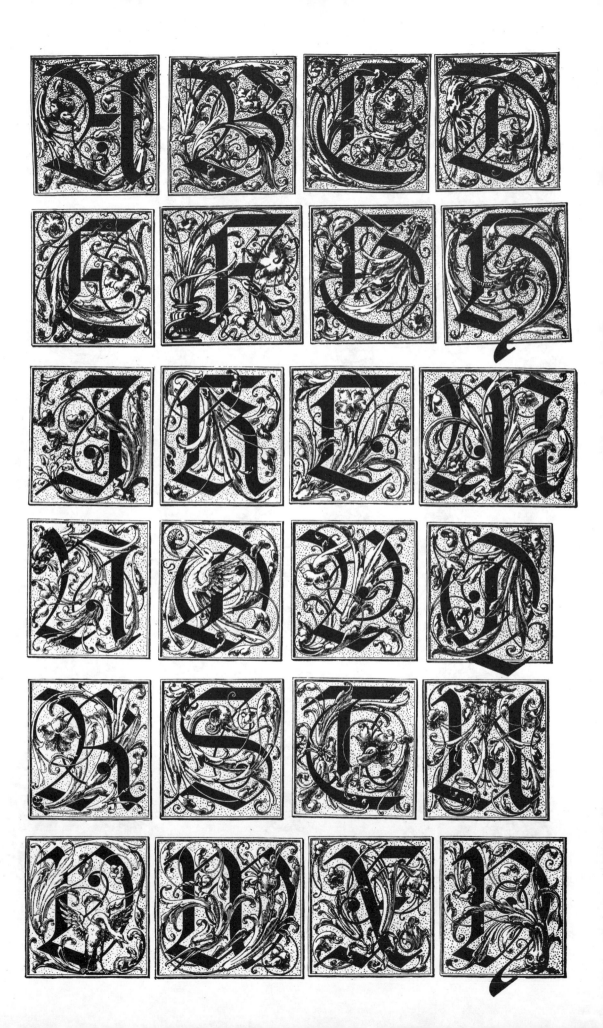

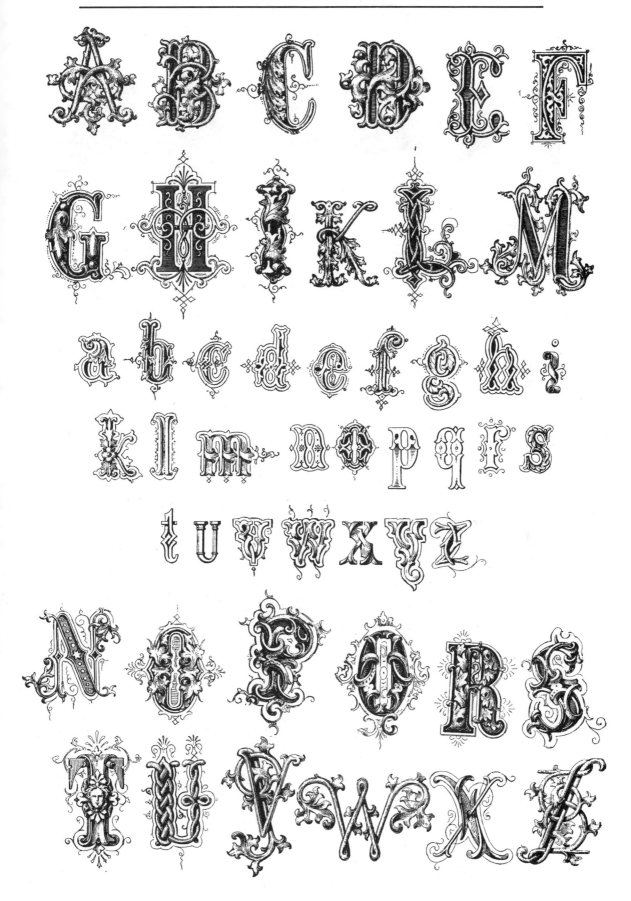

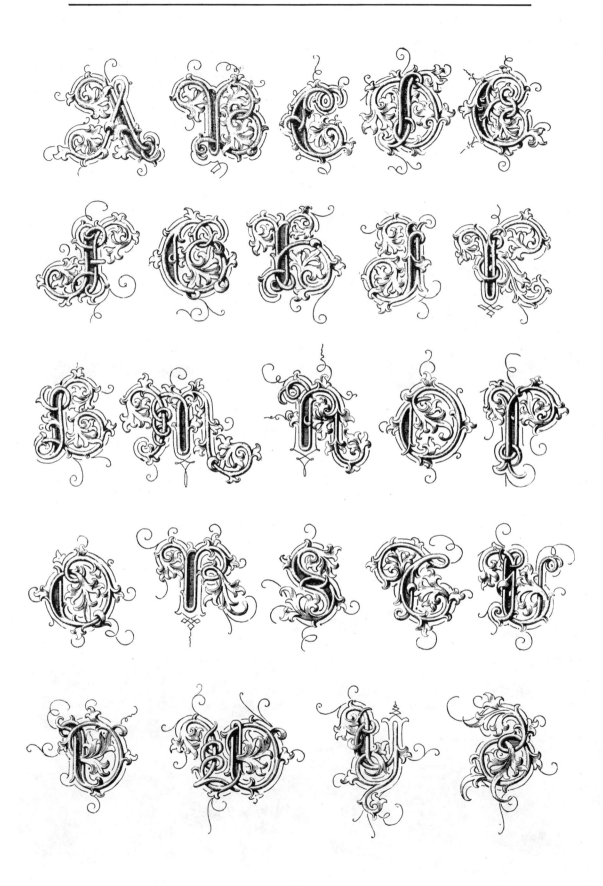

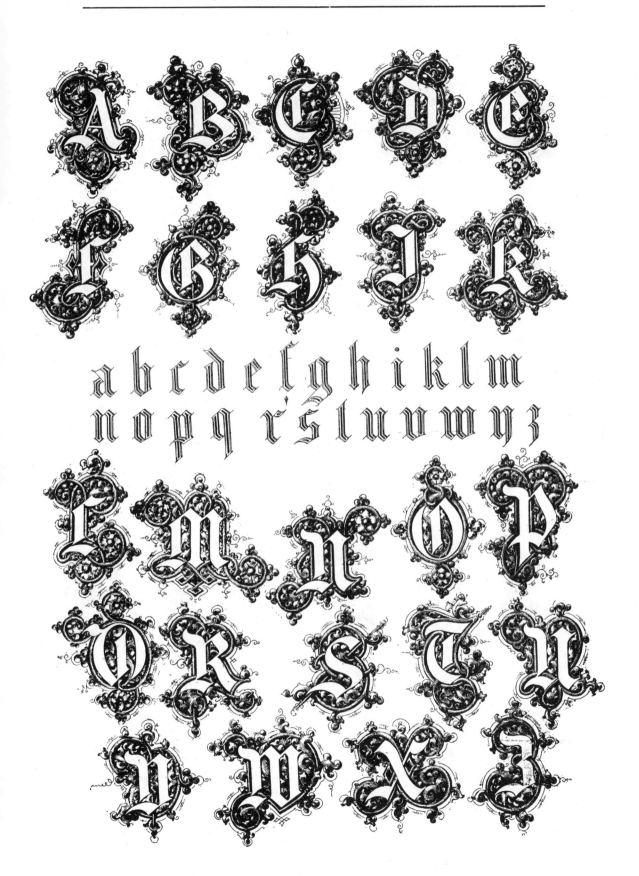

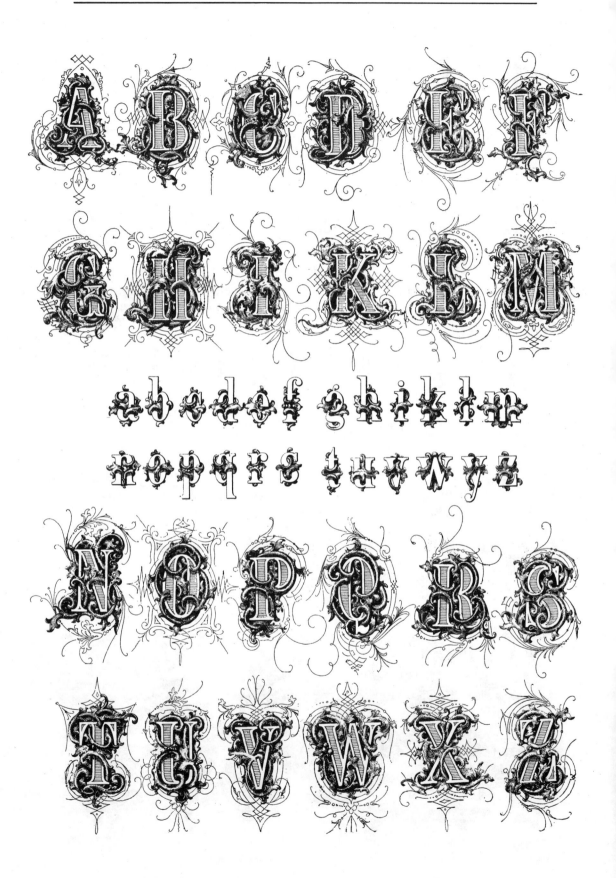

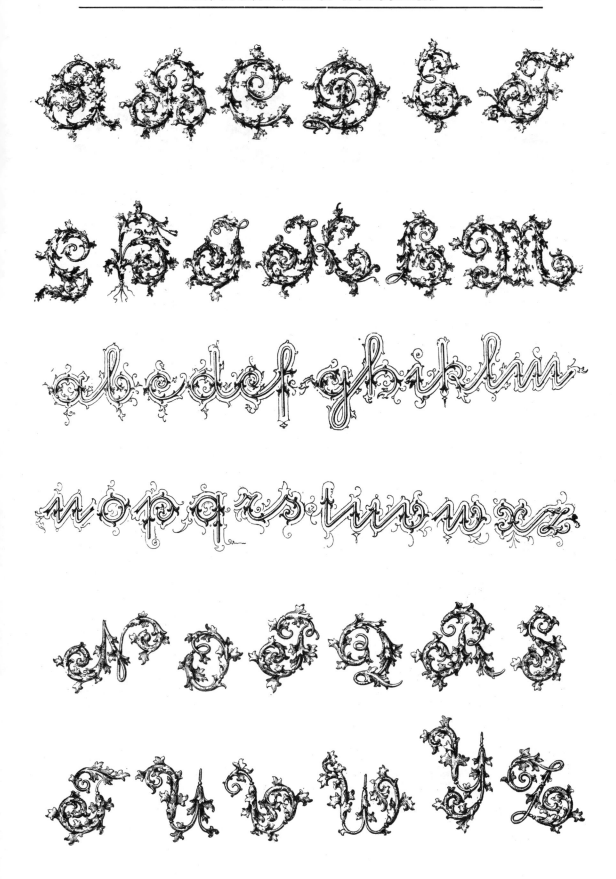

ROMAN CAPITALS AND FIGURES

ABCDEFGHIJK
LMNOPQRSTUV
WXYZ&Œ
abcdeffghijklmnopqr
æ stuvwxyz & œ
1234567890ll

TYPES OF THE 11TH, 12TH AND 16TH CENTURIES

GERMAN GOTHIC

ENGLISH GOTHIC

AM B C D E FG
H I K L M N O P Q
R S T U V W X Y Z
T O Z

13th CENTURY MANUSCRIPT. WESTMINSTER ABBEY

A B C D E F G H I
K L M N O P Q R S T
A T V X Y Z O

14th CENTURY MANUSCRIPT. BRITISH MUSEUM

A A B C D E F G H
I K L M N O P Q
R S T V W X Y Z

RICHARD II, 1400. WESTMINSTER ABBEY

ABCDEFGHIHL
MNOPQRST
ZZ

FROM 8th CENTURY MANUSCRIPT BRITISH MUSEUM

AABCCDEFGHH
JLMNHNOPGSS
SSSTQUYZZ

FROM 9th CENTURY MANUSCRIPT ANGLO-SAXON. BATTEL ABBEY

ABCDEFGHIJ
KLMNNOPQRST
UVXYZ.ÆM

FROM 10th CENTURY MANUSCRIPT. BRITISH MUSEUM

ABCDEFGHIK
LMNOPQRSTU
VWXYZ

FROM 12th CENTURY
MANUSCRIPT IN
BRITISH MUSEUM

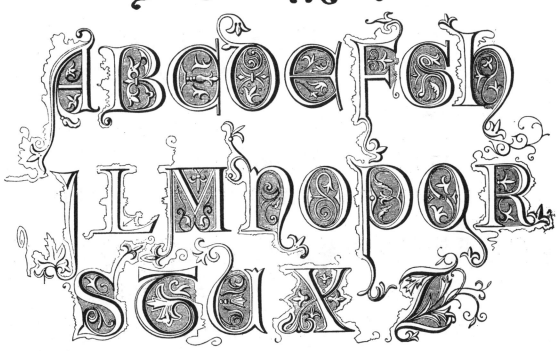

12th CENTURY. FROM THE MAZARIN BIBLE

ABCDEFGHI
KLMNOPQRS
GUVWXYZ

FROM 13th CENTURY MANUSCRIPT IN BRITISH MUSEUM

ABCDEFGHIKLMNOP
QRSTU 123456 VWXYZ.
78 abcdefghijklmnopqrstuvwxyz.90

ROUND ALPHABET

ABCDEFGHIKLMNOPQRSTUVWXYZ
12345 abcdefghiklmnopqrstuvwxyz 67890

ENGLISH ALPHABET

ABCDEFGHIKLMNOPQR
12345 STUVWXYZ 67890

FRENCH ELZIVIR

ABCDEFGHIKLMNOPQR
12345 STUVWXYZ 67890
abcdefghiklmnopqrsstubwxyz

OLD GOTHIC

ABCDEFGHIKLMNOPQRST
12345 UVWXYZ 67890
abcdefghiklmnopqrsstuuwxyz

OLD CHURCH GOTHIC

ABCDEFGHIKLMNOPQRSTUVWXYZ
12345 abcdefghiklmnopqrsstuvwxyz 67890

OLD GERMAN ITALICS

АБВГДЕЖЗИІКЛМНОПРСТУФХЦЧШЩЪЫЬѢЙЭЮЯѲѴ
абвгдежзиіклмнопрстуфхцчшщэюяѳѵйъыѣь

RUSSIAN ALPHABET

ΑΒΓΔΕΖΗΘΙΚΛΜΝΞΟΠΡΣΤΥΦΧΨΩ
αβγδεζηϑικλμνξοπρϛςτυφχψω

GREEK ALPHABET

MODERN GERMAN

MODERN GREEK

$A\ \alpha$	$B\ \beta$	$\Gamma\ \gamma$	$\Delta\ \delta$	$E\ \varepsilon$	$Z\ \zeta$	$H\ \eta$	$\Theta\ \theta\ \vartheta$	$I\ \iota$
A—Alpha.	B—Beta.	G—Gamma.	D—Delta.	Ĕ—Epsilou.	Z—Zeta.	Ē—Eta.	TH—Theta.	I—Iota.

								Final
$K\ \varkappa$	$\Lambda\ \lambda$	$M\ \mu$	$N\ \nu$	$\Xi\ \xi$	$O\ o$	$\Pi\ \pi$	$P\ \varrho$	$\Sigma\ \sigma\ \varsigma$
K—Kappa.	L—Lambda.	M—Mu.	N—Nu.	X—Xi.	Ŏ—Omikron.	P—Pi.	R—Rho.	S—Sigma.

$T\ \tau$	$\Upsilon\ \upsilon$	$\Phi\ \varphi$	$X\ \chi$	$\Psi\ \psi$	$\Omega\ \omega$
T—Tau.	U or Y—Upsilon.	PH—Phi.	CH—Chi.	PS—Psi.	O—Omega.

T—Teth	Ch—Cheth	Z—Zain	V—Vau	H—He	D—Daleth	G—Gimel	B—Beth	A or O—Aleph
		final		final			final	

E—Ain	S or soft C—Samech	N—Nun	M—Mem	L—Lamedh	K—Caph	I, J, Y or U—Yod
final					final	

T—Tau	Sh—Shin	R—Resh	K or Q—Koph	TZ or Soft Ch—Tsadhe	P—Pe	F—Pe
				final	final	

MODERN HEBREW

PART II.

MONOGRAMS

ARRANGED ALPHABETICALLY

To designate any Monogram or Figure specify page and number.

THE COMPLETE ALPHABET

1 AA

2 AA

3 AA

4 AA

5 AA

6 AA

7 AA

8 AA

9 AA

10 AA

11 AA

12 A. A. A.

13 A B

14 AA

15

16 AB

17 A A

18 A A

19 A A S

20 AA

21 A B

1   A B

2   A B

3   AAW

4   A B l

5   A C

6

7   A C

8   A B C

9   A C

10   A . B . Y .

11   A B C

12   AB

13   ABC

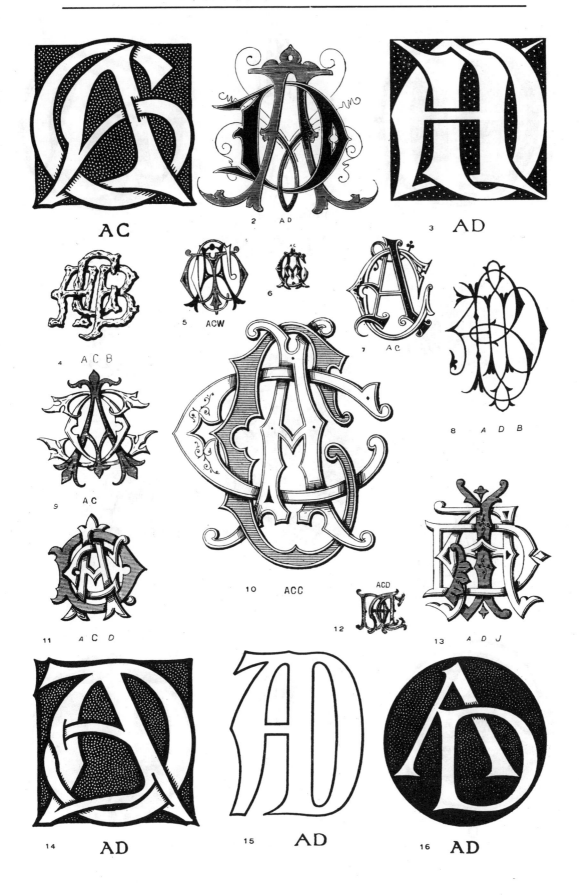

AC

2 AD

3 AD

4 ACB

5 ACW

6

7 AC

8 ADB

9 AC

10 ACC

11 ACD

12 ACD

13 ADJ

14 AD

15 AD

16 AD

1   AD

2   AD

3   AD

4   AD

5   AD

6   AD

7   AD

8   AD

9   AD

10   AD

11   AD

12   AD

13   AD

A E

2   A E A

3   A E

A E

4

A E

5   6   A E

7   A E

8   AE

9   AEI

10   AEI

11   A E.

12   AEI

13   A E

A. E.

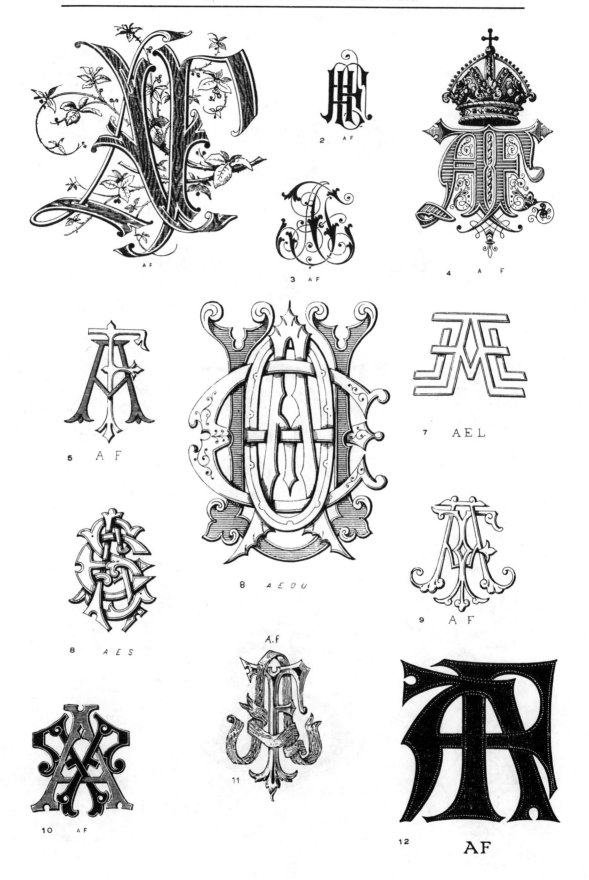

AF

2   AF

3   AF

4   AF

5   A F

7   AEL

8   AEOU

8   AES

9   A F

A.F

10   AF

11

12   AF

1 A.F.L.

2

3 A G

4 AG

5 A G

6 A G

7 A G

8 A G

9 AG

10 A G

11 A G

12 A G K

13 A.G.H.M

14 A G

15 A.G.N

16 AGP

1 A.G.R
2 A.G.W
3 A.G.Y.
4 A.G.Y.
5 A H
6 A H
7 AH
8 AH
9 A H
10 AH
11 AH
12
13 A H
14 A H D
15 A H
16
17 A H
18 A.H.M.
19 AH
20 A H F.
21 A.H.R.
22 A I

1 AI

2 AI

3 AI

4

5 AJ

6 AJ

7 AJ

8 AJ

9 AJ

10 AJT

11

12 A.J.D.

13 AJ

14 A.J.M.

15 A.J.D

16 A K

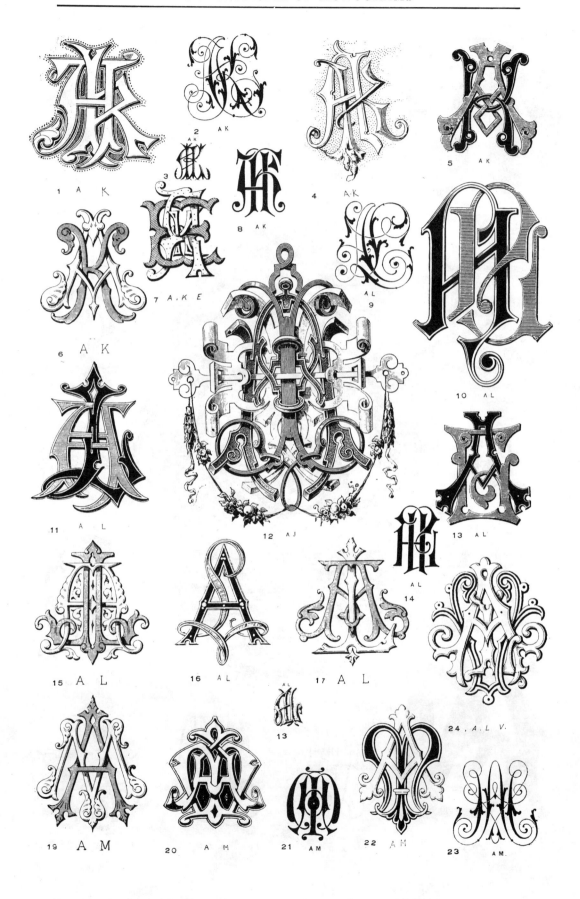

1   A·K

2   AK

AK

3

4   A·K

5   AK

6   A K

7 A.K E

8 AK

9   AL

10   AL

.11   A L

12 AJ

13   AL

14   AL

15 A L

16 AL

17 A L

13

19   A M

20   A M

21 AM

22 AM

23   AM

24 , A.L V.

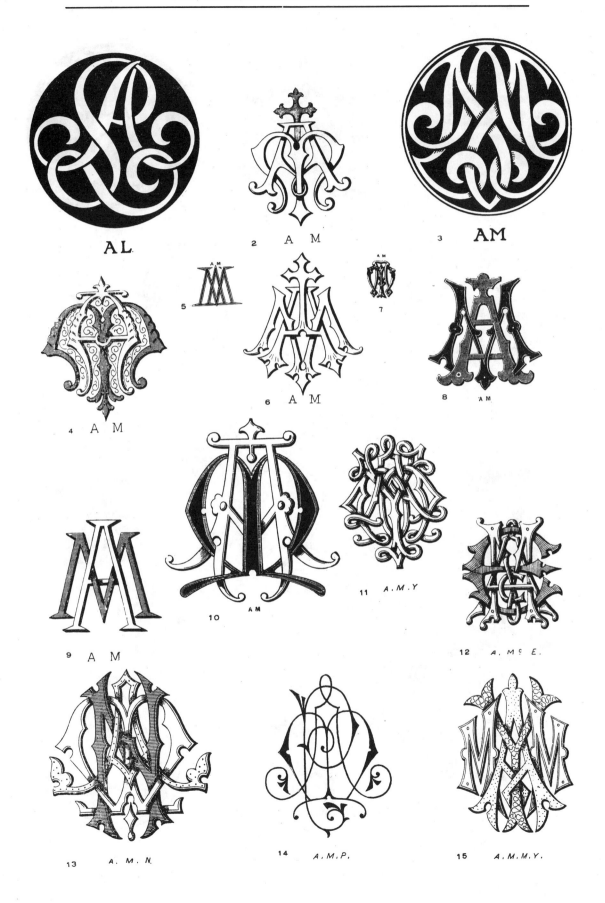

AL.

2   A M

3   AM

4   A M

5   AM

6   A M

7

8   A M

9   A M

10

11   A.M.Y

12   A. Mc E.

13   A. M. N.

14   A.M.P.

15   A.M.M.Y.

1   A N

2   A N G

AN
3

5
AN

6
AN

4   A N

7   A N

8   AN

9   A . N W

10   A N

11   A O

12   AN

13   AN

14   AN

15   AO

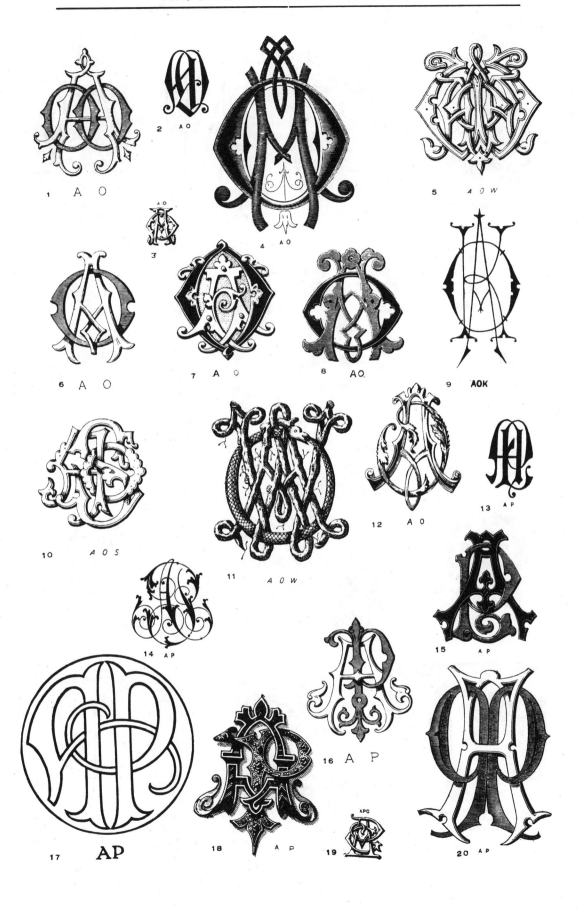

1   A O

2   A O

3   A O

4   A O

5   A O W

6   A O

7   A O

8   A O.

9   AOK

10   A O S

11   A O W

12   A O

13   AP

14   AP

15   AP

16   A P

17   AP

18   A P

19   APG

20   AP

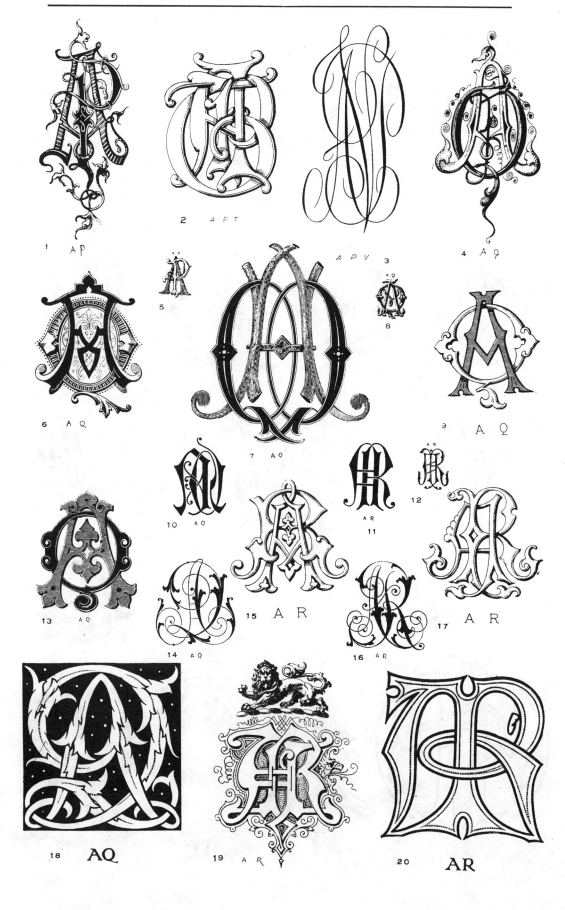

1   A P

2   A P T

A P V   3

4   A Q

5   A P

6   A Q

7   A Q

8   A Q

9   A Q

10   A Q

11   A R

12   A R

13   A Q

14   A Q

15   A R

16   A R

17   A R

18   **AQ**

19   A R

20   **AR**

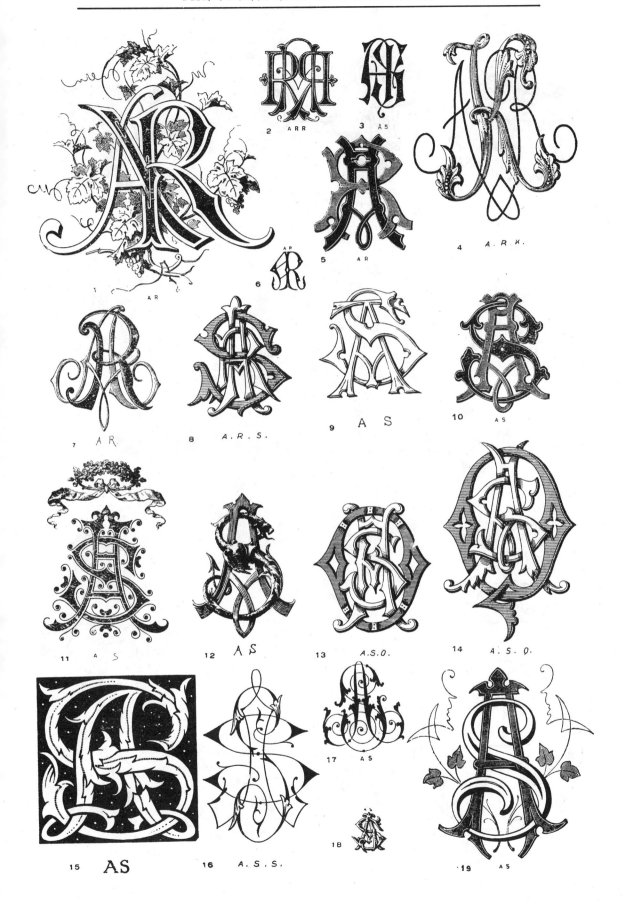

1 AR

2 ARR

3 AS

4 A.R.K.

5 AR

6

7 AR

8 A.R.S.

9 A S

10 AS

11 A S

12 AS

13 A.S.O.

14 A.S.Q.

15 AS

16 A.S.S.

17 AS

18

19 AS

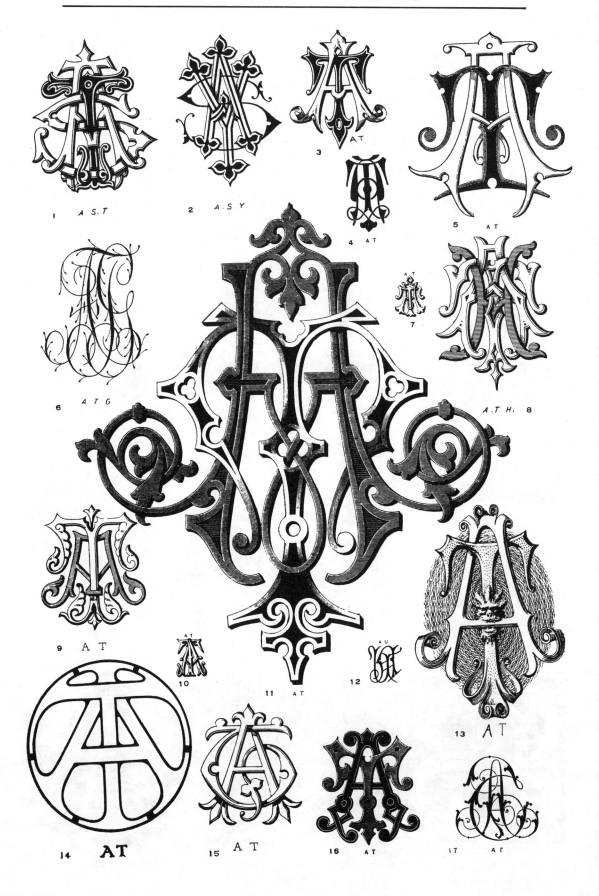

1 A.S.T

2 A.S.Y.

3 AT

4 AT

5 AT

6 ATG

7

A.T.H. 8

9 AT

10

11 AT

12

13 AT

14 AT

15 AT

16 AT

17 AT

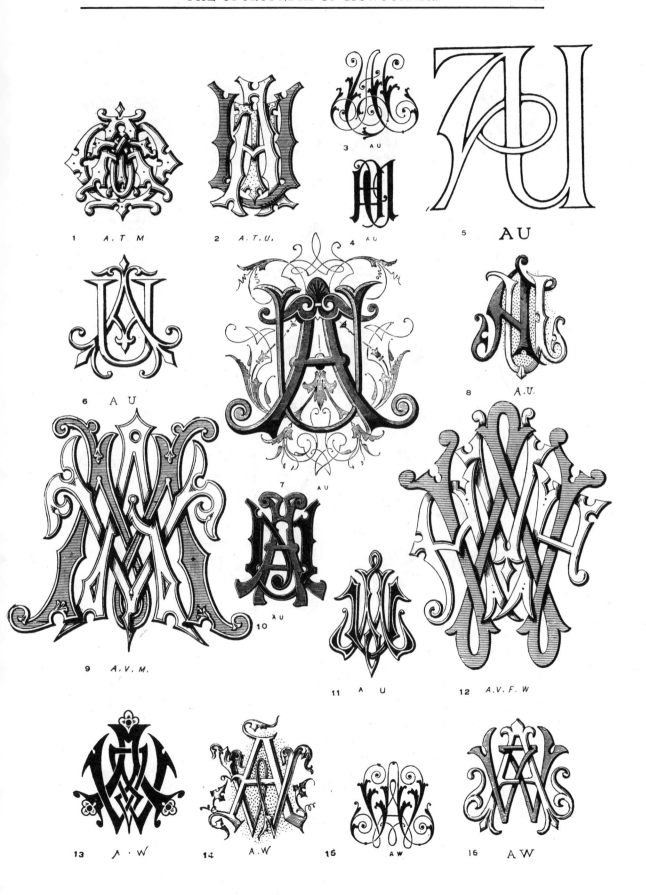

1   A. T. M

2   A. T. U.

3   AU

4   AU

5   AU

6   AU

7   AU

8   A. U.

9   A. V. M.

10   AU

11   A U

12   A. V. F. W

13   A . W

14   A. W

15   AW

16   A W

1 A V

2 A V

3 A V

4 A V

5 A V

6 A V

7 A V

8 A V

9 A V

10 A W

11 A W E

12 A V

13 A W

14 A W

15 A W

1 AW

2 A.W.S.

3 AWP

4 AX

5 AX

6 AX

7 AX

8 AY

9 AX

10

11 AY M.

12 AY

13 AY

14 AX

15 AY

16 AY

17 AZ

18 AZ

19 AY

1   A Z

2   A Z

3   AZ

4   AZ

5   AZ

6   A Z

7   A&B

8   A Z

9   A & M.D

10   AGNES.

11   ABCL

12   A&Cº

13   A & R.W.

14   Albert.

Agnes.

Amour.

"Alice"

ALBERT
Couronne de Duc

ALICE

1 Anna.

2 DAVID

3 ELIZA.

4 EMILY.

5 Emma.

6 DAVID

7

8 ANNIE

9

1   BA

2   B A

3   BB

4   B B

5   B A

6   B A

7

8   B

9   B B

10   B B

11   B B

12   B B

13   B B

14   BBA

15   B A

BBD

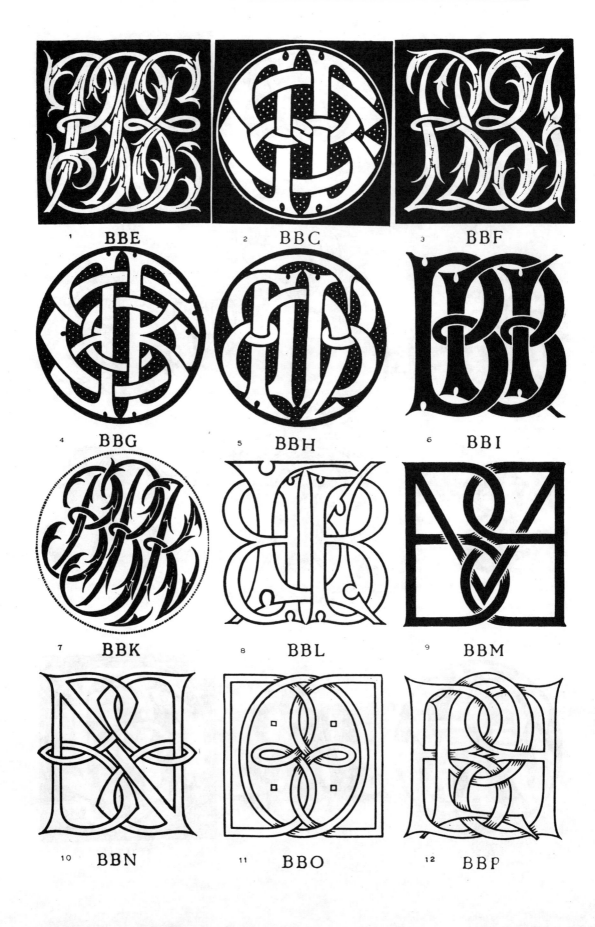

1   BBE 2   BBC 3   BBF

4   BBG 5   BBH 6   BBI

7   BBK 8   BBL 9   BBM

10   BBN 11   BBO 12   BBP

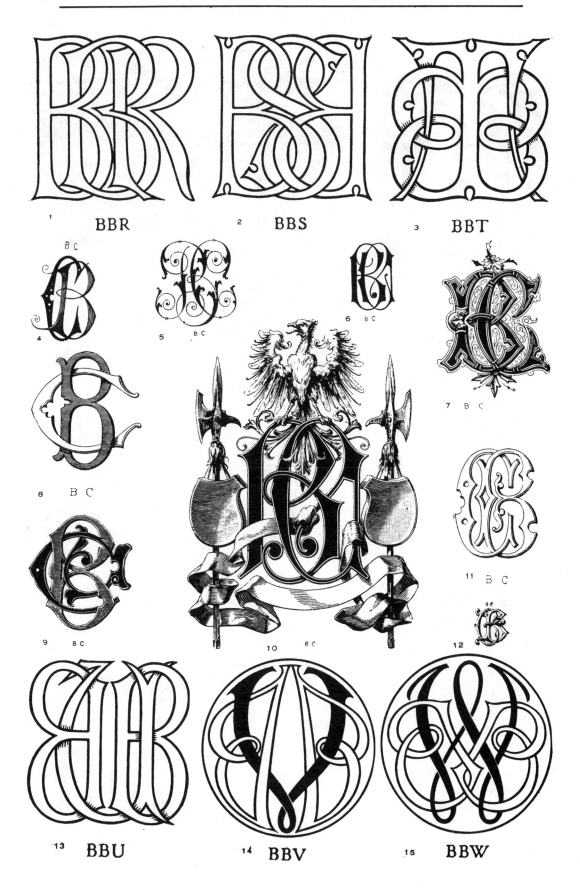

1   BBR
2   BBS
3   BBT

4   B C
5   B C
6   B C
7   B C

8   B C
9   B C
10   B C
11   B C
12   B C

13   BBU
14   BBV
15   BBW

BC

2   B C D

'3   'B C D D

4

5   B C E

6   B C B

7   B C D

8   B.C.L.

9   BCD

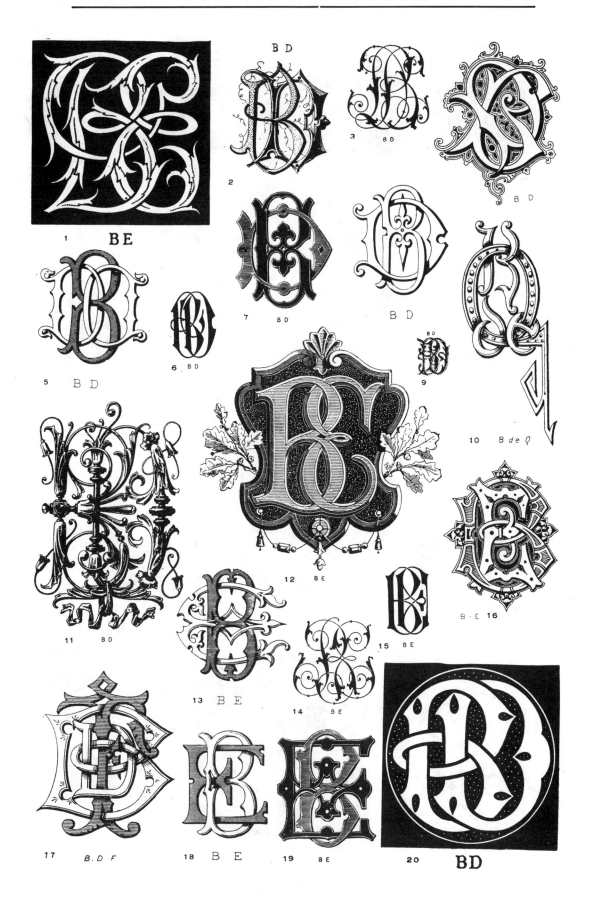

1   BE

B D

2

3   B D

B D

5   B D

6   B D

7   B D

B D

9

10   B de Q

11   B D

12   B E

13   B E

14   B E

15   B E

B·E 16

17   B. D F

18   B E

19   B E

20   **BD**

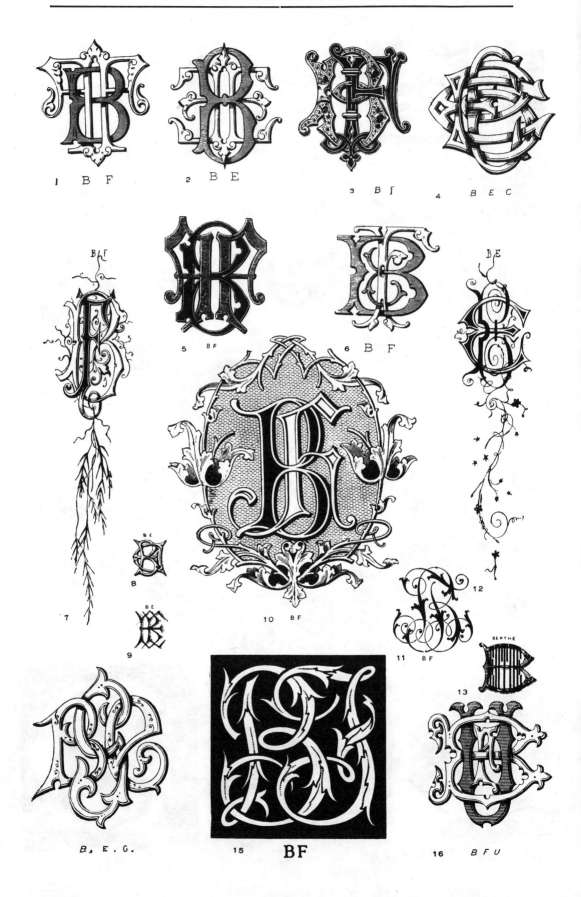

1   B F

2   B E

3   B F

4   B E C

5   B F

6   B F

B E
7

B E
8

B E
9

10   B F

11   B F

12

13   BERTHE

B, E, G.

15   BF

16   B F U

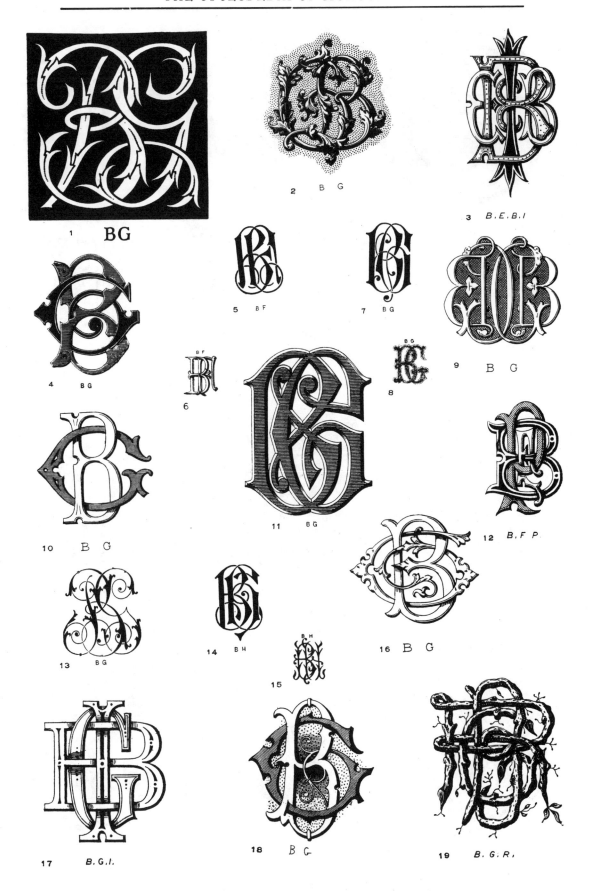

1 BG

2 B G

3 B.E.B.I

4 BG

5 BF

6 Bf

7 BG

8 BG

9 B G

10 B G

11 BG

12 B.F.P.

13 BG

14 BH

15 BH

16 B G

17 B.G.I.

18 B G

19 B.G.R.

1 **BH**

2 B H

3 B H

4 B H

5 B H

6 B I

7 B H

8 B H

9 B H

10 B H

11 **BJ**

12 B I

13 **B I**

14 B I

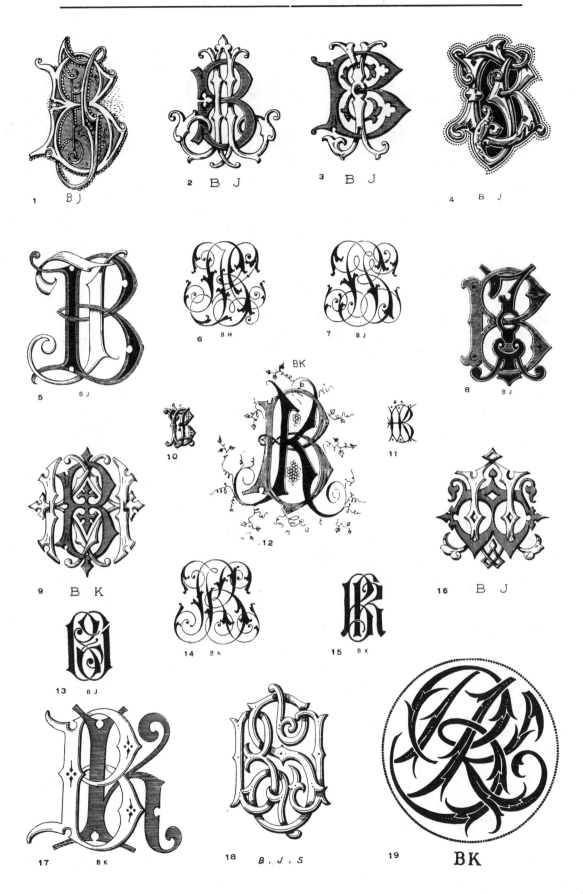

1   B J

2   B J

3   B J

4   B J

5   B J

6   B H

7   B J

8   B J

9   B K

10

11

12

13   B J

14   B K

15   B K

16   B J

17   B K

18   B . J . S

19   BK

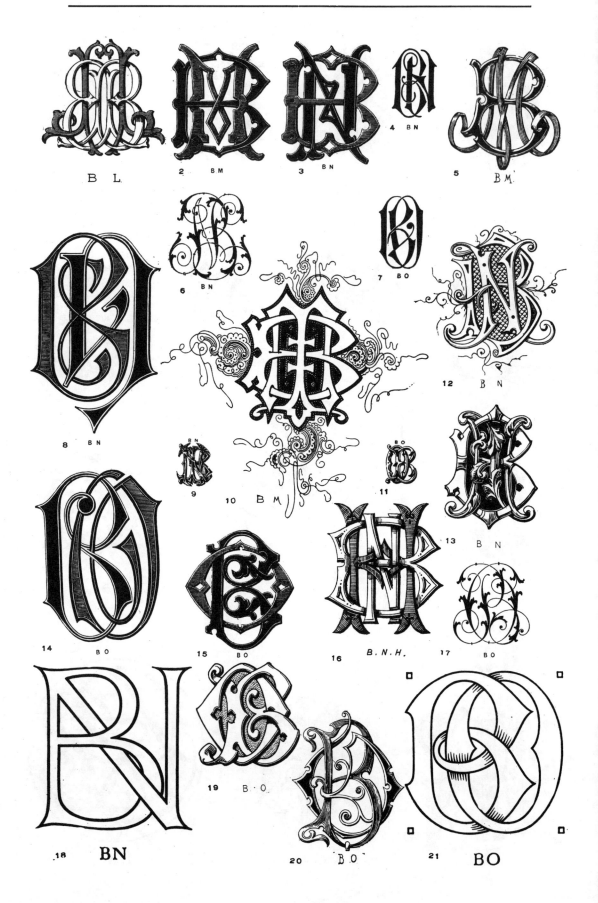

B L.

2   B M

3   B N

4   B N

5   B M

6   B N

7   B O

8   B N

12   B N

9

10   B M

11   B O

13   B N

14   B O

15   B O

16   B. N. H.

17   B O

18   BN

19   B O

20   B O

21   BO

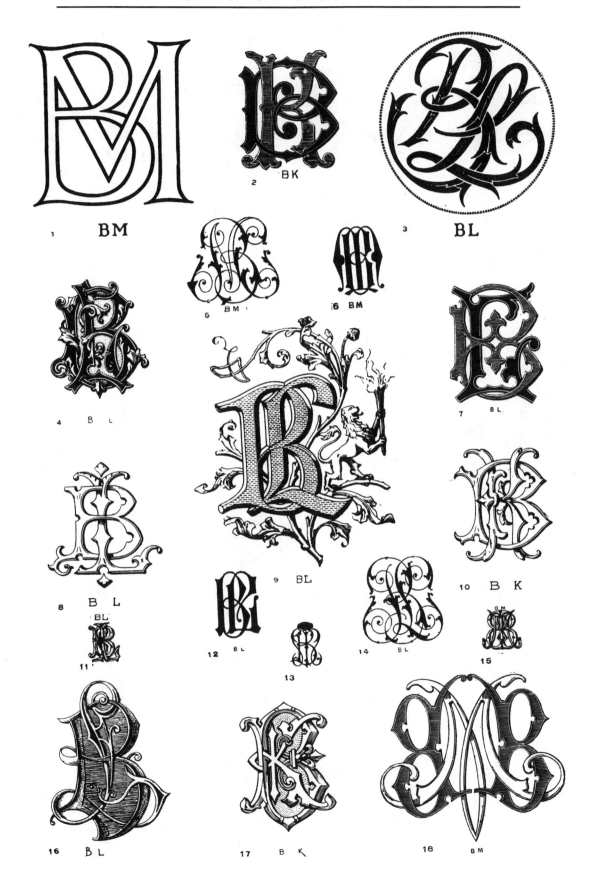

1 BM

2 BK

3 BL

5 BM

6 BM

4 B L

7 BL

8 B L

9 BL

10 B K

11

BL

12 BL

13

14 BL

15 BM

16 BL

17 B K

18 BM

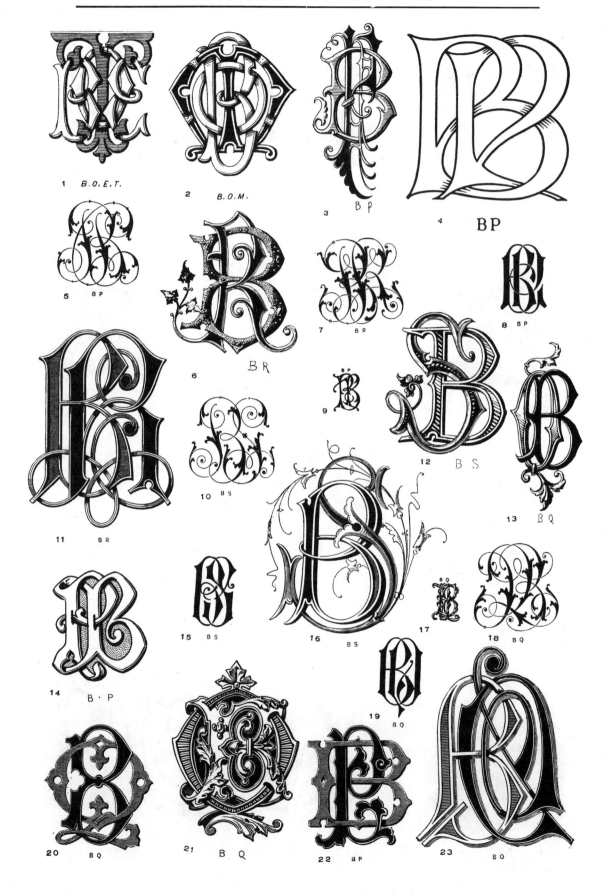

1 B. O. E. T.

2 B. O. M.

3 B P

4 BP

5 B P

6 B R

7 B R

8 B P

9 B P

10 B S

11 B R

12 B S

13 B Q

14 B · P

15 B S

16 B S

17 B Q

18 B Q

19 B Q

20 B Q

21 B Q

22 B P

23 B Q

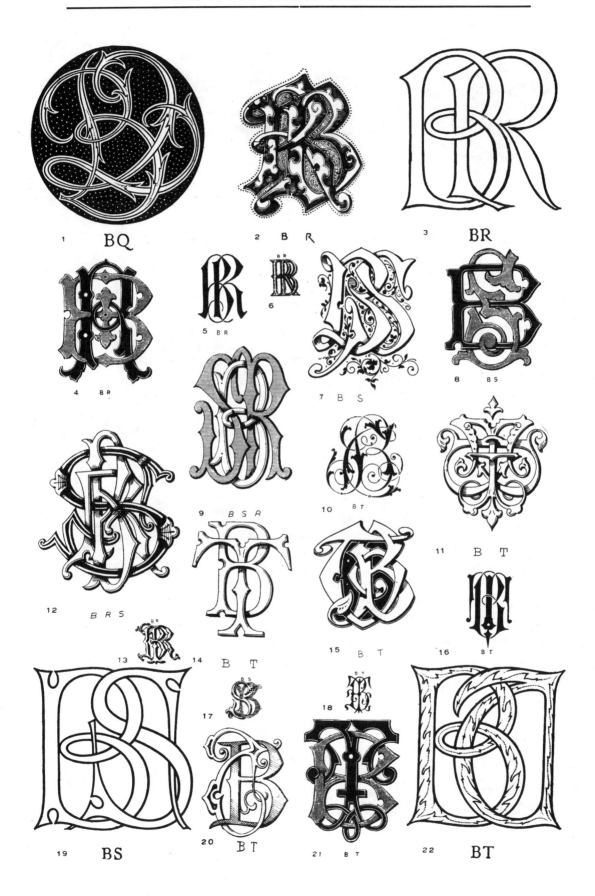

1 BQ

2 B R

3 BR

4 BR

5 BR

6

7 B S

8 BS

9 B S R

10 B T

11 B T

12 B R S

13 B R

14 B T

15 B T

16 B T

17 B S

18 B T

19 BS

20 B T

21 B T

22 BT

1   B T

2   B U

3   B U

4   B U

5   B U

6   B U

7   B U

8   B V

9   B V

10   B T

11   B U

12   B V

13   B U

14   B V

15   B U

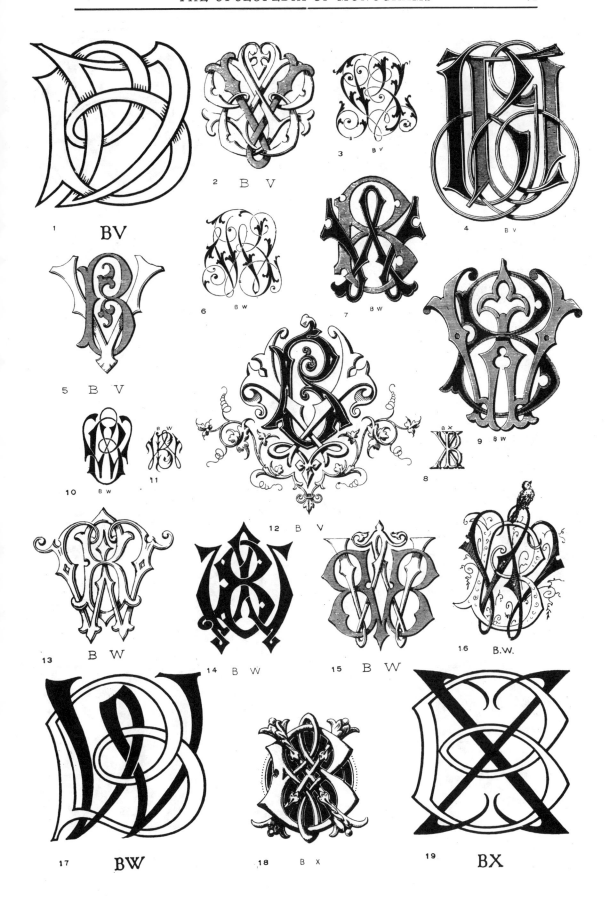

1   BV

2   B V

3   B V

4   B V

5   B V

6   B W

7   B W

8   B V

9   B W

10   B W

11   B W

12   B V

13   B W

14   B W

15   B W

16   B.W.

17   BW

18   B X

19   BX

1 B X
2 B X
3 B X
4 BY
5 B Y
6 B Z
7 B Z
8 B Y
9 BZ
10 B Z
11 B Z
12 B Y
13 B Z
14 B Z
15 B Z
16 B&A
17 B Z
18 B&C
19 BY

1 BENOIT

2 B & Co.

3 Betti.

BLANCHE

4

5 BELLA.

6 BENJAMIN D.

7 BETSY.

8 B & Co

9 Bertha.

10 Bernard

1 CA

2 ICA

3 CA

4 CA

5 C A B.

6 CA

7 C. A. M.

8 C A. F

9 C B.I

10 C A H. H

11 C. B. E. A.

12 CB

13 C

14 C B

15 C B

16 C B

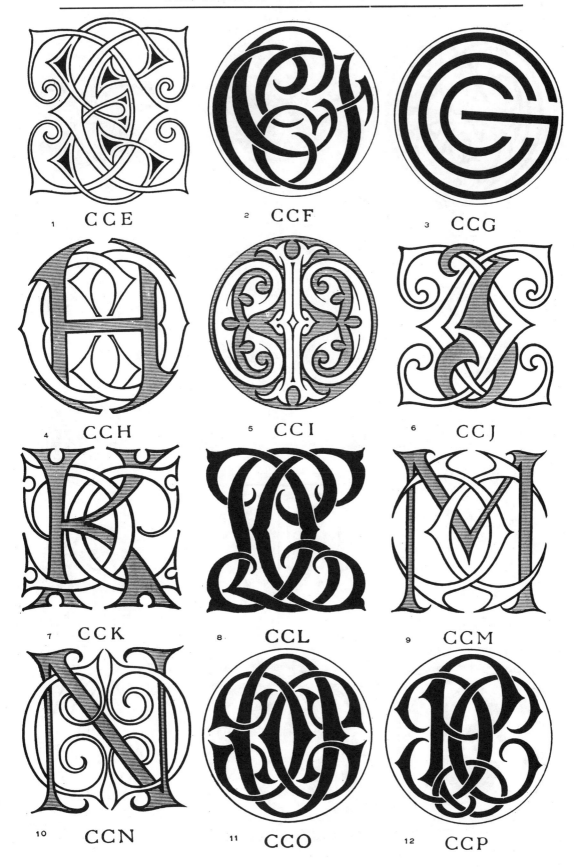

1 C C E

2 C C F

3 C C G

4 C C H

5 C C I

6 C C J

7 C C K

8 C C L

9 C C M

10 C C N

11 C C O

12 C C P

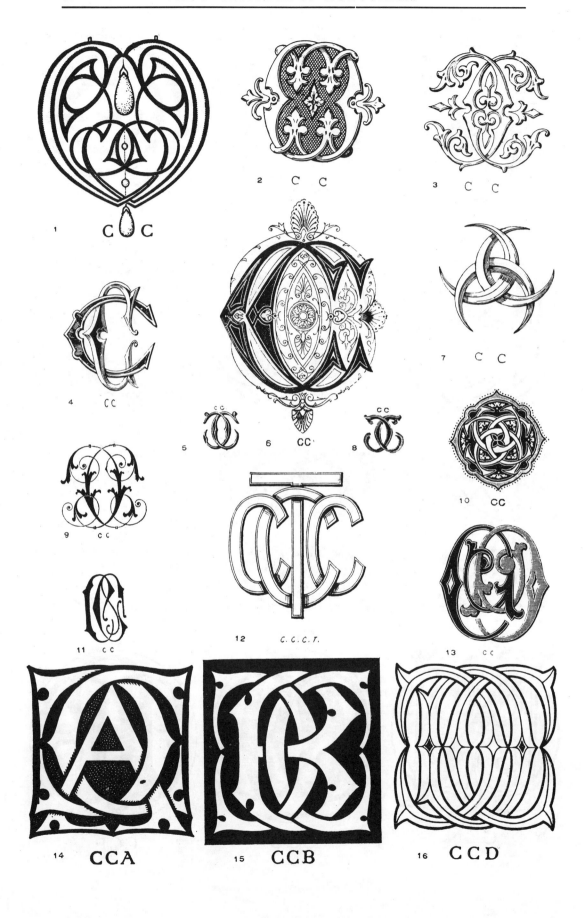

1   C C

2   C C

3   C C

4   CC

5   C C

6   CC

7   C C

8   C C

9   C C

10   CC

11   C C

12   C. C. C. T.

13   C C

14   **CCA**

15   **CCB**

16   **CCD**

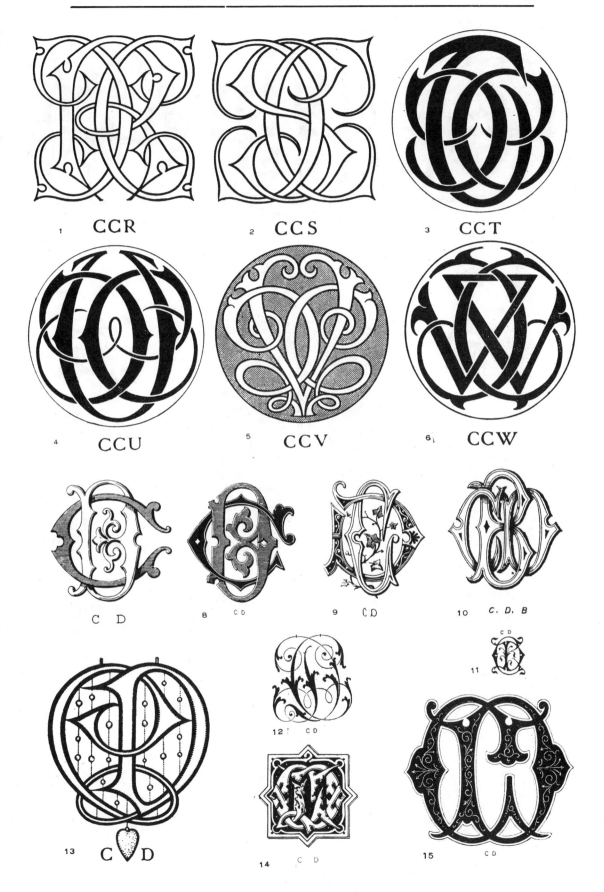

1 CCR

2 CCS

3 CCT

4 CCU

5 CCV

6 CCW

C D

8 C D

9 C D

10 C. D. B

11 C D

12 C D

13 C D

14 C D

15 C D

1   C D E

2   CDE

3   C E

4   CE

5   CE

6   C   E

7   C D E

8   CE

9   CE

10

11   C E

12   C. E. C.

13   CE

14   C. E.

15   C E

1   C. E. D

2   C E D

3   C. E. G.

4   C. E. O.

5   C. E. W.

6   C F

7

8   C. F

9

10   C F

11   C F

12   C F

13   CF

14   CFS

15   C. F. T.

1 C G

2 **CG**

3 C G

4 C G

5 C G

6 C G

7 CG

8 C. G. J. I.

9

10

11 C H

12 G. G. S

13 C H

14 C H

15

16 C H

17 **CH**

18 C H

19 C H

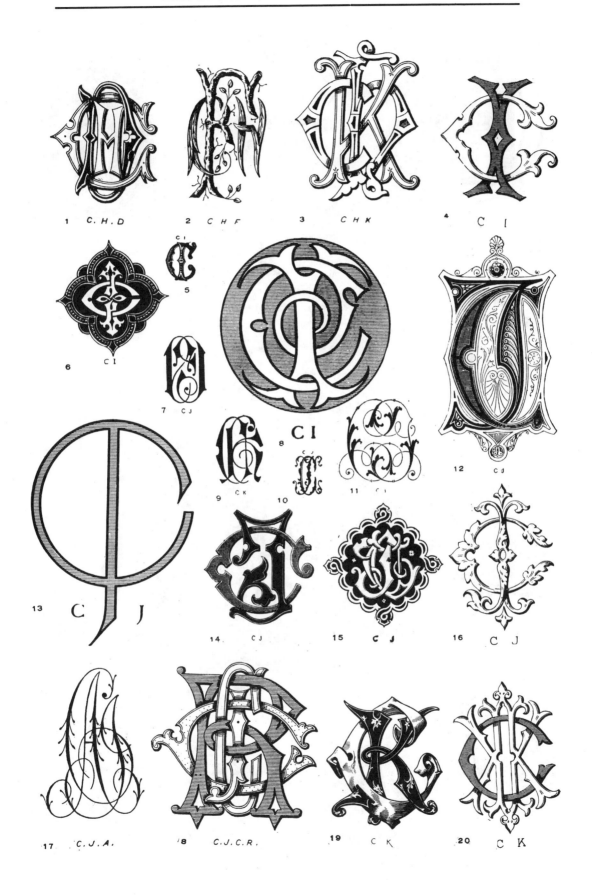

1 C.H.D
2 C H F
3 C H K
4 C I
5 C I
6 C I
7 C J
8 C I
9 C K
10
11 C I
12 C J
13 C J
14 C J
15 C J
16 C J
17 C.J.A.
18 C.J.C.R.
19 C K
20 C K

1 CK

2 C K

3

4

5 C K

6 C K

7 C K

8 C L

9 C. K. S

10 C L

11 C L

12 C L

13 C. K. Y. M.

14

15 C L

16 C. K. B.

1 CL

2 C L

3 CM

4 C M

5

6 CM

7 CM

8

9 C M

10 CM

11 CN

12 CM

13

14 CN

15 C M

16 C N

17 C M

18 CM

19 C.M.T.

20 C N

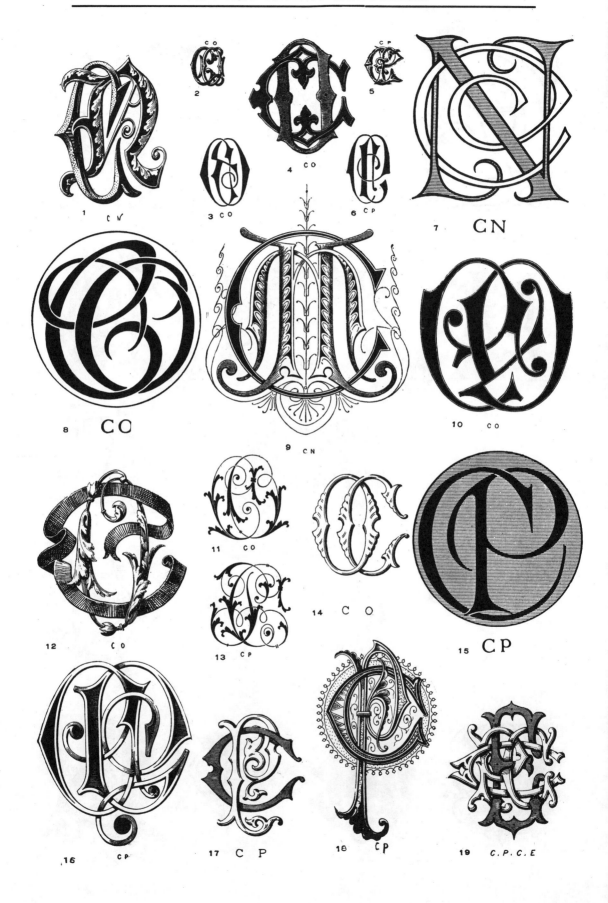

1   C V

2

3 C O

4   C O

5   C P

6   C P

7   CN

8   CO

9   C N

10   C O

11   C O

12   C O

13   C P

14   C O

15   C P

16   C P

17   C P

18   C P

19   C . P . C . E

1 CP

2 CQ

3 CQ

4 CQ

5 CQ

6 CR

7 CQ

8 CQ

9 CQ

10 CR

11

12 CR

13 CR

14 CR

15 CR

16 CR

17 C. R. M.

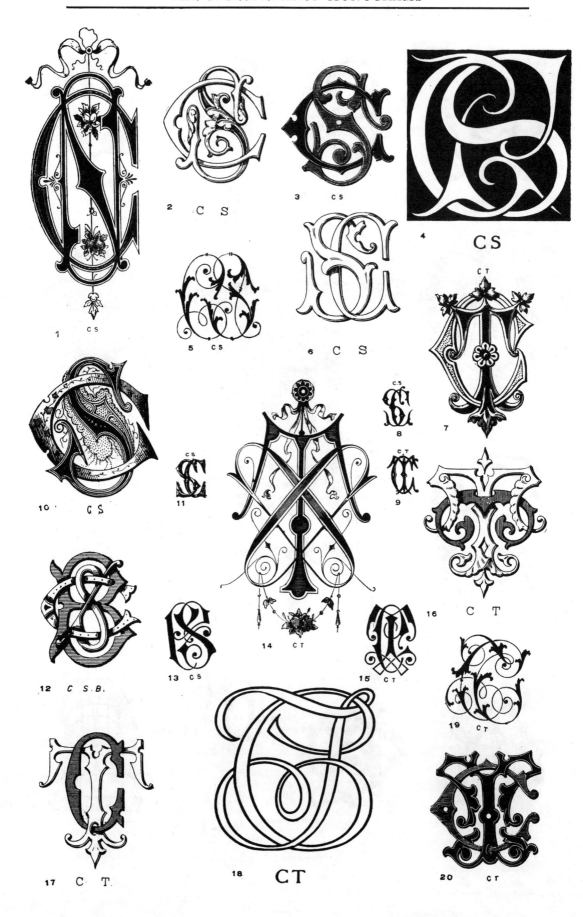

1   C S

2   C S

3   C S

4   CS

5   C S

6   C S

7   C T

8   C S

9   C T

10   C S

11

12   C S B.

13   C S

14   C T

15   C T

16   C T

17   C T

18   CT

19   C T

20   C T

1   C.T.R.

2   C U

3   C U   4   C V

5   C U

6   C U

8

7

9   C V

18   C V

10

11   C V

12   C U

13   C V

14   C W

15   C V

16   C V

17   C V

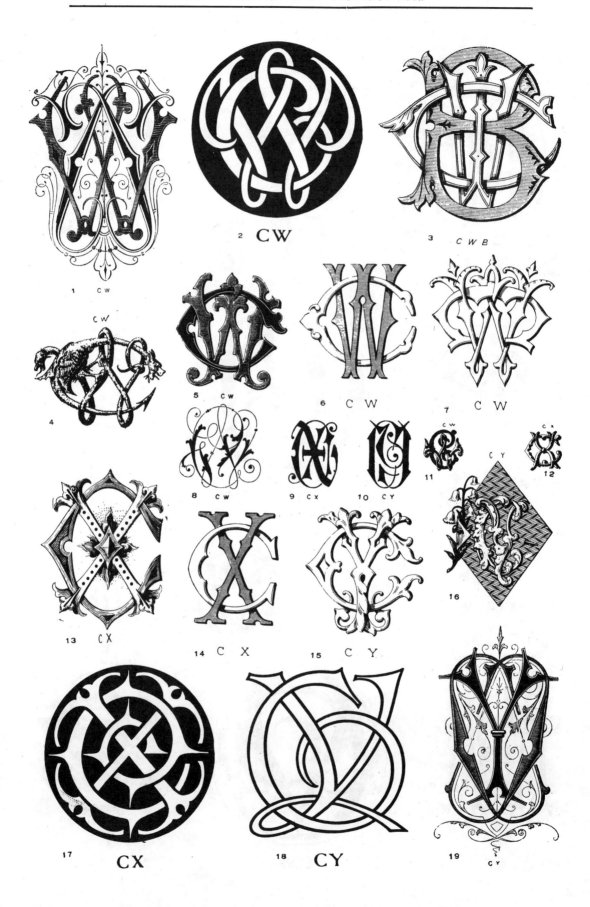

1   C W

2   C W

3   C W B

C W

4

5   C W

6   C W

7   C W

8   C W

9   C X

10   C Y

11   C W

C Y

12   C X

13   C X

14   C X

15   C Y

16

17   CX

18   CY

19   C Y

1 CZ

2 c z

5 *CARRIE.*

6 C Z

7 Cz

8 Cz

9 cz

10 cz

17

11 C&B

12 C&Co

13 cz

14 C&Co

15 Carl

16 C&D

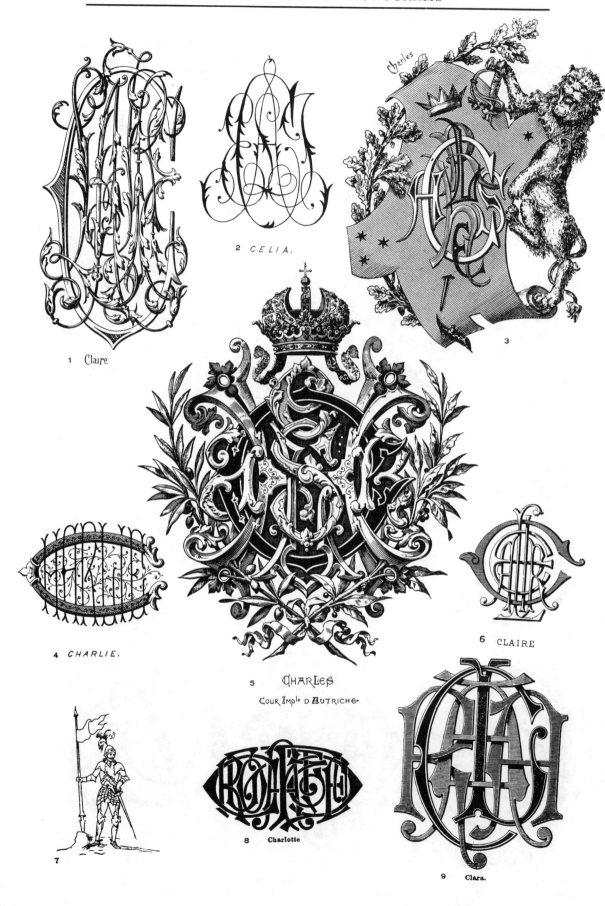

1 Claire

2 CELIA.

3

4 CHARLIE.

5 CHARLES
Cour Impl. d'Autriche

6 CLAIRE

7

8 Charlotte

9 Clara.

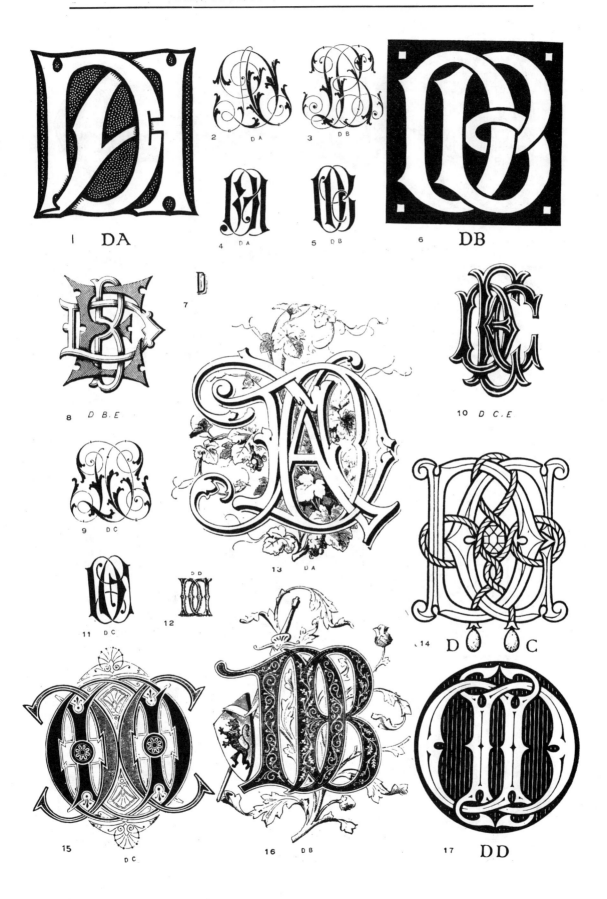

1 DA

2 DA

3 DB

4 DA

5 DB

6 DB

D

7

8 D B.E

9 DC

10 D C.E

11 DC

12 DD

13 DA

14 D C

15 DC

16 DB

17 DD

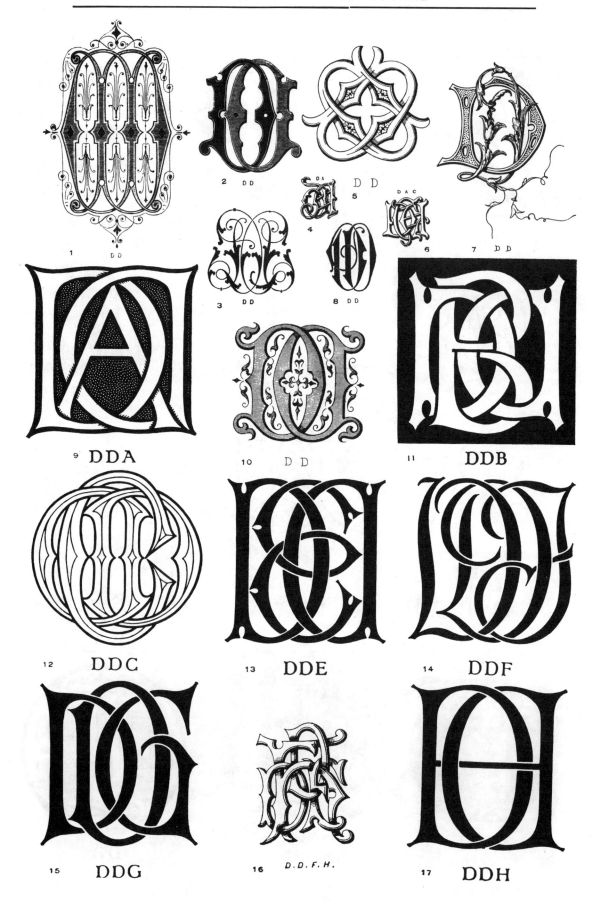

1   D D

2   D D

3   D D

4   DA

5   D D

6   DAC

7   D D

8   D D

9   DDA

10   D D

11   DDB

12   DDC

13   DDE

14   DDF

15   DDG

16   D.D.F.H.

17   DDH

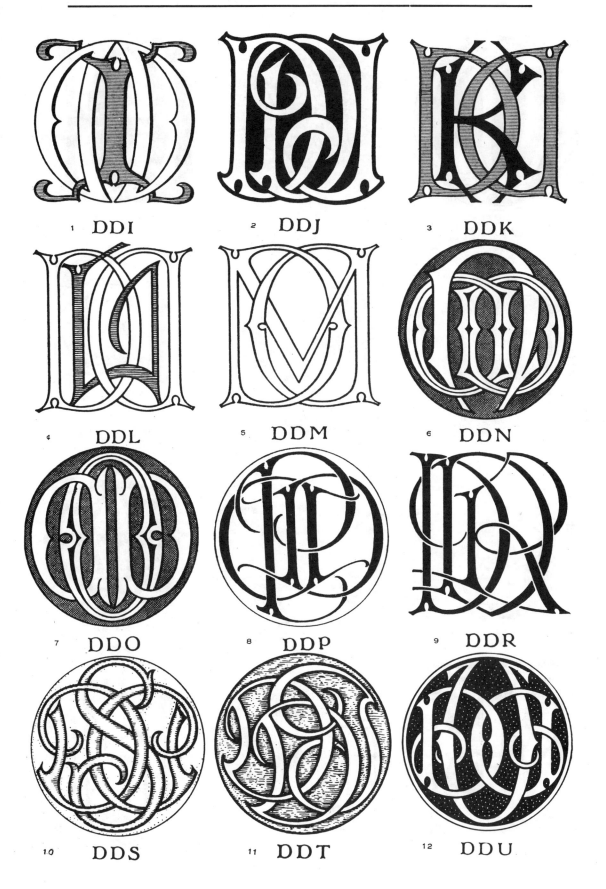

1 DDI

2 DDJ

3 DDK

4 DDL

5 DDM

6 DDN

7 DDO

8 DDP

9 DDR

10 DDS

11 DDT

12 DDU

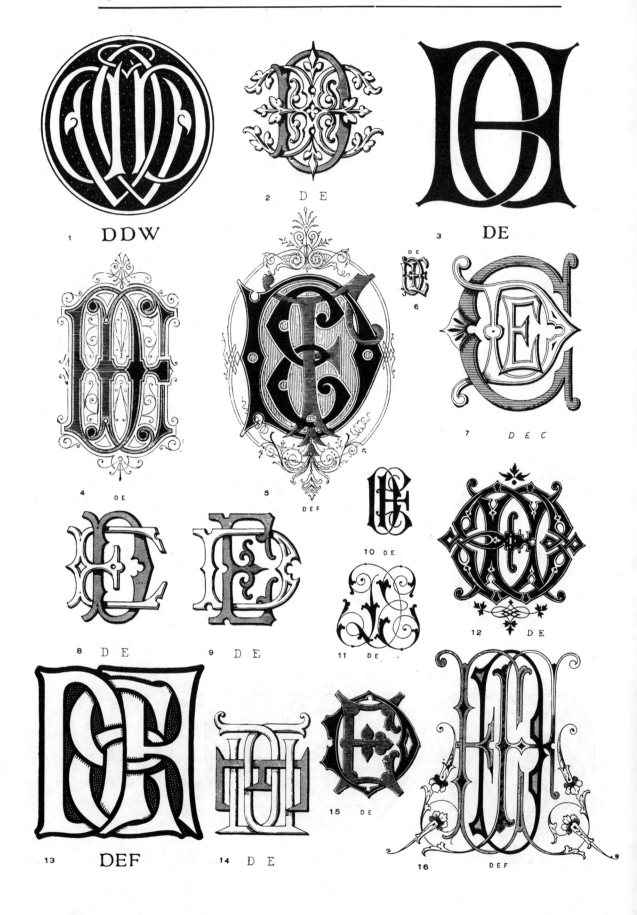

1   DDW

2   D E

3   DE

4   D E

5   D E F

6   D E

7   D E C

8   D E

9   D E

10   DE

11   D E

12   D E

13   DEF

14   D E

15   D E

16   D E F

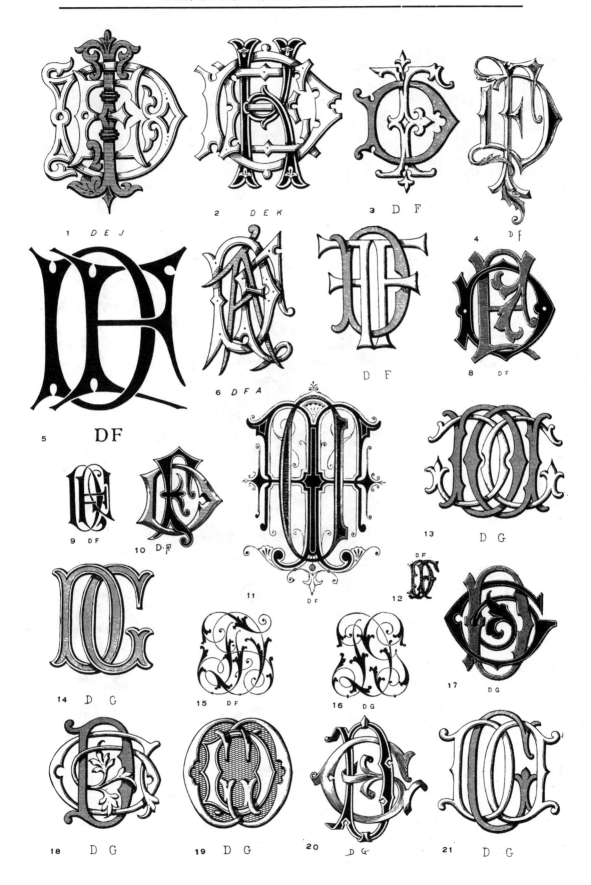

1   D E J

2   D E K

3   D F

4   D F

5   **DF**

6   D F A

7   D F

8   D F

9   D F

10   D·F

11   D F

12   D F

13   D G

14   D G

15   D F

16   D G

17   D G

18   D G

19   D G

20   D G

21   D G

1 DG

2 D G

3 DG

4 D G

5 D G K.

6 D G M

7

8

9 D H

10 D H

11 D G.

12 D H

13 D H

14 D H

15

16 D h

17 DH

18 DGR

19 D H

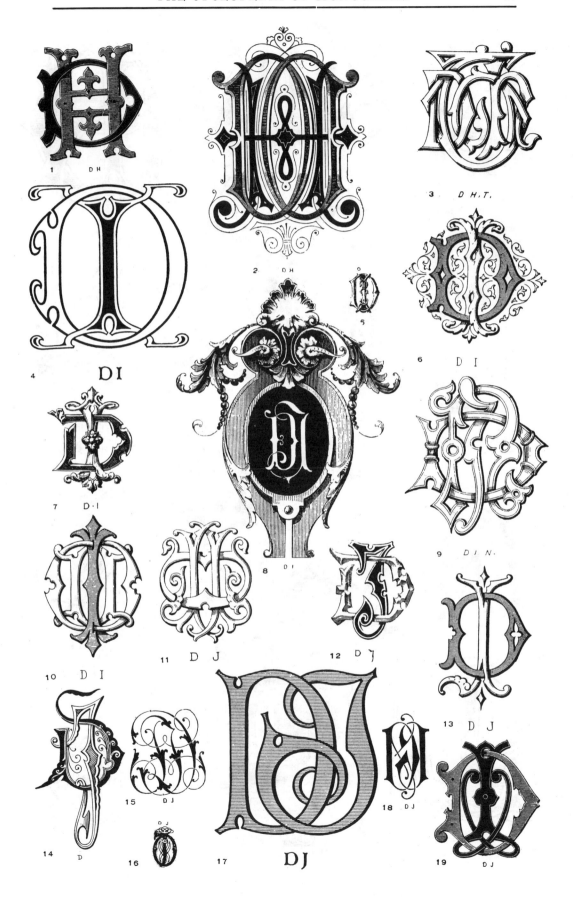

1   D H

3   D H. T.

2   D H

5   D

6   D I

4   D I

7   D·I

9   D I N.

8   D I

11   D J

12   D J

10   D I

13   D J

15   D J

18   D J

14   D

16   D J

17   D J

19   D J

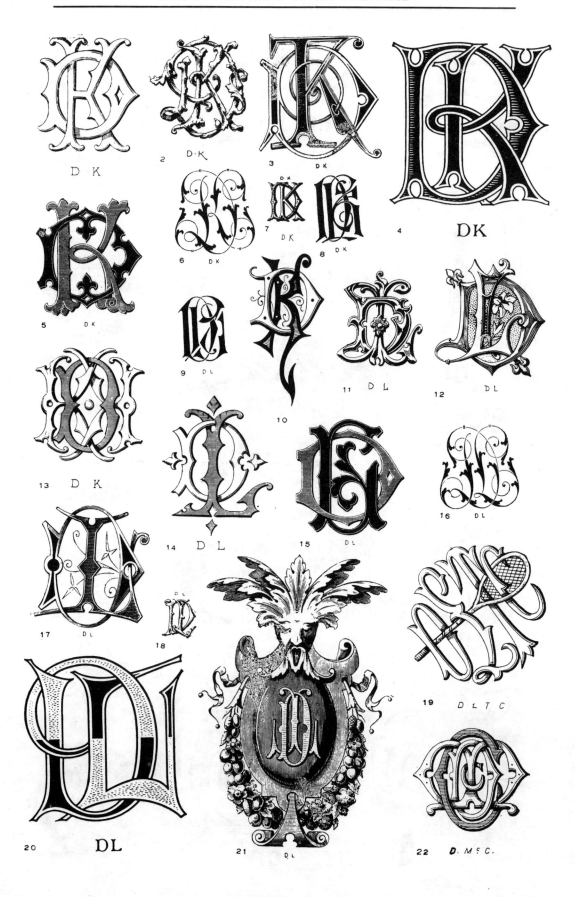

D K

2   D·K

3   DK

4   DK

DK

5   DK

6   DK

7   DK

8   DK

9   DL

10

11   DL

12   DL

13   D K

14   D L

15   DL

16   DL

17   DL

18

19   DLTC

20   DL

21   DL

22   D·MᵑC.

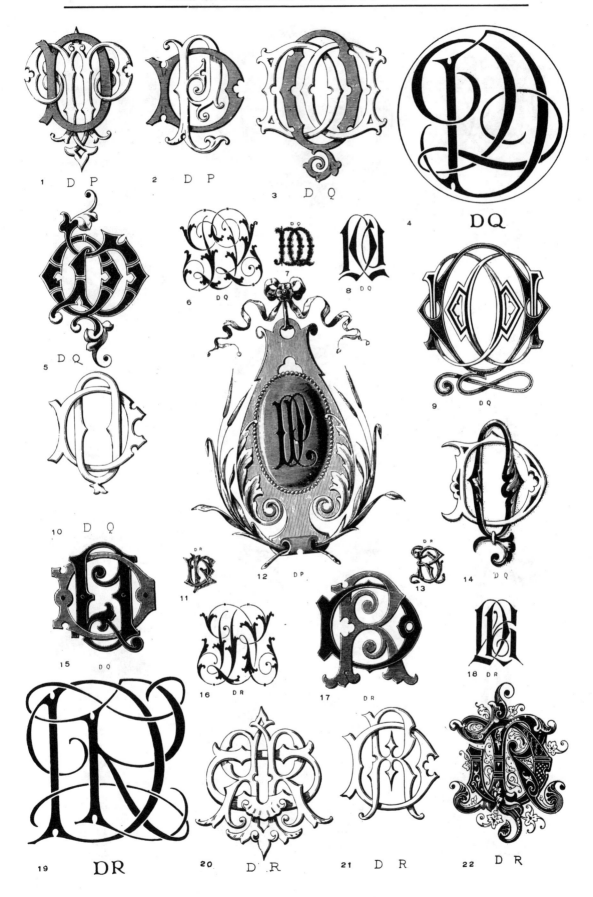

1 D P

2 D P

3 D Q

4 DQ

5 D Q

6 D Q

7

8 D Q

9 DQ

10 D Q

11 D R

12 D P

13

14 D Q

15 D Q

16 D R

17 D R

18 D R

19 DR

20 D R

21 D R

22 DR

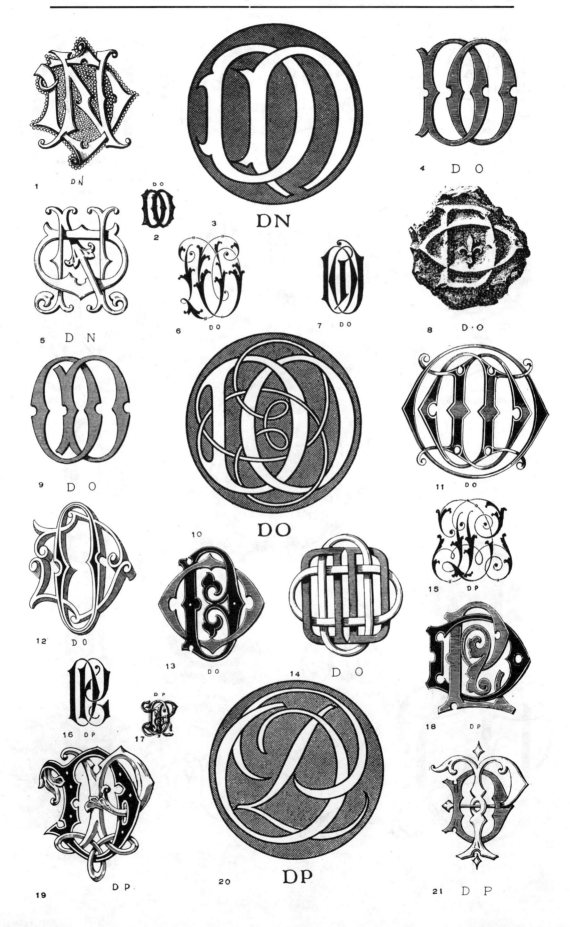

1   D N

2   D O

3   DN

4   D O

5   D N

6   D O

7   D O

8   D·O

9   D O

10   DO

11   D O

12   D O

13   D O

14   D O

15   D P

16   D P

17   D P

18   D P

19   D P

20   DP

21   D P

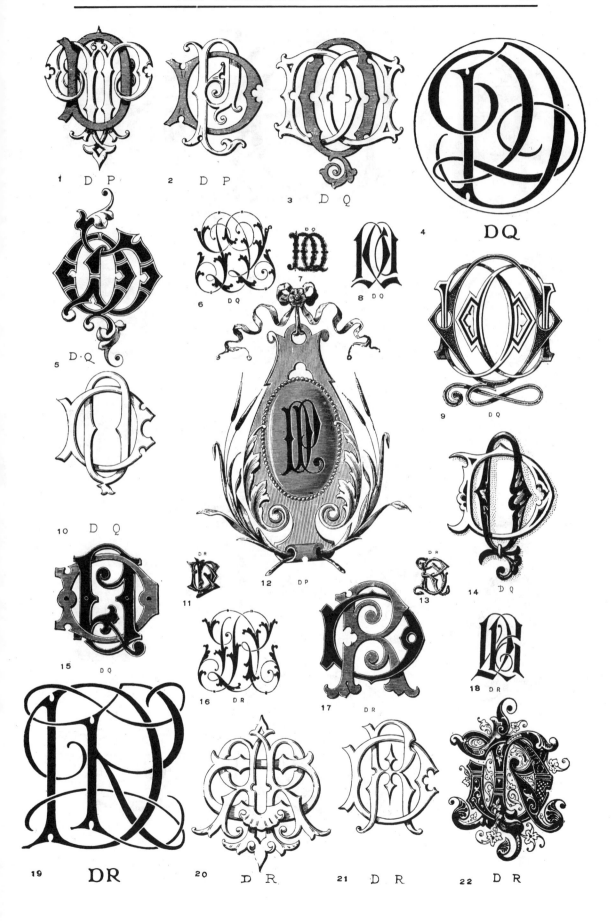

1 D P

2 D P

3 D Q

4 DQ

5 D·Q

6 DQ

7

8 DQ

9 DQ

10 D Q

11 D R

12 D P

13 D R

14 D Q

15 DQ

16 D R

17 D R

18 D R

19 DR

20 D R

21 D R

22 D R

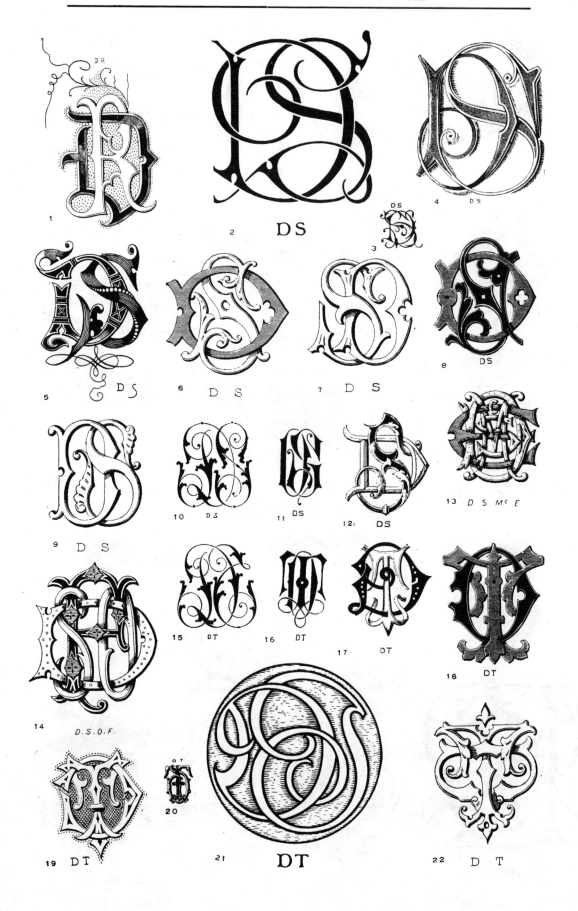

1

2 DS

3 DS

4 DS

5 D S

6 D S

7 D S

8 DS

9 D S

10 D S

11 DS

12ı DS

13 D S Mᶜ E

14 D.S.O.F

15 DT

16 DT

17 DT

18 DT

19 DT

20 DT

21 **DT**

22 D T

1 D T

2 D T

3 D U

4 DU

5 D U

6 D U

7 D U

8 D U

9 D U

10 D U

11 D U

12 D V

13 D V

14 D V

15 D V

16 D V

17 D V

18 DV

19 D V

20 D V

21 D V

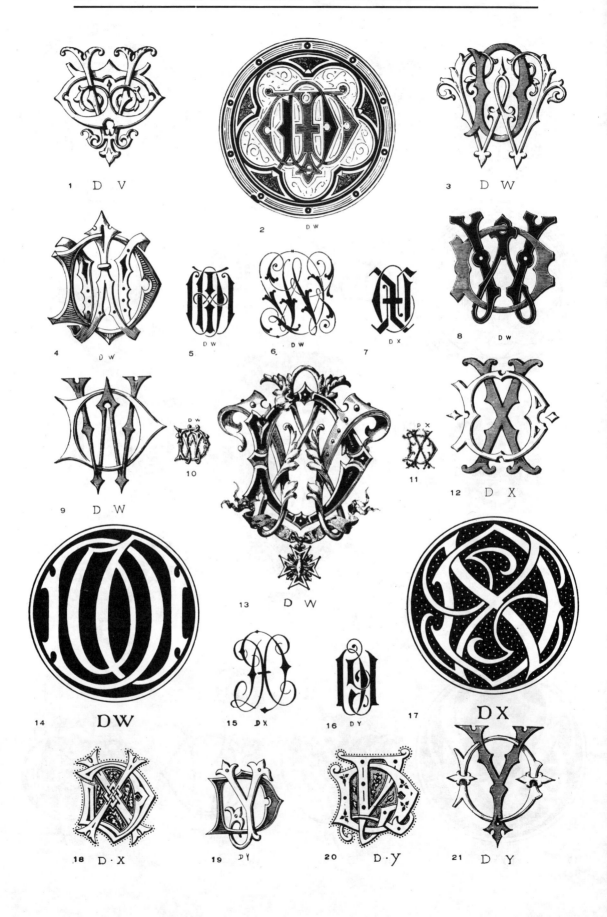

1 D V

2 D W

3 D W

4 D W

5 D W

6 D W

7 D X

8 D W

9 D W

10 D W

11 D X

12 D X

13 D W

14 D W

15 D X

16 D Y

17 D X

18 D · X

19 D Y

20 D · Y

21 D Y

1 DY

2 D Z

3 D Z

4 D Z

5 D Z

6 D Y

7 D Z

8 D Z

9 D Z

10 D Z

11 D&C

12 DAVID

13 DORA

14 D Z

15 DESIRE

16 Daniel.

17 D&Co

18 D&Co

19 D&E

1   E A

2   E

4

5   E A

3   E A

6   E A P

7   EAP

8   EBB

9   EB

10   E B

11   E B. N

12   E B

13   EBB

14   E B

15   E C

16   E C

18   E. C. B.

19   E C

20.   E.C.C.

21   E.C E

22   E.C McD

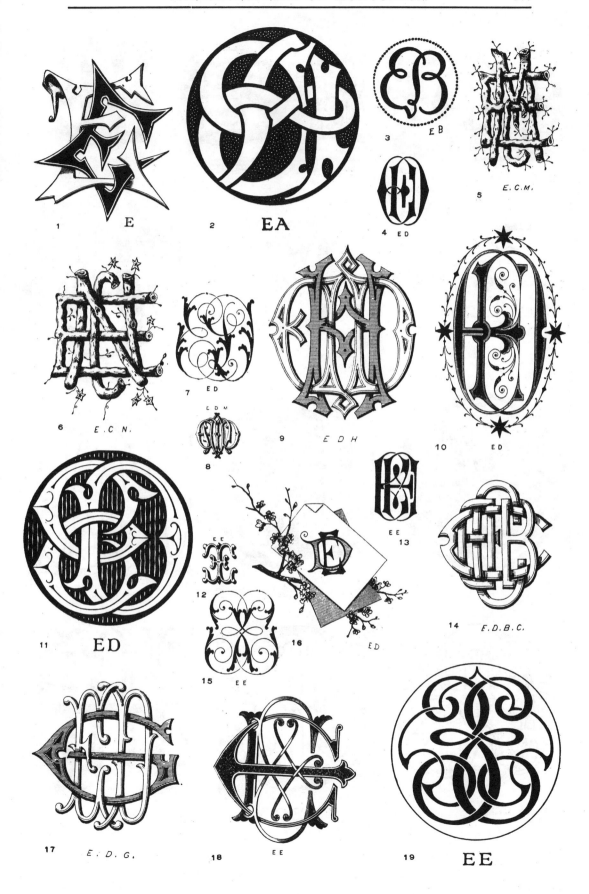

1   E

2   EA

3   E B

4   E D

5   E.C.M.

6   E.C.N.

7   E D

8   E D M

9   E D H

10   E D

11   ED

12   E E

13   E E

14   F.D.B.C.

15   E E

16   E D

17   E.D.G.

18   E E

19   EE

1 E E

2 E E

3 E E

4 EE

5 E E

6 E E

7 EEA

8 EEB

9 EED

10 EEF

11 EEC

12 EEG

13 EEH

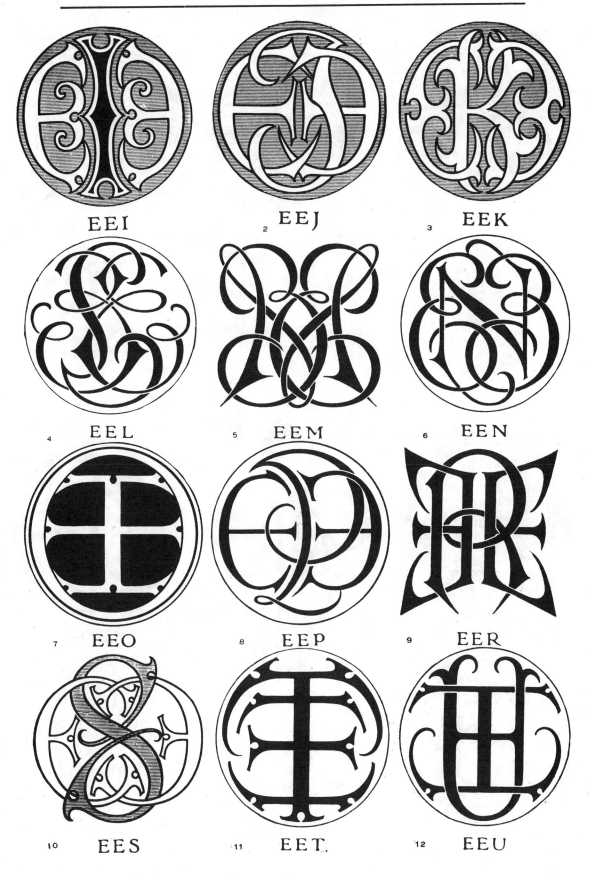

EEI

2 EEJ

3 EEK

4 EEL

5 EEM

6 EEN

7 EEO

8 EEP

9 EER

10 EES

11 EET

12 EEU

1   EEW

2   E F

3   EF

4   E F

5   E F

6   E F

7   E F

8   E F

9   E F

10   E F

11   E F

12   E F G

13   E F G

14   EFG

15   E. F. J.

16   E G

17   E. F. Q.

E C

2   E G   3   E G

4   E G

5   E G

7

6   E G

E C

8   E G

9   E G

10

13   E G

E G C.

14

E G J

15

12   E G H

16   E H

17   E H

11   E . G . I .

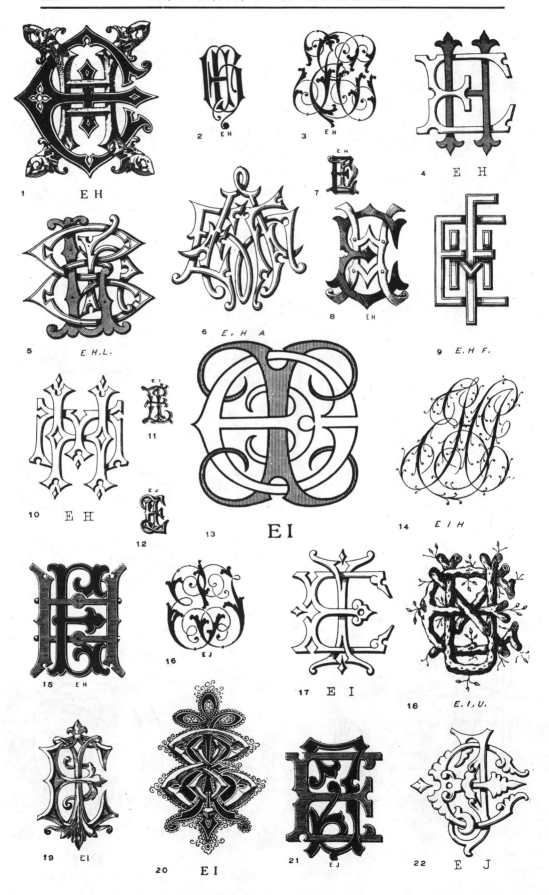

1   E H

2   E H

3   E H

4   E H

5   E H L.

6   E. H A

7   E H

8   E H

9   E. H F.

10   E H

11   E I

12   E J

13   E I

14   E I H

15   E H

16   E J

17   E I

18   E. I. U.

19   E I

20   E I

21   E J

22   E J

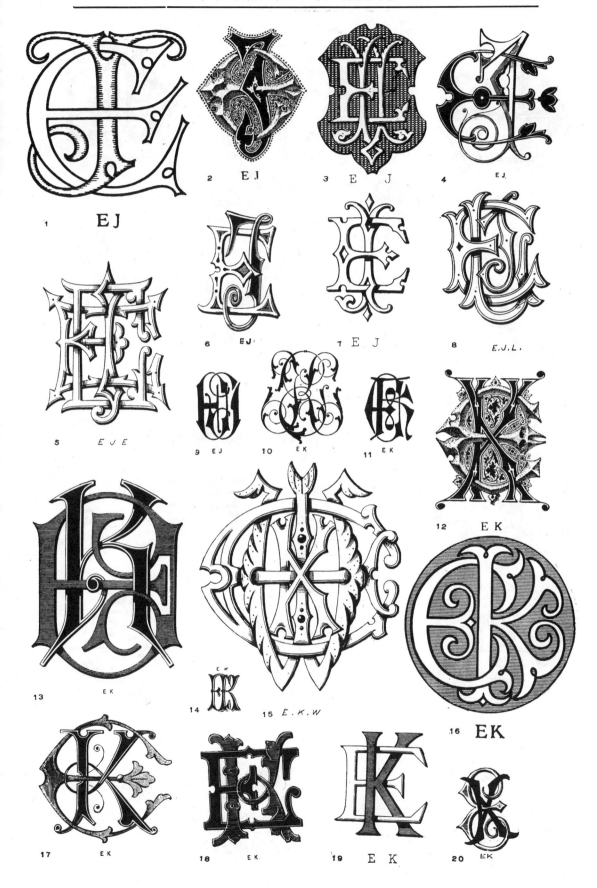

1   E J

2   E J

3   E J

4   E J.

5   E J E

6   E J

7   E J

8   E. J. L.

9   E J

10   E K

11   E K

12   E K

13   E K

14   E K

15   E. K. W

16   E K

17   E K

18   E K

19   E K

20   E K

1   EL

2 EL

3   EL

4

5   E L

6   E L

7   EL

8   EL

9   E L

10   EL

11   EMTLE

12   E L D

13   E L F

14   EL

15   E L J

16   E.L.M.

17   E.M.B.S

18   E.L.P.

9   EM

20   E M

21   E M

22   EM

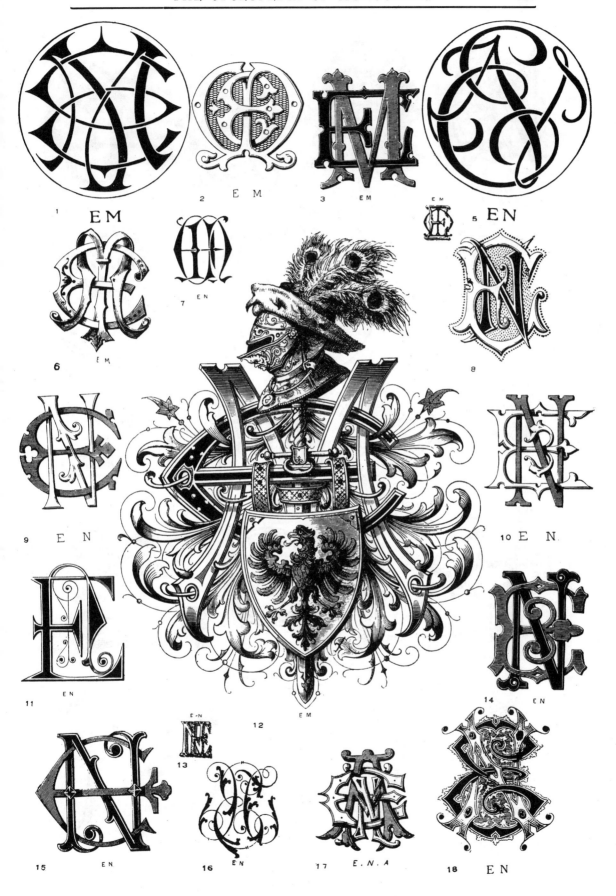

1   E M

2   E M

3   EM

4   EM

5   EN

6   E M

7   E N

8

9   E N

10   E N

11   E N

12   E M

13   E N

14   E N

15   E N

16   E N

17   E. N. A

18   E N

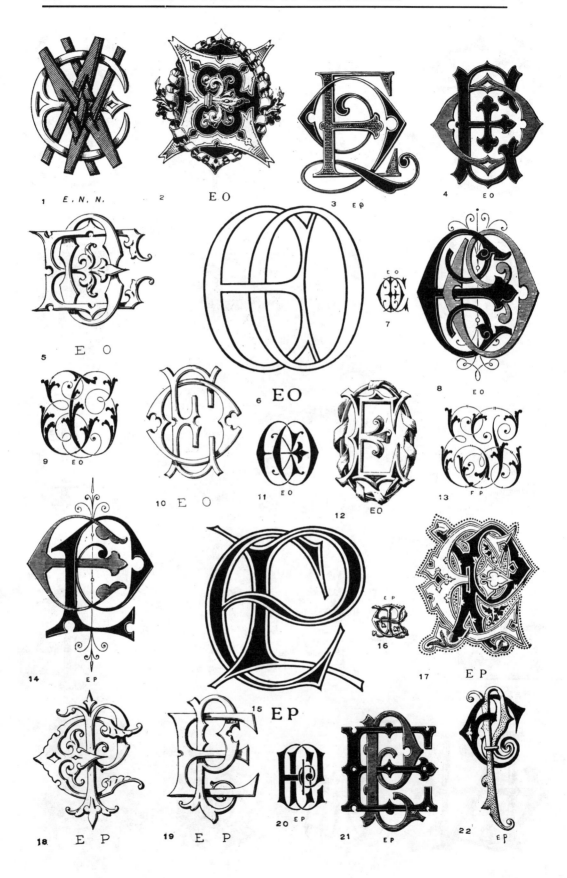

1   E. N. N.

2   E O

3   E P

4   E O

5   E O

6   E O

7   E O

8   E O

9   E O

10   E O

11   E O

12   E O

13   F P

14   E P

15   E P

16   E P

17   E P

18   E P

19   E P

20   E P

21   E P

22   E P

EPF

2   E Q

3

4   EQ

5   EPX

6   ER

7   E Q

8   E Q

9   ER

10   ER

11   EQ

12   EQ

13   ER

14

15   ER

16   EQ

17   E R

18   E R

19   ER

20   E R

21   ERS

22   E R

1   E R W

2   E S

3   ES

4   E S

5   ES

6   E S

7   ES

8   ES

9   ER   AS

10   ES

11   EST

12   ES

13   E.S.R.

14   ES

15   E.S.T.

16   E.S.G.

1 E T

2 E T

3 E T

4 E T

5 E T

6 E T

7 E T

8 E T

9 E T

10 E T A

11 E T C

12 E T S W.

13 E U

14 E T T

15 E U

17 E T

18 E U

19 EU

20 E U

21 E T K

1   E U

2   E U

3   E U

4   E V

5   E

6   E V

7   E V

8   E V

9   E V

10   EV

11   E V

12   E V

13   E V

14   E V

15   EW

16   E W

17

18   E W

19   E W

20   E W

E W

2 E W

3 E W

4 E W

5 EX

6 EX

7 E X

8 E X

9 E Y

10 E X

11 E Y

12 E Y

13 EY

14 E Y

15 E Y

16 E Y

17 E Y

18 E Z

19 E Z

20 EZ

1   E Z

2   E Z

3   E Z

4   E Z

5

6   E Z

E & Co   8

E & D   9

E & F

EUGENE   10

ESTHER   11

EMILE   12   E & G. M.

13

15   Elisabeth

14   Edgar.   16   EDITH

1

2 F

3 FA

4 FA

5 FA

6 FA

7 F A G

8 FB

9 FB

10 FC

11 FC

12 FC

13 FB

14 FB

15 FC

16 FD

17 FD

18 FD

19 FD

1 F E

2 FE

3 FE

4 F.D.L

5 FE

6 FE

7 F. E D.

8 F. E. O

9 F F

10 F F

11 FF

12 FF

13 F.F

14 FF

15 FF

16 FF

17 F F

18 F F

19 FF

1   F. G. D. W.

2   F G

3   F G

4   F G

5   F G H

6   F H

7   FG

8   F G

9   F H

10   F H

11   F G

12   FC

13   F G

14   F H

15   F H

16   F G H

17   F H

18   F. G. Q.

1 FH

2 F H

3 F H

4 F H

5 FI

6 F H

7 F J

8 F I

9 F I I

10 F I

11 F J

12 F J

13 F J

14 F J

15 F J

16 FJ

17 F. J. I. (Franz Josef 1.)

18 F J I

19 F J

1 F.J.S.

2 FK

3 F K

4 FK

5 F K

6 FK

7 F L

8 FL

9 FK

10

11 F K

12 FL

13 F L

14 F L

15 FL

16

17 F L

18 FL

19 F L

20 FL

21 F M

22 FM.

1 FM

2 FM

3 FM

4 FM

5 FM

6 FM

7 F M

8 F M H.

9 F N

10 FM

11

12 F N

13 F N

14.   F N

15

16 F N

17 FN

18 F. N. H. W.

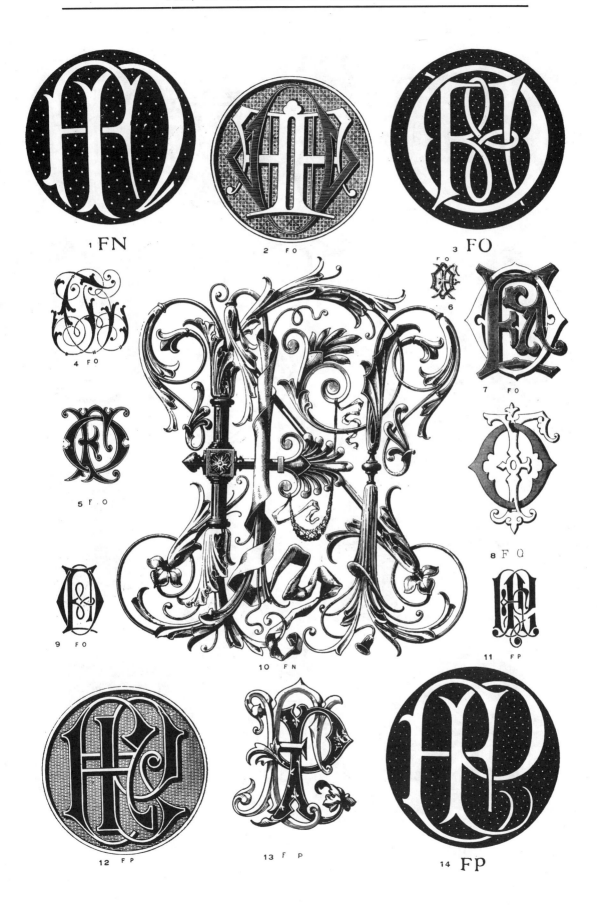

1 FN

2 FO

3 FO

4 FO

5 F O

6 FO

7 FO

8 F O

9 FO

10 FN

11 FP

12 FP

13 F P

14 FP

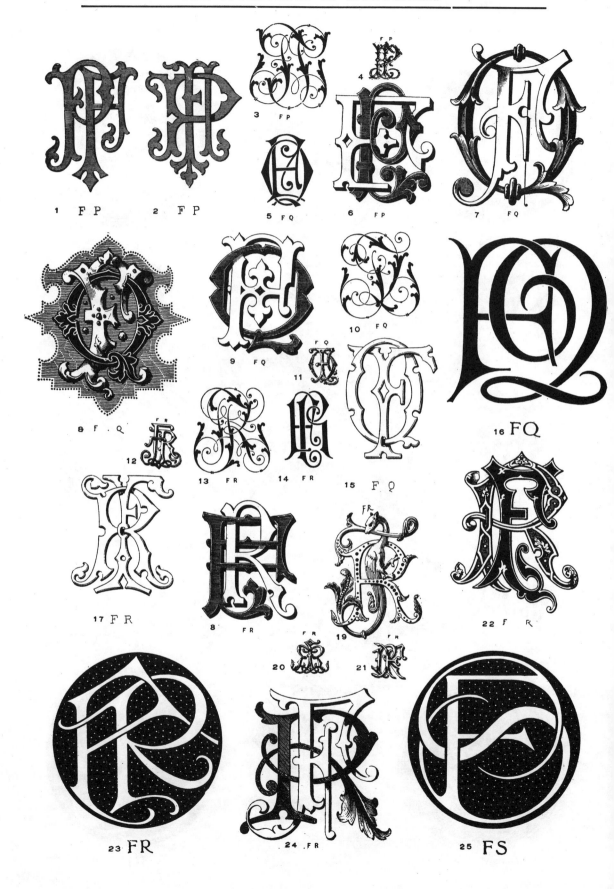

1   F P

2   F P

3   F P

5   F Q

4   F P

6   F P

7   F Q

8   F . Q

9   F Q

10   F Q

11   F Q

12   F R

13   F R

14   F R

15   F Q

16   FQ

17 F R

8   F R

19   F R

20   F R

21   F R

22   F   R

23   FR

24   FR

25   FS

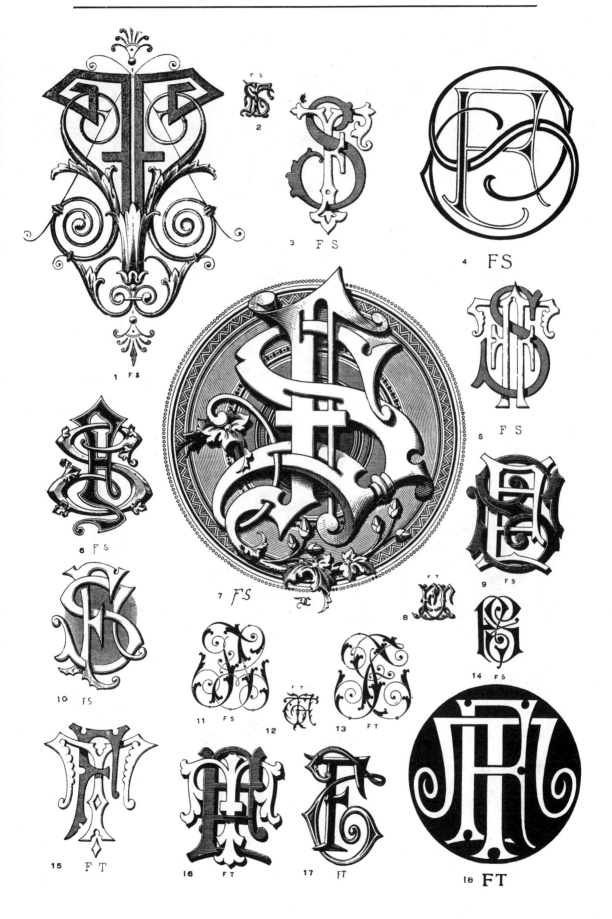

1 F S

F S
2

3 F S

4 FS

5 F S

6 F S

7 FS

8 F T

9 F S

10 FS

11 F S

12 F T

13 F T

14 F S

15 F T

16 F T

17 F T

18 FT

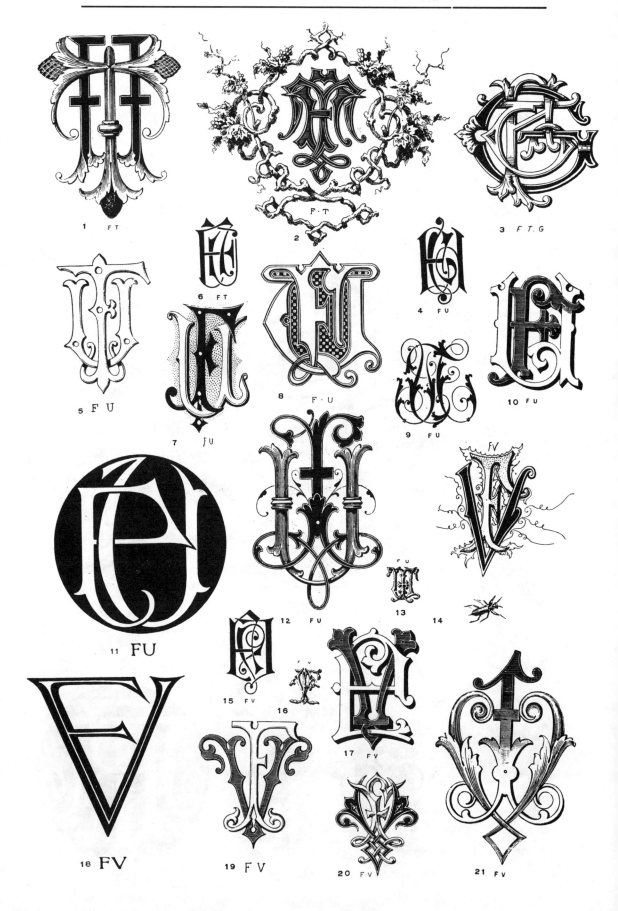

1 FT

2 F·T

3 F·T·G

4 FU

5 FU

6 FT

7 FU

8 FU

9 FU

10 FU

11 FU

12 FU

13 FU

14

15 FV

16 FV

17 FV

18 FV

19 FV

20 FV

21 FV

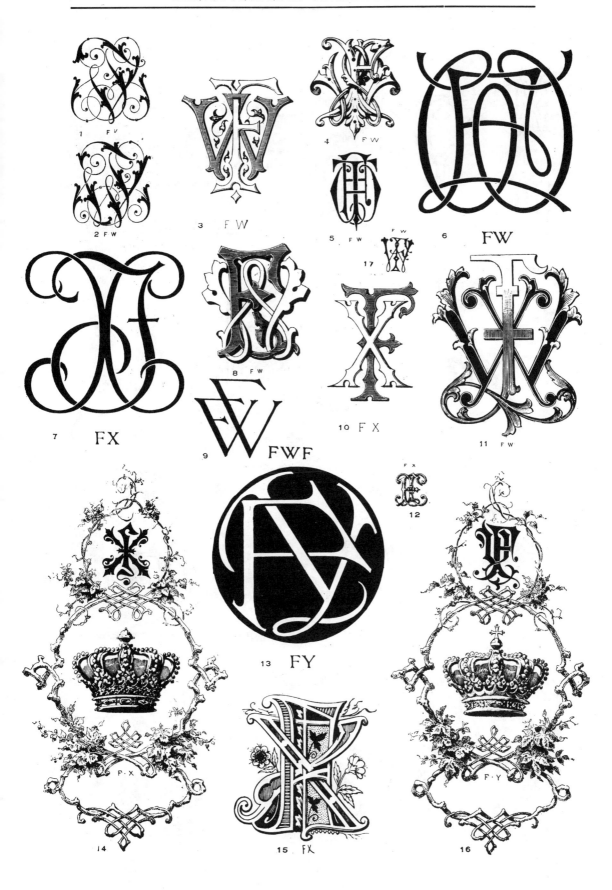

1 FV

2 FW

3 FW

4 FW

5 FW

6 FW

7 FX

8 FW

9 FWF

10 FX

11 FW

12 FX

13 FY

14

15 FX

16

17 FW

1 FX
2 FY
3 FY
4 FZ
5 FY
6 FZ
7 FY
8 FANNY
9 FZ
10 FZ
11 FRANCIS
12 FZ
13 FZ
14 FZ
15 FZ
16 FZ
17 F&E
18 F&G
19 F&CO
20 F&CO

1 FANNY.

2 FLORA.

3 Flora.

4 FREDERIC

5 FRANCES H.B.

1   GA

2   GA

3

4   GA

5   GA

6   G.A.A.W.

7   GA

8   G.A.C.R.

9   G.A.L.

10   G.A.M.

11   G A M

12   GB

13   G.A.Y.

14   G.B

15   GB

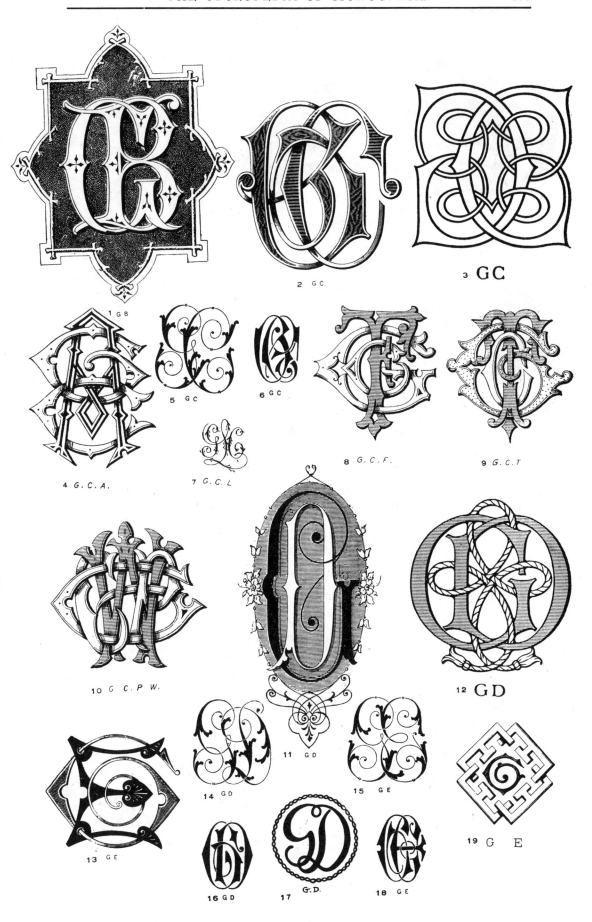

1 G B

2 G C.

3 GC

4 G.C.A.

5 GC

6 GC

7 G.C.L

8 G.C.F.

9 G.C.T

10 G C.P.W.

11 GD

12 GD

13 GE

14 GD

15 GE

16 GD

17 G.D.

18 GE

19 G E

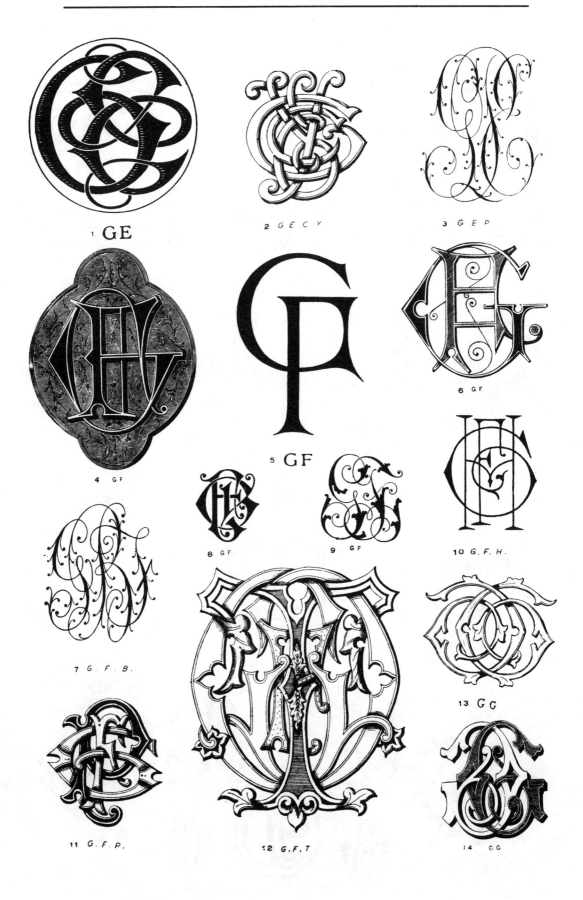

1 GE

2 G E C Y

3 G E P

4 G F

5 GF

6 GF

7 G . F . B .

8 GF

9 GF

10 G. F. H.

11 G . F . P .

12 G.F.T

13 G G

14 G G

1 GG

2 CG

3

4 GG

5 CG

6 GG

7. GG

8 CG

9 GGA

10/ GH

11 GH

12 GH

13 GH.

14 G.H.E.

15 GH

16 GH

17

18 G.H.F.L.

19 GHJ

1 G H N.

2 G. H P.

3 G H R

4 G I

5 GI

6 G. I E

7 G I D.

8 G J

9 G J

10 G J

11 C J

12 G I

13 G J

14 G J

15 G J

16 G J

1   G J

2   G J

3   G . J . F

4   G . J . A .

5   G J

6   G . J . L . V .

7   G K

8   G K

9   G K

10   GK

11   G . K . F . A .

12   G K

13   G K

14   G K

15   G L

16   G L

1   G L

2   G L

3   GL

4   G L

5   G L

6

7   G L H R

8   GM

9

10   GM

11   G M

12   G L N H

13   G M

14   GM

15   G M

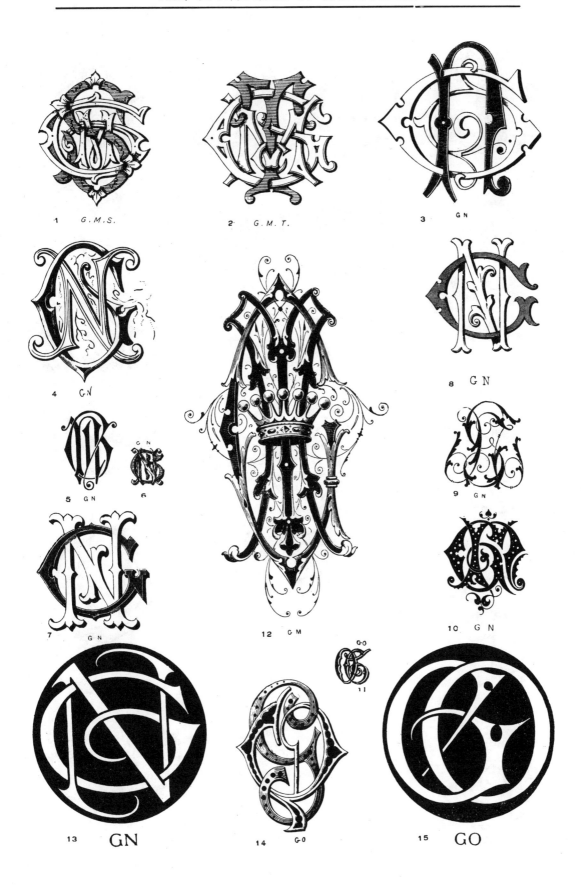

1   G.M.S.

2   G.M.T.

3   G N

4   G N

8   G N

5   G N   6

9   G N

7   G N

12   G M

10   G N

11

13   GN

14   G O

15   GO

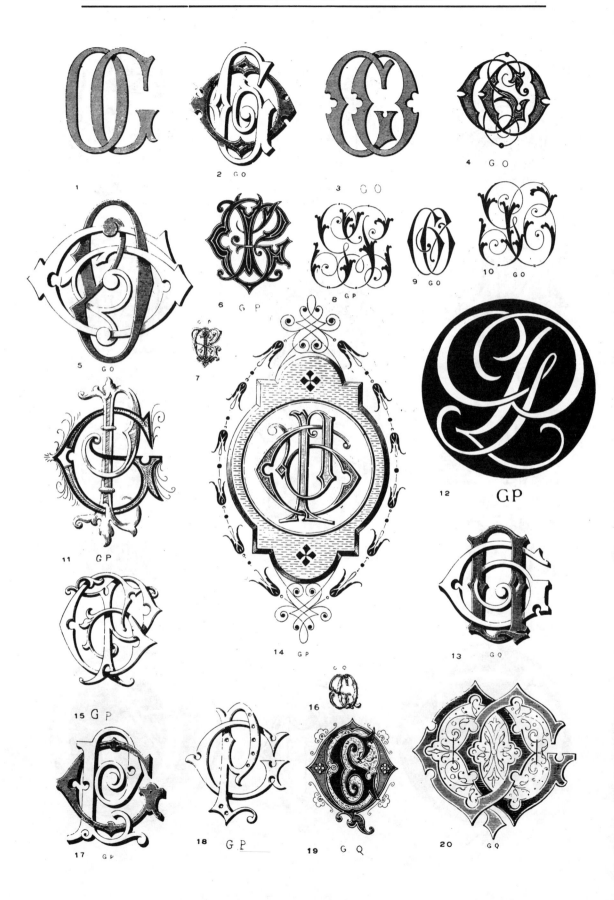

1

2 G O

3 G O

4 G O

5 G O

6 G P

7

8 G P

9 G O

10 G O

11 G P

12 GP

13 G O

14 G P

15 G P

16

17 G P

18 G P

19 G Q

20 G Q

1 G Q

2 GQ

3 GQ

4 GQ

5 GR

6 GR

7 GR

8 GR

9 GR   10 GR

11 GR

12 GR

13 GR

14 GS

15 G.R.C.Y.

16 GS

17 G.R.F.

1 G S

G S

2

3   G S

4   *G.S.P*

5   *G S M*

6   *G S U*

7   G S

8 G S

9   G S

10   GT

11   G T

12   G T

13   G T

14

15   G T

16   G T

G T

2 G T

3 G T

4 G T

5 G.T.O.A

6 GU

7 GU

8

9 GU

10 G U

GU

12 G U

13 GU

14

15 G V

16 G V

17 G V

18 G V

GV

3 GW

5 GV   2 G V   6 GV

4 G W

7 GW

8 GX

GW   10 GW

12 GW

11 G Y

14 G W

15   16 G X   17 G·Y   18 G·X

13 GW   G Y

19 GX   20 G Y   21 GY

GZ

2   G Y. N.

3   GZ

4   GZ

5   GZ

6   GZ

7   G Z

8   GZ

9   G and B.

10   G Z

11   G&F

12

13   G&H

14   G&CO

15   G&CO

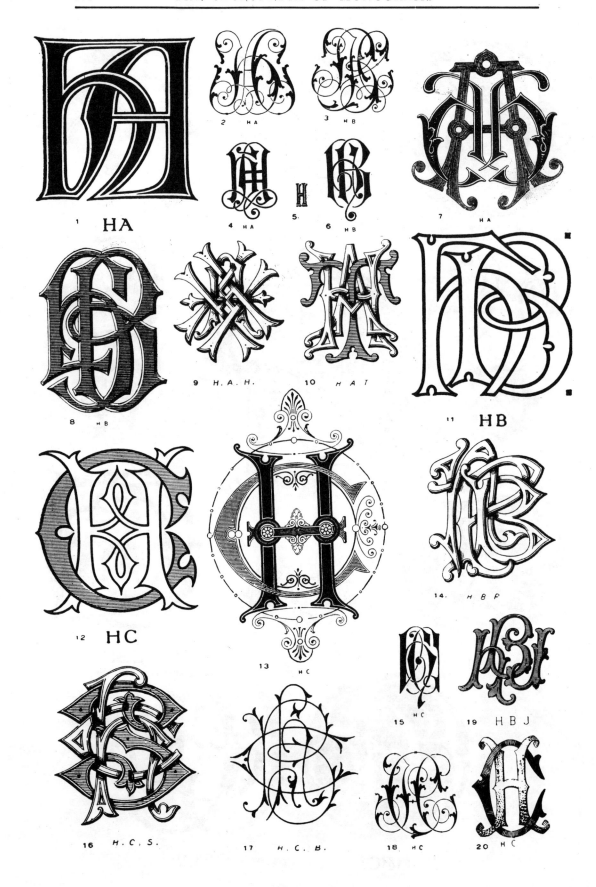

1   HA

2   H B

3   H B

4   HA

5   H

6   H B

7   HA

8   H B

9   H. A. H.

10   H A T

11   HB

12   HC

13   H C

14   H B P

15   H C

16   H. C. S.

17   H. C. B.

18   H C

19   H B J

20   H C

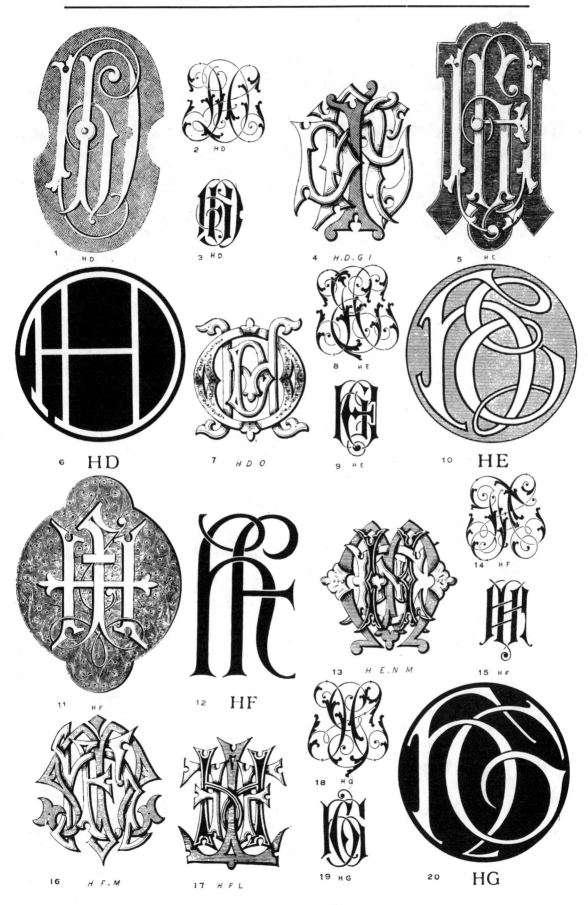

1 HD

2 HD

3 HD

4 H.D.G I

5 HE

6 HD

7 HDO

8 HE

9 HE

10 HE

11 HF

12 HF

13 HE.NM

14 HF

15 HF

16 HF.M

17 HFL

18 HG

19 HG

20 HG

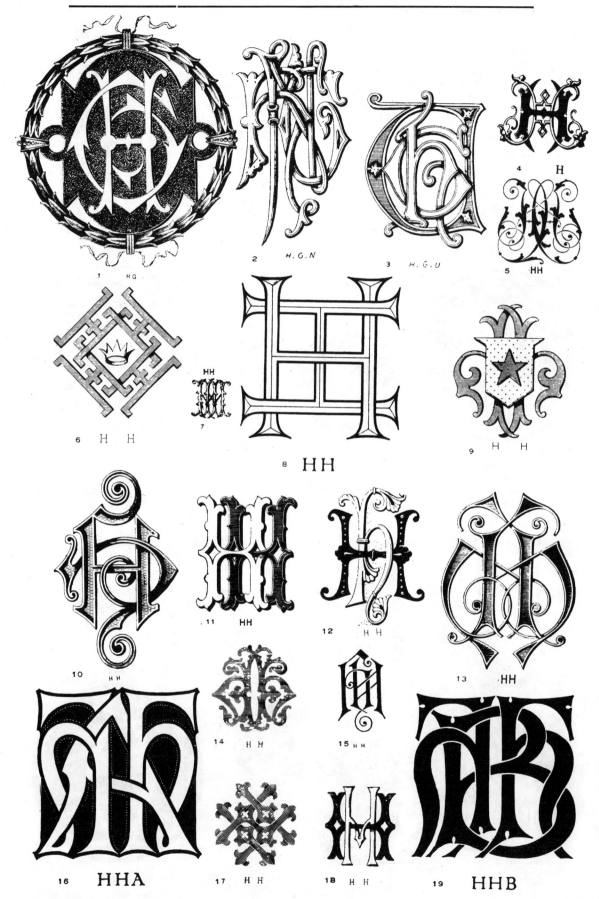

1 HG

2 H.G.N

3 H.G.U

4 H

5 HH

6 H H

7 HH

8 HH

9 H H

10 H H

11 HH

12 H H

13 HH

14 H H

15 H H

16 HHA

17 H H

18 H H

19 HHB

1 HHP 2 HHR 3 HHS

4 HHT 5 HHU 6 HHW

7 HI 8 HJ 9 HIJ

11 HJ 12 H·I 13 HJ 14 HJ 10 15 HJ

1 HJK

2 HJ

3 HJ

4 HJE

5 HJ

6 HK

7 HJ

8 HK

9 HJK

10 HK

11 HK

12 HK

13 HK

14 HL

15 HK

16 HK

17 HL

18 HL

19 HK

HL

21 HL

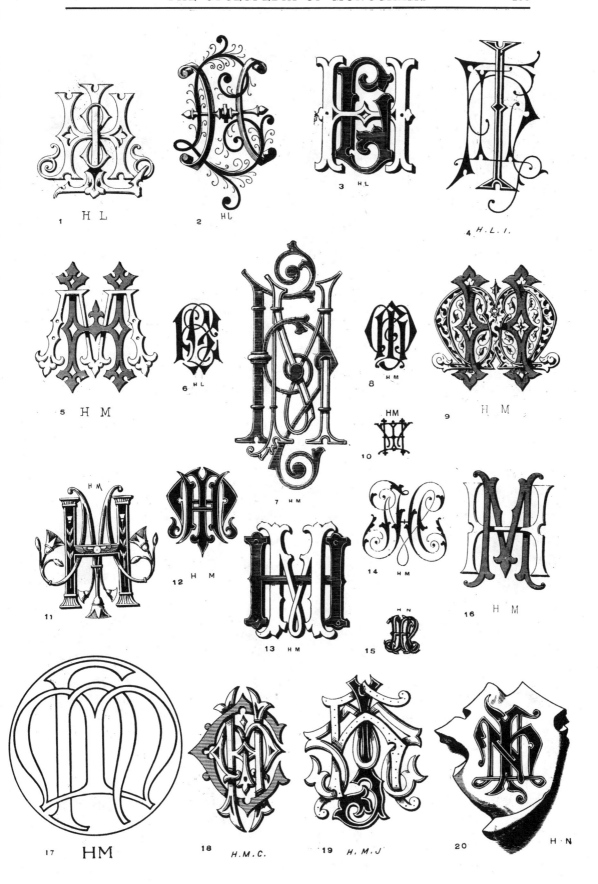

1 H L
2 HL
3 HL
4 H.L.I.
5 H M
6 HL
7 HM
8 HM
9 H M
10 HM
11 HM
12 HM
13 HM
14 HM
15 HN
16 H M
17 HM
18 H.M.C.
19 H.M.J
20 H·N

1   HN
2
3   HN
4 HN
5
6 HN
7 HN
8 HN
9 H.N.H.
10 HO
11 HO
12 HO
13 HO
14 HNF.
15 HO
16 HO
17 HO
18 HO
19 HO
20 HO

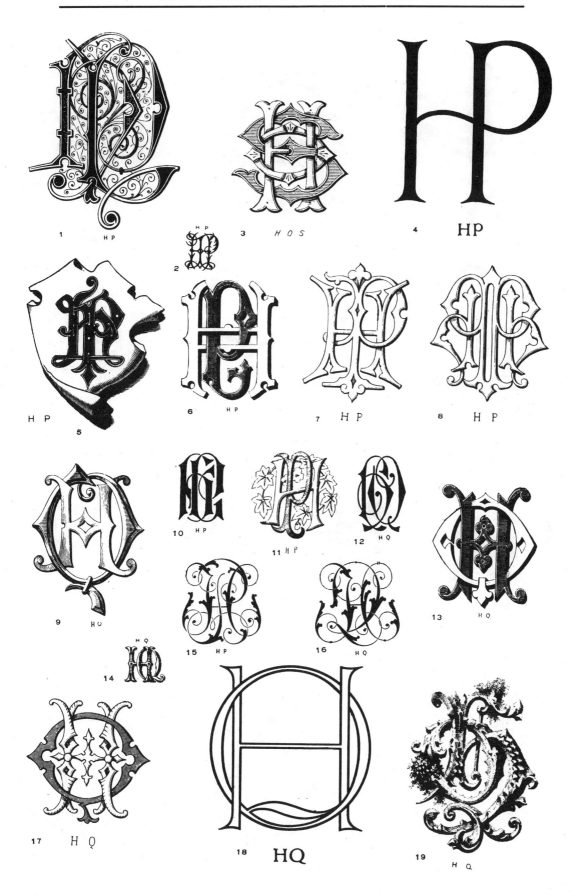

1   H P

2

3   *H O S*

4   HP

H P
5

6   H P

7   H P

8   H P

9   H Q

10   H P

11   H P

12   H Q

13   H Q

14   H Q

15   H P

16   H Q

17   H Q

18   HQ

19   H Q

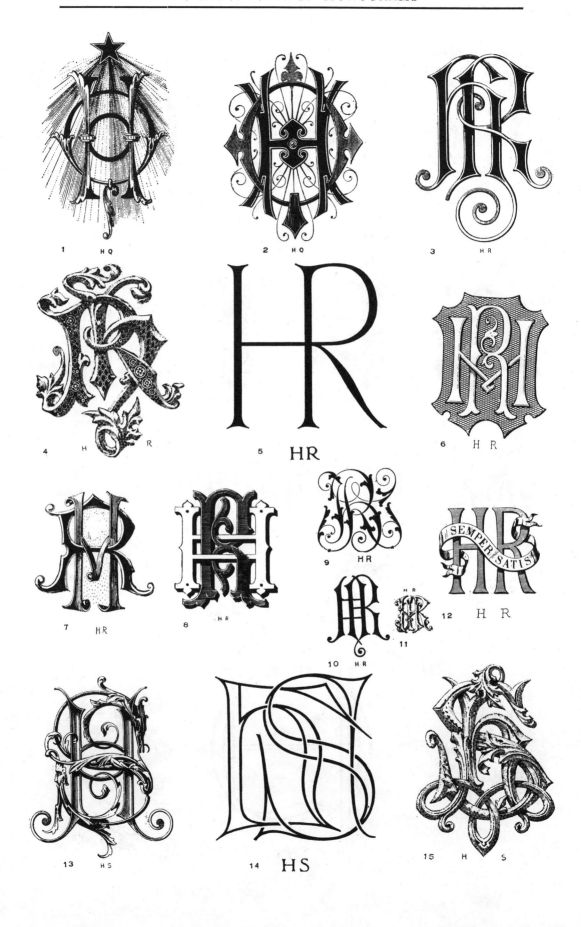

1   HQ

2   HQ

3   HR

4   H   R

5   HR

6   HR

7   HR

8   HR

9   HR

10   HR

11

12   H R

13   HS

14   HS

15   H   S

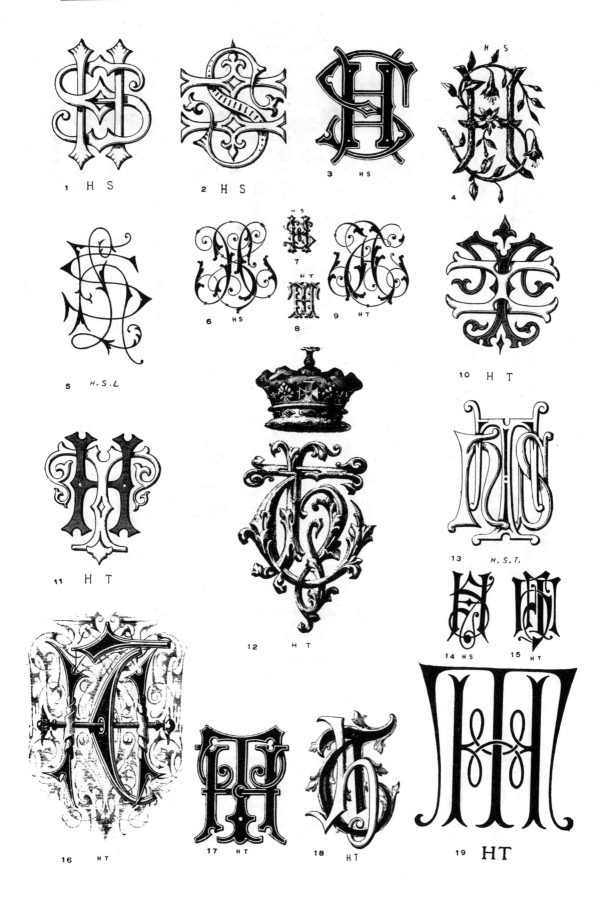

1 H S
2 H S
3 H S
4
5 H.S.L
6 H S
7
8
9 H T
10 H T
11 H T
12 H T
13 H.S.T.
14 H S
15 H T
16 H T
17 H T
18 H T
19 H T

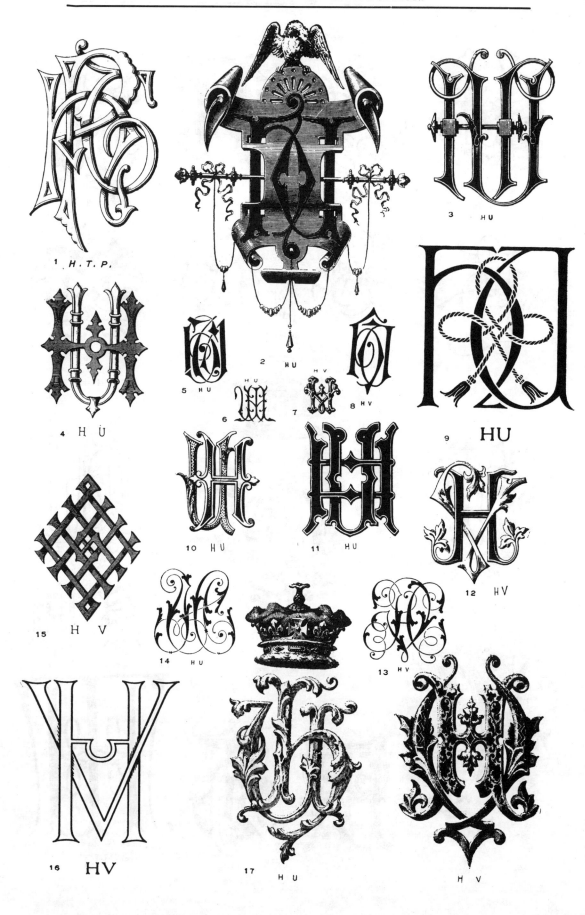

1   H. T. P.

2   HU

3   HU

4   H U

5   HU

6

7

8   HV

9   HU

10   HU

11   HU

12   HV

13   HV

14   HU

15   H V

16   HV

17   HU

HV

1   H V

2   H V

3   H W

4   HW

5   H V

6   HW

7   H W

8   H W

9   H W

10   H W

11   H · W

12   H.W.E.

13   HWL

14   H.W.Y.

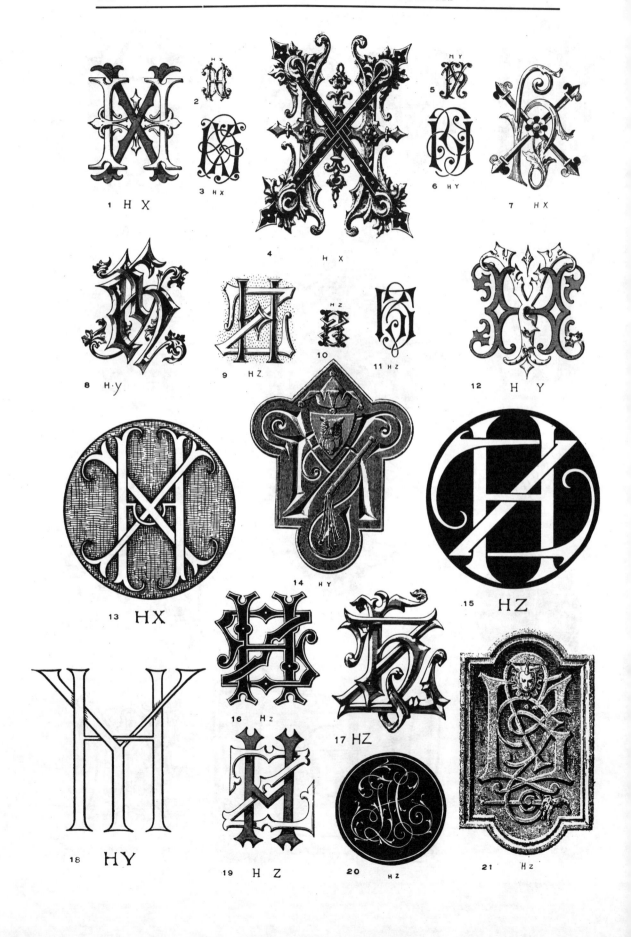

1 H X

2

3 HX

4   H X

5

6 H Y

7   H X

8 H·Y

9   H Z

10

11 H Z

12   H Y

13   HX

14   H Y

15   HZ

16   Hz

17 HZ

18   HY

19   H Z

20   HZ

21   Hz

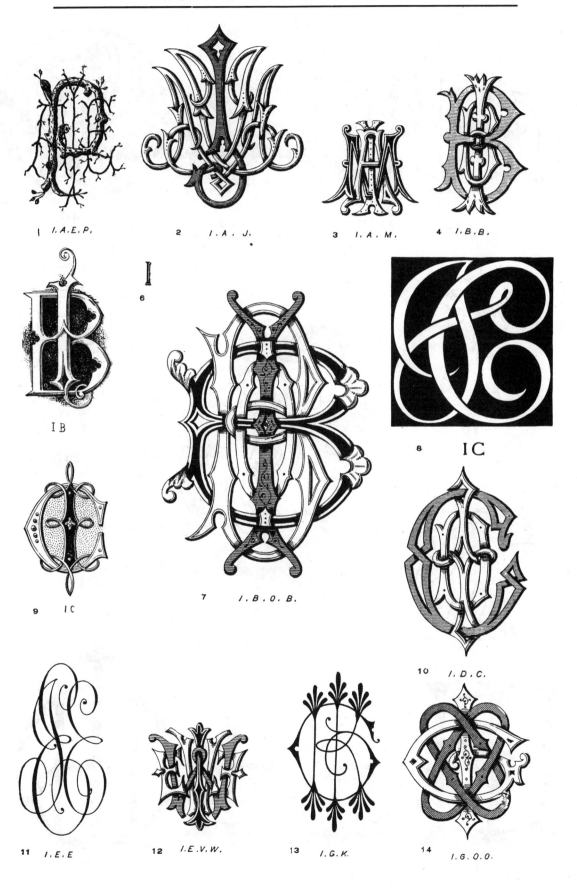

1   *I.A.E.P.*

2   *I.A.J.*

3   *I.A.M.*

4   *I.B.B.*

I B

6   I

8   IC

9   IC

7   *I.B.O.B.*

10   *I.D.C.*

11   *I.E.E*

12   *I.E.V.W.*

13   *I.G.K.*

14   *I.G.O.O.*

1 *I. G. R*   2 IHC   3   4 IHC

5 *I H E*   6 IHS

7 IHS   8 *I H S*   9 IHS

10 IHS   11 IHS   12 IHS   13 IHS

1 I J
2 I J
3 I J
4 I J
5 I K
6 I J
7
8 I K
9 I K
10 I K
11 I K
12 I L
13 I L
14 I J K
15 M I
16 I M
17 I L
18 I M
19 I L
20 I M
21 I. M. O
22 I. M. H. M.

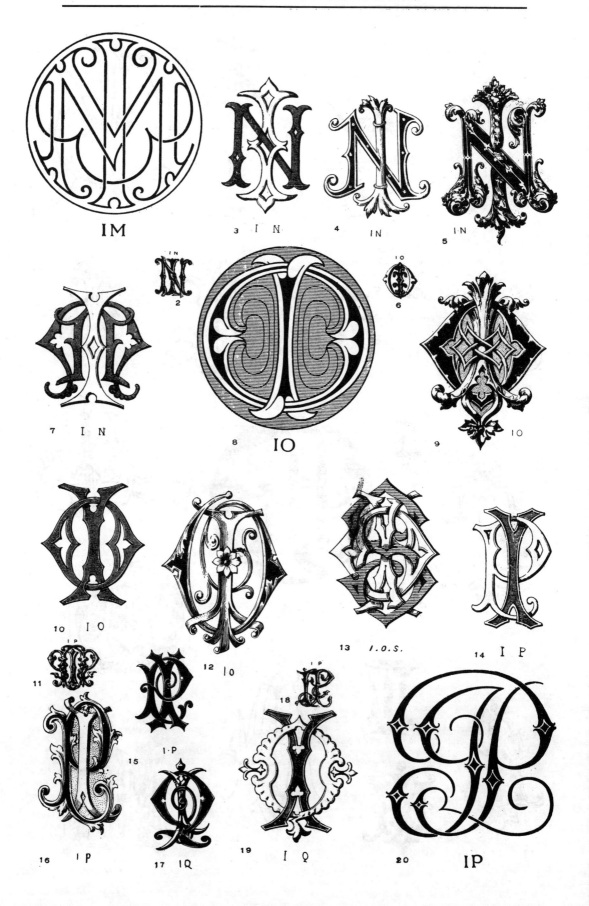

IM

3 I N

4 IN

IN
5

IN
2

7 I N

8 IO

10
6

10
9

10 I O

12 IO

13 *I.O.S.*

14 I P

11

15

18

16 I P

17 IQ

19 I Q

20 IP

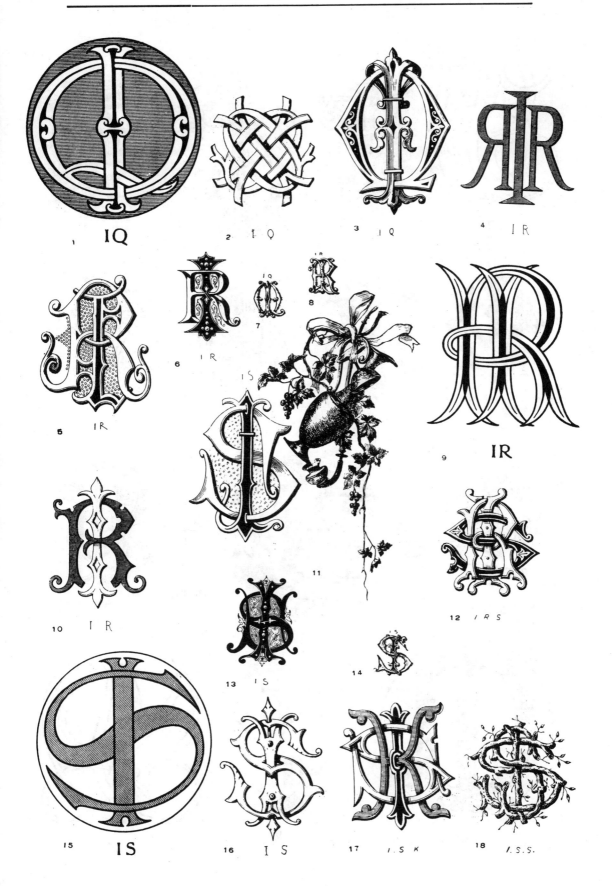

1 IQ
2 IQ
3 IQ
4 IR
5 IR
6 IR
7 IQ
8 IR
9 IR
10 IR
11 IS
12 IRS
13 IS
14 IS
15 IS
16 IS
17 ISK
18 I.S.S.

IT

2 IT

3

4 IT

5 IV

6 IU

7 IU

8 IV

9 IT

10

11 IU

12 IU

13 IV

14 IV

15 IU

16 IW

IV

1 IW

2 IW

3 IW

4 IW

5 I X

6 IX

7 IY

8 IX

9 IZ

10 IY

11 IZ

12 IY

13 I Y

14 IZ

15 I Z

16 I&Co

17 IZ

18 IY

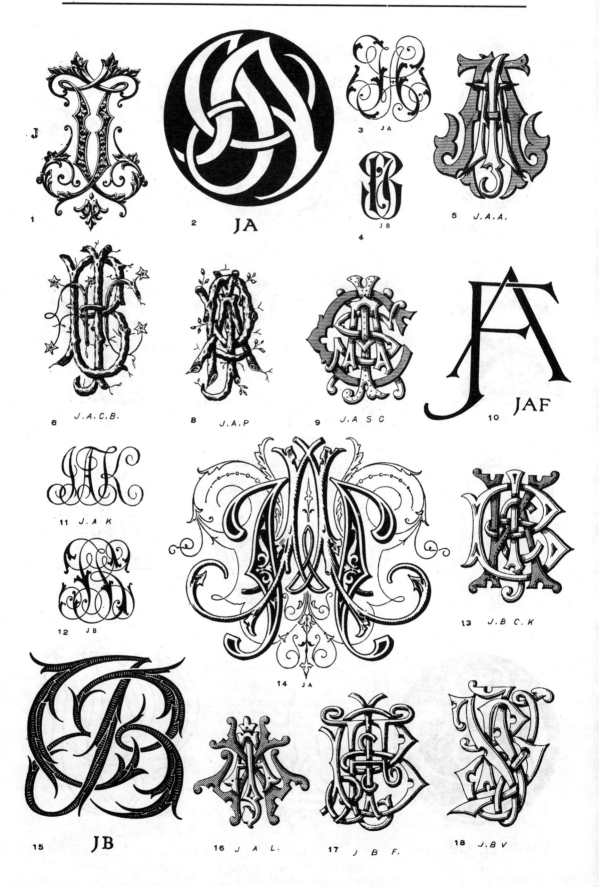

1   J

2   JA

3   JA

4   J B

5   J.A.A.

6   J.A.C.B.

8   J.A.P

9   J.A.S C

10   JAF

11   J.A K

12   J B

13   J.B C.K

14   JA

15   JB

16   J A L.

17   J B F.

18   J.B V

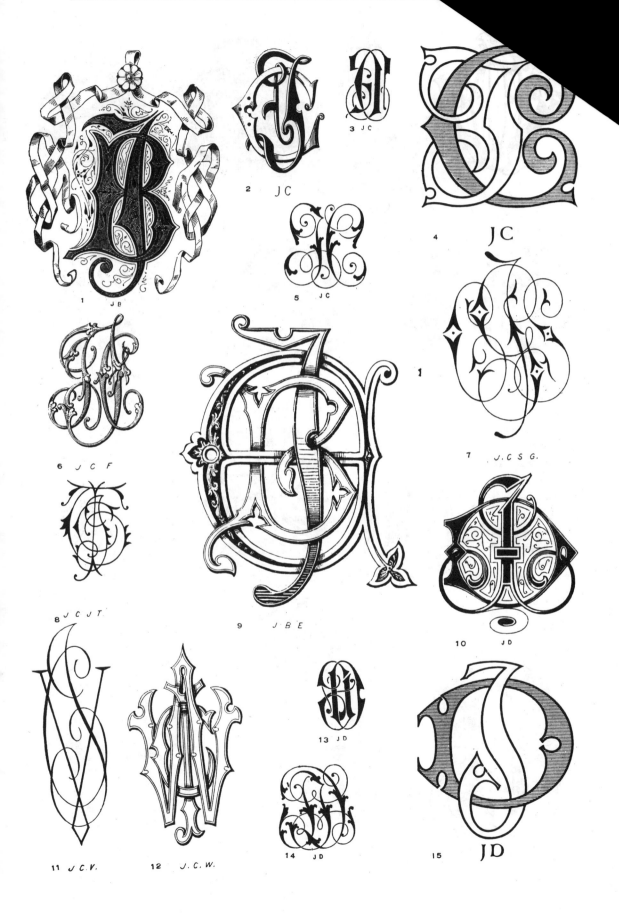

1   J B

2   J C

3   J C

4   J C

5   J C

6   J C F

7   J C S G.

8   J C J T

9   J B E

10   J D

11   J C V.

12   J. C. W.

13   J D

14   J D

15   J D

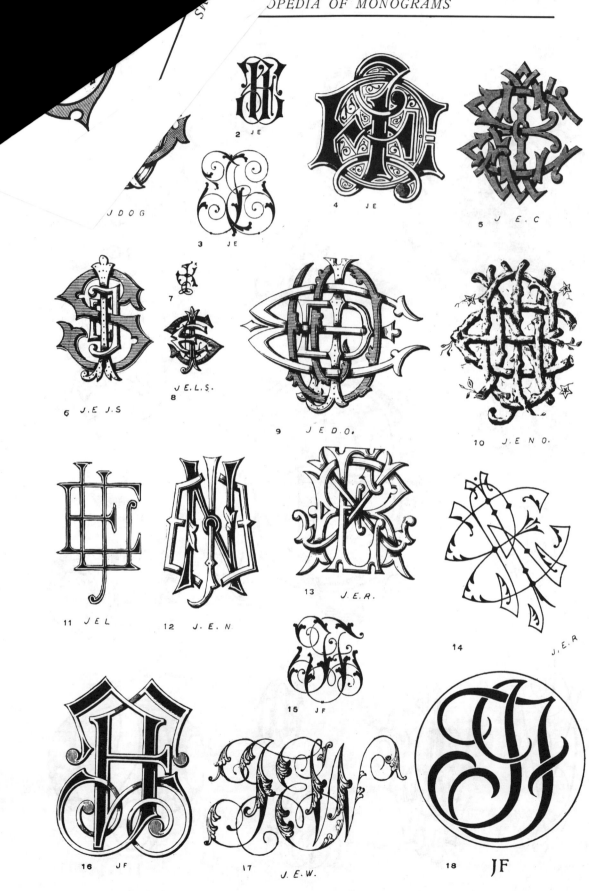

2 J E

J D O G

3 J E

4 J E

5 J. E. C.

6 J.E J.S

7

J.E.L.S.
8

9 J E D O.

10 J.E N O.

11 J E L

12 J. E. N.

13 J. E. R.

14 J. E. R

15 J F

16 J F

17 J. E. W.

18 JF

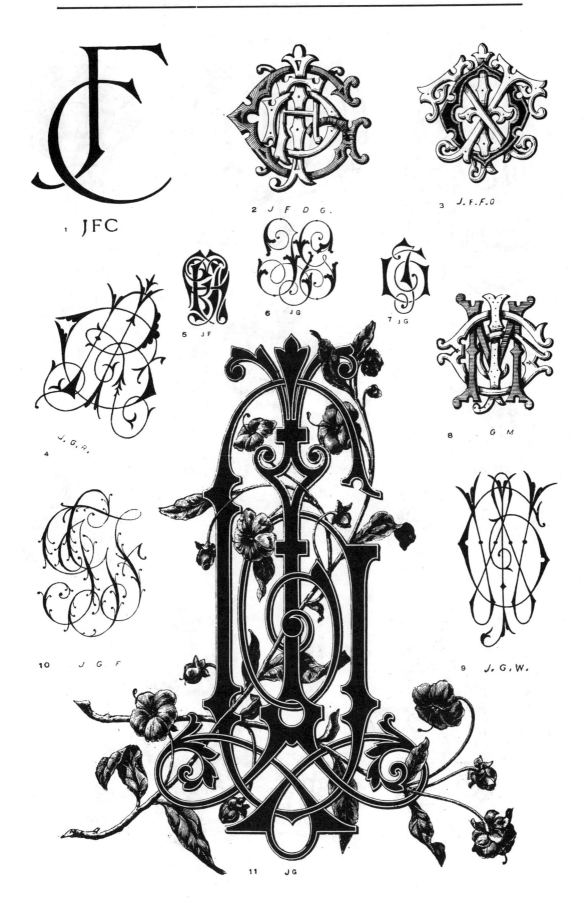

1 JFC

2 J F D G.

3 J.F.F.O

5 JF

6 JG

7 JG

4 J.G.R.

8 G M

10 J G F

9 J.G.W.

11 JG

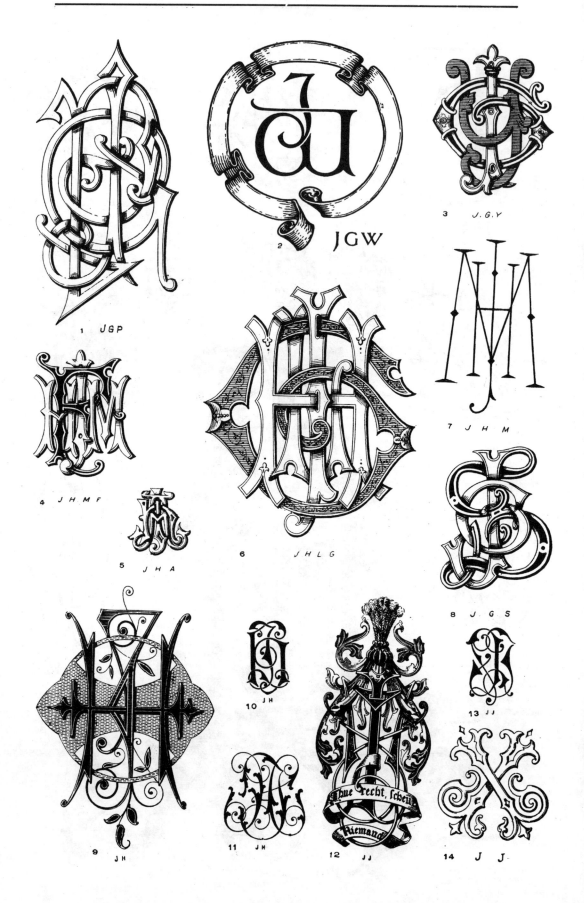

1 J G P

2 JGW

3 J. G. Y

4 J H M F

5 J H A

6 J H L G

7 J H M

8 J G S

9 J H

10 J H

11 J H

12 J J

13 J J

14 J   J

1　J K

2　JL

3　J K

6　J K

4　JL

5　J L

7　J K

8　J L

9　JL

11　JL

13　J K L

10　J K

12　J M

14　J M

15　J L

16　JL

17　J K

18　J M

19　J M

20　JL

21　J. MᶜL.

22　J M

23　J M

JO

2 *J.O.Y.*

3 *J.O.S*

4 J P

5 J P

6 J Q

7 J P

8 J P

9 *J.P.H.*

10 J P

11 J P

12 J P

13 J Q

15 J Q

16 J P

17 *J.P.L*

18

19 J Q

JP

20 JQ

21 *J.P.T.*

22 J Q

23 J Q

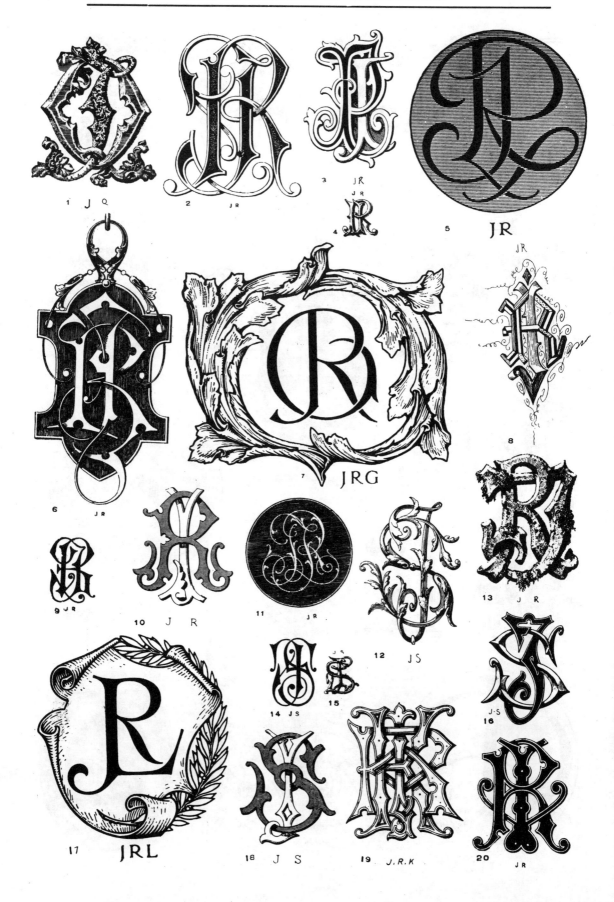

1 J Q

2 JR

3 JR

4 JR

5 JR

6 JR

7 JRG

8 JR

9 JR

10 J R

11 JR

12 JS

13 J R

14 JS

15

16 J·S

17 JRL

18 J S

19 J.R.K

20 JR

1 JS

2 J S

3 J S

4 J.S.M.

5 JT

6 JS

7 JS

8 JT

9 JSN

10 JT

11 J T

12 JT

13 J T

14 JT

15 J.T.W.

16 JT

17 JU

18 JT

19 JU

20 JT

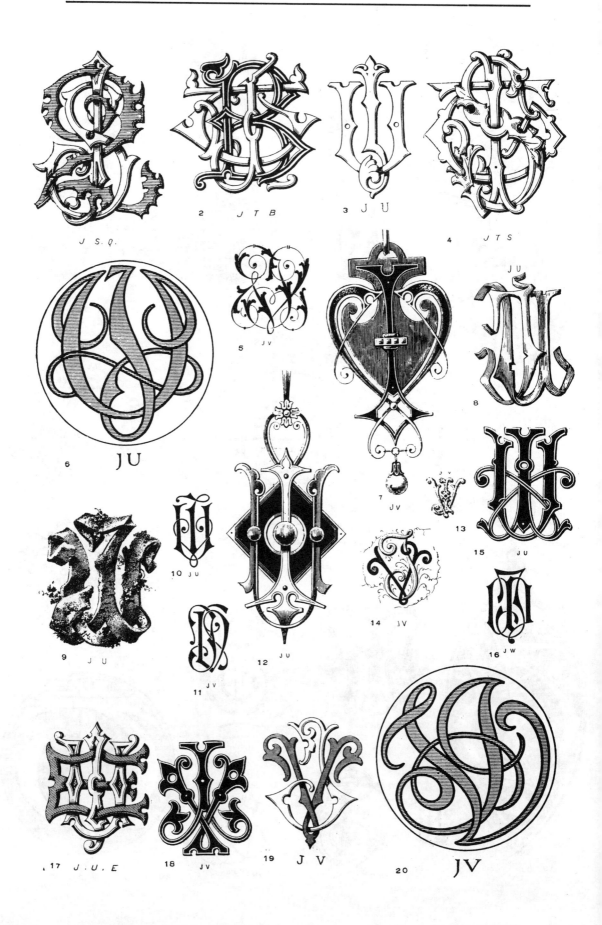

J S Q.

2   J T B

3   J U

4   J T S

J U

5   J V

6   J U

7   J V

8

9   J U

10   J U

11   J V

12   J U

13

14   J V

15   J U

16   J W

,17   J . U . E

18   J V

19   J V

20   J V

1   J W

2   J V

3   J W

4   J W

5   J W

6   J.W.P.

7   J W

8   J W

9   J X

10   J.W.H

11   J X

12   J Y

13   J X

14   J W

15   J Y

16   J W

17   J X

18   J X

19   J Y

20   J X

1   JY

2   J W

3   J Y

4   J Z

5   JZ

6   J Z.

7   J & Co

8   JZ

9   JAMES S

10   J Z

11   J.Y.

12   J & Co

13   JAMES Z

14   JZ

15   J & R

16   J & K

17   JACK.

18   J Z

19   JZ

20   JZ

1 KA

2 KA

3 KB

4 KA

5 K

6 KB

7 KA

8 KB

9 KB

10 KC

11 KC

12 KC

13 KC

14 KC

15 KD

1   K C T

2   K D

3   K D

4   K E

5   K D

6   KD

7   KE

8   K E

9   K F

10   K E

11   KF

12   K F

13   K F

14   K G

15   KG

16   KH

17   K G

18   K G

19   K H

20   K H

1   KH

2   KJ

3   KI

4   K.H.MᶜE.

5   KJ   6   KJ

7   KK   8   KK

9   KK   10   KK   11   K K

15   KK

12   KK   13   K K   14   K K   16   KK

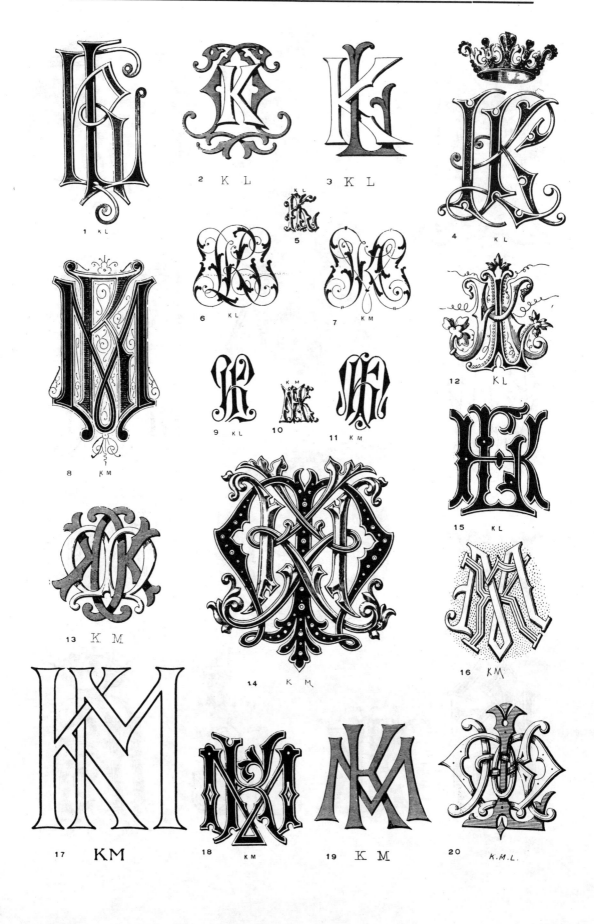

1 K L

2 K L

3 K L

4 K L

5

6 K L

7 K M

8 K M

9 K L

10

11 K M

12 K L

13 K M

14 K M

15 K L

16 K M

17 KM

18 K M

19 K M

20 K.M.L.

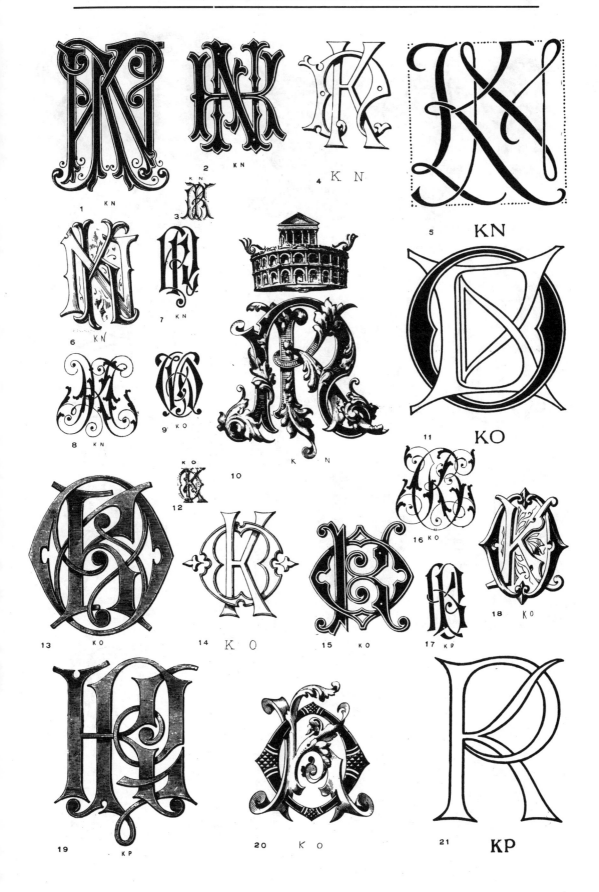

1 KN

2 KN

3

4 K N

5 KN

6 KN

7 KN

8 KN

9 KO

10

11 KO

12 KO

13 KO

14 KO

15 KO

16 KO

17 K9

18 KO

19 KP

20 KO

21 KP

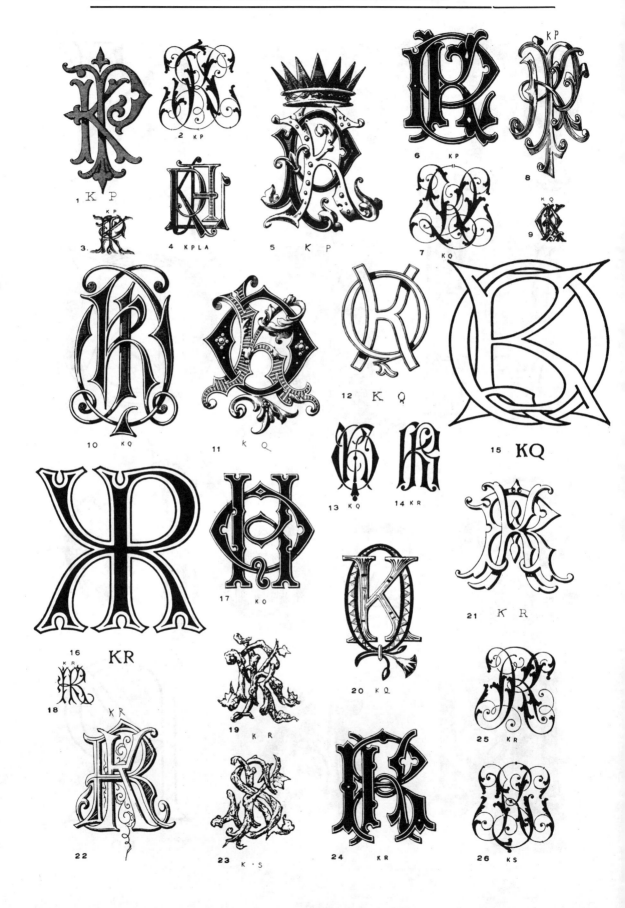

1 K P
2 KP
3 KP
4 KPLA
5 KP
6 KP
7 KQ
8 KP
9 KQ
10 KQ
11 KQ
12 KQ
13 KQ
14 KR
15 KQ
16 KR
17 KQ
18 KR
19 KR
20 KQ
21 KR
22
23 K·S
24 KR
25 KR
26 KS

KS

2 K S

3 K S

4 K S

5 K S B

6

7 K S

8 K T

9 K T

10 K. T. D

11 k T

12 K I

13

14 KT

15 K T

16 K T

1 K. T. G.

2 K. T. I.

3 K U

KU

5 K U

6 K U

7 K U

8 K U

Cᵐᶜ Mˡᵉ de la V.-de VERSAILLES

9 K U

10 K V

11 K U

12 K V

13 K U

14 K V

15 K V

16 K V

17 K V

18

19 K V

20 K V

21 K V

22 K W

23 K W

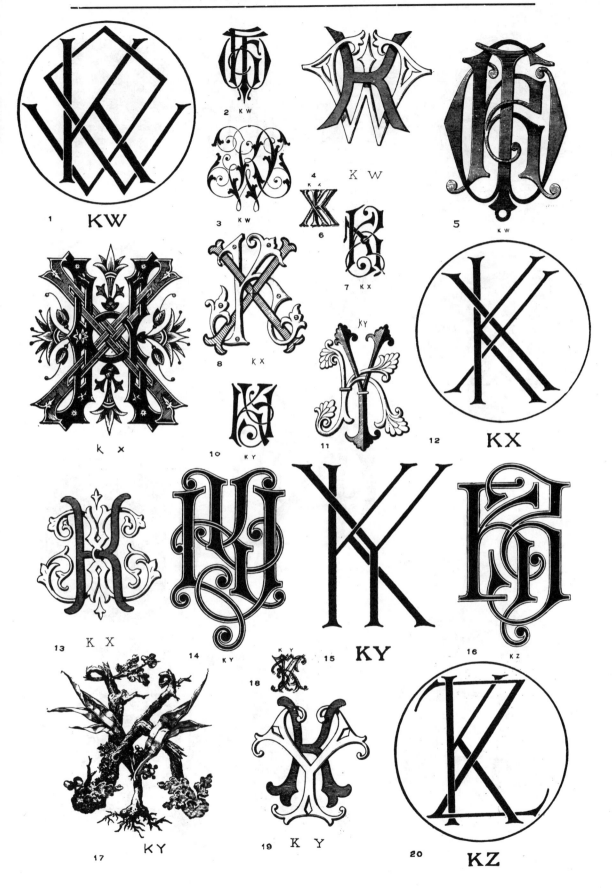

1   KW

2   KW

3   KW

4   KW

5   KW

6

7   KX

8   KX

k x

10   KY

11

12   KX

13   KX

14   KY

15   KY

16   KZ

17   KY

18

19   KY

20   KZ

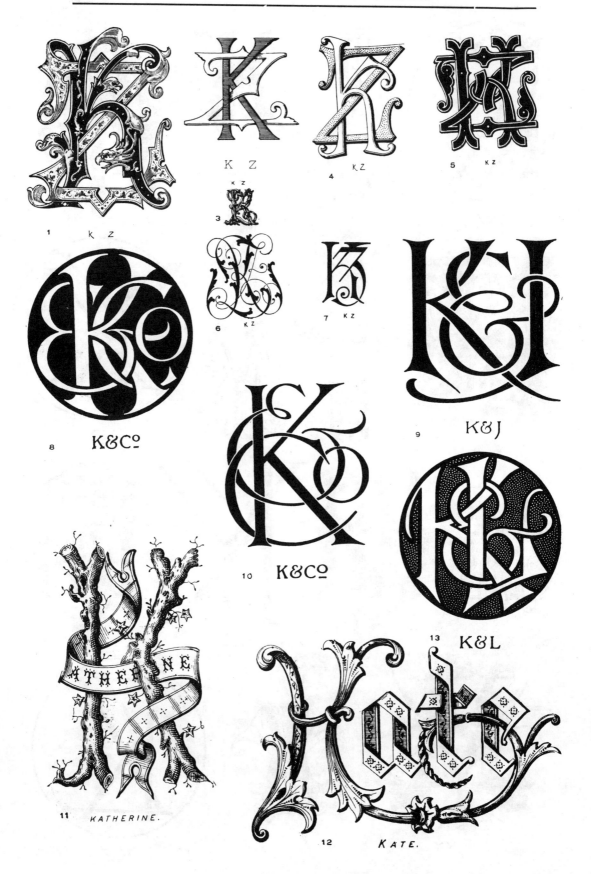

1 K Z

K Z

3 K Z

4 K Z

5 K Z

6 K Z

7 K Z

8 K&Cº

9 K&J

10 K&Cº

11 KATHERINE.

12 KATE.

13 K&L

1 L

2 L

3 LA

4 LA

5 L.A.F

6 LA

7 LB

8 LB

9 LA

10 LB

11 LC

12 LB

13 LC

14 LD

15 LC

16 LD

17 LC

18 L.E.R.O.

19 LD

20 LC

LE

2 L E C

LE 3

5 LE

4 LF

6 LG

9 LE

7 LG

10 LF

8 LD

11 L.E.B.

12 L.G.D.

13 LF

LF

2 LG

3 LFA

LFA

4 L.H.A.P

5 LH

6 LH

7 LJ

8 LH

10 LG

9 LH

11 LF

1   LJ

2   LK

3   LJ

4   L L

5   LL

6   LK

7   L L

8   LK

9   LL

10   LM

11   LL

12   LJ

13   LL

14   LL

15   LL

16   L. K. N. G.

17   LL

18   LL

1 L M

2 LM

3 L M

4 LM

5 LM

6 LN

7 L.M.W.

8

9 LN

10 LM

11 LN

12 LN

13 L N

14 L N

15

16 LN

17 L N F

18 LN

19 LO

20 LO

21 LO

22 L N

23 LO

24 LO

25 LO

26 LO

LP

2   LO

3   L P

4   LPP

5   L O

6   LP

7   LP

8   L P

9   LP

22   L P

11   L P

10   LP

12   LP

13   LP

14   L P

15

16   L Q

17   L Q

18   LP

19   L Q

20   L Q

21   L Q

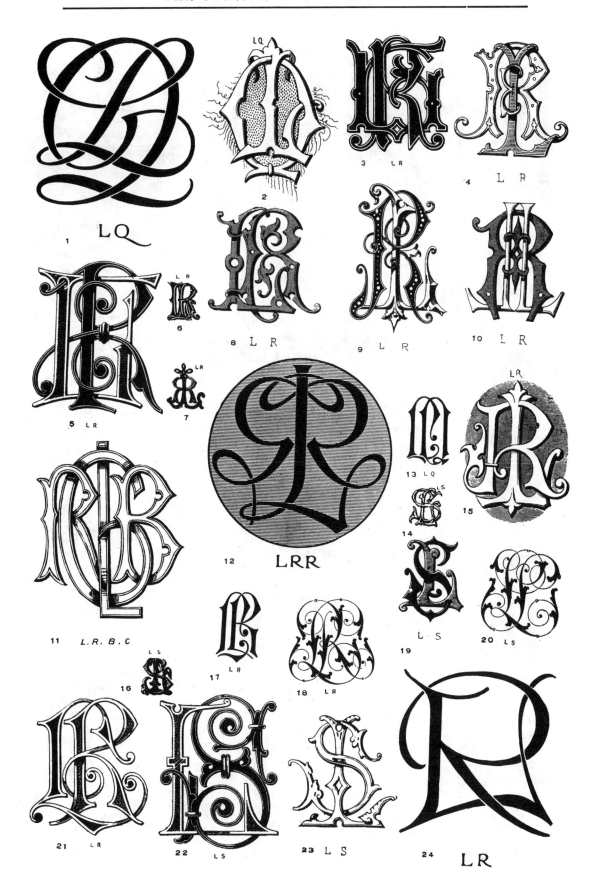

1 LQ

2

3 LR

4 L R

5 LR

6 LR

7 LR

8 LR

9 L R

10 LR

11 L.R.B.C

12 LRR

13 LQ

14 LS

15 LR

16 LS

17 LR

18 LR

19

20 LS

21 LR

22 LS

23 LS

24 LR

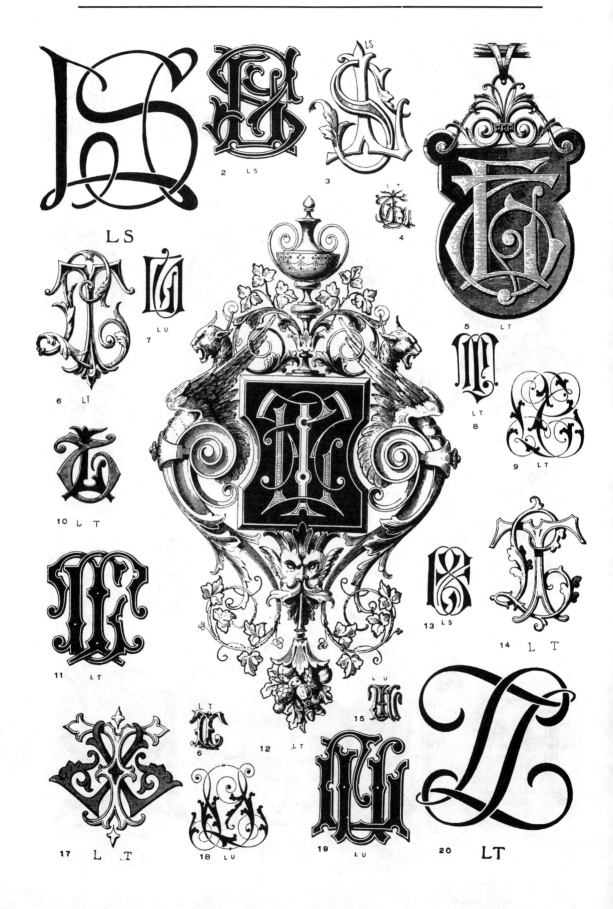

LS

2 LS

3

4 LT

5 LT

6 LT

7 LU

8 LT

9 LT

10 L T

11 LT

12 LT 6

13 LS

14 L T

15 LU

17 L T

18 LU

19 LU

20 LT

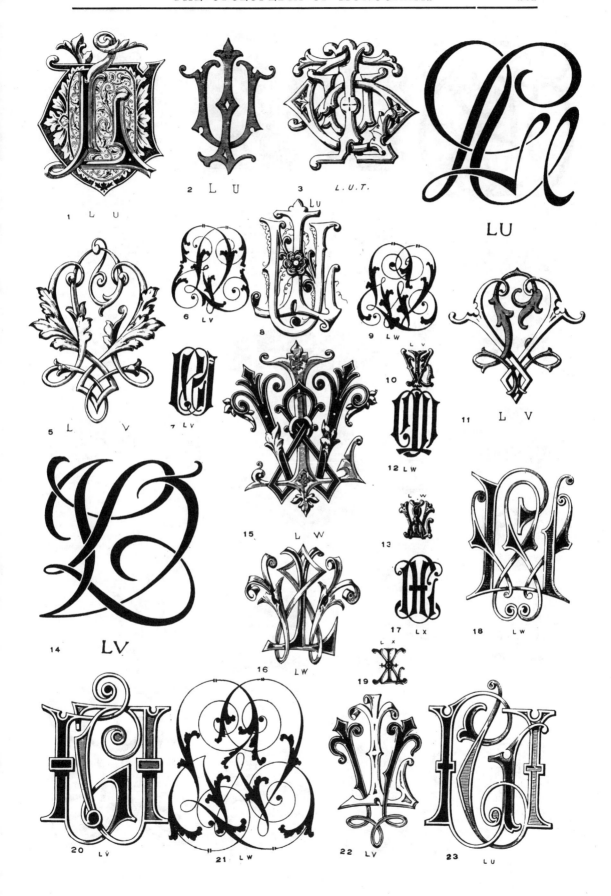

1 L U

2 L U

3 L.U.T.

LU

5 L V

6 L V

7 LV

8

9 LW

10 LV

11 L V

12 LW

13 LW

14 LV

15 L W

16 LW

17 LX

18 LW

19 L X

20 LV

21 LW

22 LV

23 LU

1   L W

2   L V

3   L W

4   L W

5   L · X

6   L Z

7   L Z

8

9

10   L Z

11   L Y

12   L Y

13   L Y

14   L X

15   L Z

16   L Z

17   L y

18

19   L Z

20   L Z

21   L Z

22   L X

1 LY

2 L&Co

3 LZ

4 L&K

5

6 LZ

7 L&Co

8 LOTTIE

9 LEWIS

10 LOUISA

11 LOUIS

12 LILY

13 LIZZIE

14 L&M

15 LENNOX.

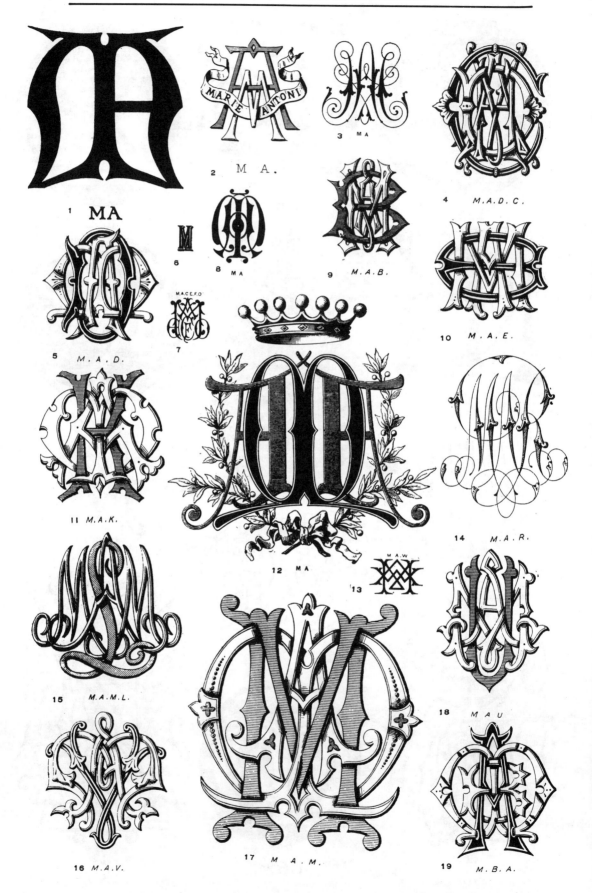

1   MA

2   M A.

3   MA

4   M.A.D.C.

5   M.A.D.

6

7   M.A.C.E.F.O

8   MA

9   M.A.B.

10   M.A.E.

11   M.A.K.

12   M A

13   M.A.W.

14   M.A.R.

15   M.A.M.L.

16   M.A.V.

17   M.A.M.

18   M A U

19   M.B.A.

1 M B
2 M B
3 M B
4 M. B. D.
5 M.B.R.V.
6 M ç C.
7 M. C. L.
8 M.C.M.R.
9 M. C. A.
10 M. C. W.
11 M C
12 MB
13 M C
14 M C
15 MC

SOUVENIR

1   M. C. I.

2   M D

3

MD

4   M. D. W.

5   M D

6   M E

7   M F

8   M. E A

9   M. E. S. D.

10   M D

11   M E

M E H

12

13   M E

14   M. E. G.

15   M. E. I.

16   M. E. N.

17   M. E. P

a   ME

19   M F

20   M F

1   MF

2   M.G.C.

3   M.F.M.F.

4   MG

5   MG

6   MG

7   MH

8   MG

9   MG

10   MHT

11   MJ

12   MH

13   M.IN

14   MJ

15   MH

16   MH

17   MJ

18   MJ

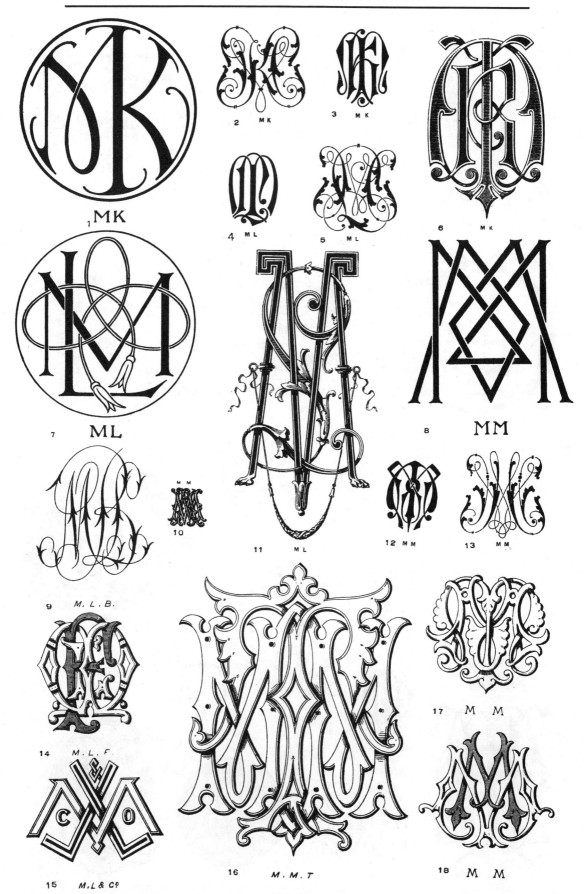

1 MK

2 MK

3 MK

4 ML

5 ML

6 MK

7 ML

8 MM

9 M.L.B.

10 MM

11 ML

12 MM

13 MM

14 M.L.F.

15 M.L & Cº

16 M.M.T

17 M M

18 M M

1 MM

2 M·M

3 M M

4 MM

5 M M

6 M M

7 MM

8 MM

9 MMA

10 MMB

11 MMC

12 MMD

13 MME

14 MMF

1 MMU

2 MMW

3 MN

4 MNO

5 MO

6 M N

7 M N

8 M N

9 M N

10 M N

11 M O

12 M · N

13 M N

14 M N

15 M O

16 M N

17 M.N.D.

18 M O

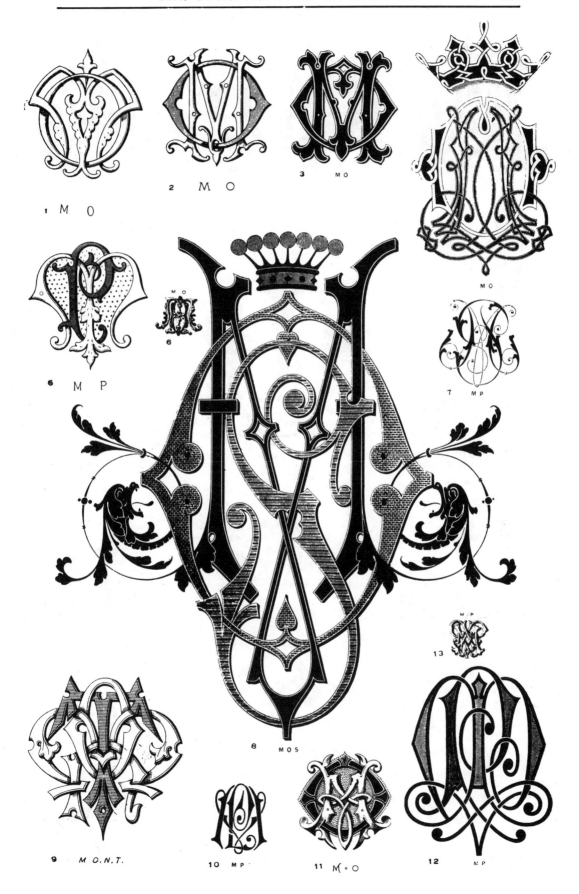

1 M O

2 M O

3 M O

M O

5 M P

6 M O

7 M P

8 M O S

9 M O N T

10 M P

11 M O

12 M P

13 M P

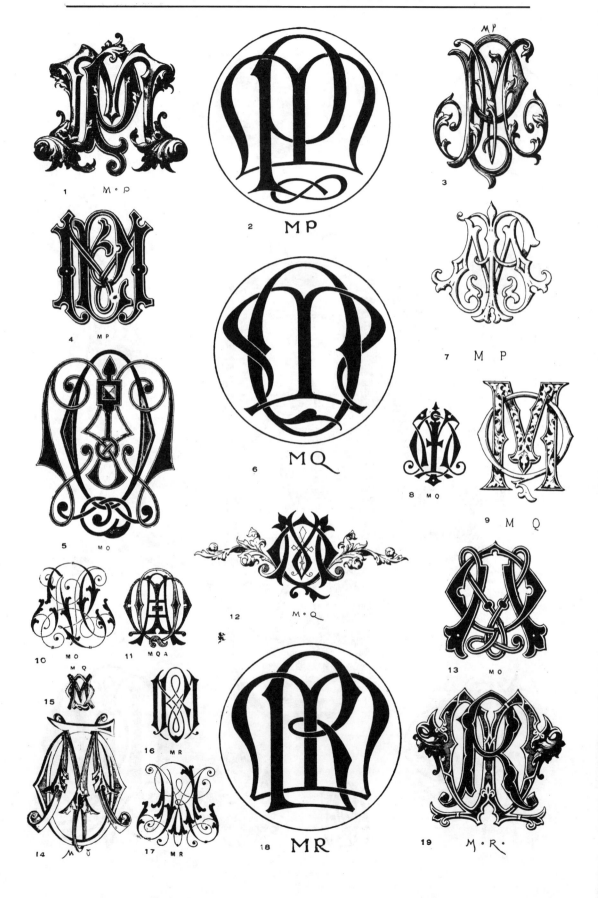

1   M ○ P

2   MP

3

4   MP

5   M O

6   MQ

7   M P

8   MQ

9   M Q

10   MO

11   MQA

12   M ○ Q

13   MO

14   M ○

15

16   MR

17   MR

18   MR

19   M ○ R ○

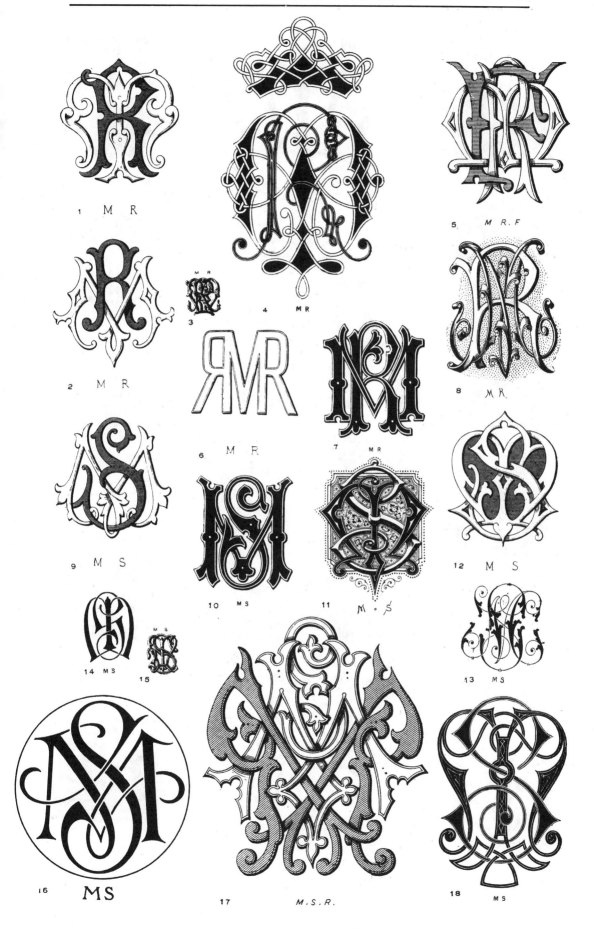

1 M R

5 M R F

2 M R

3 MR

4 MR

6 M R

7 MR

8 M R

9 M S

10 MS

11 M S

12 M S

14 MS

15 MS

13 MS

16 MS

17 M S R

18 MS

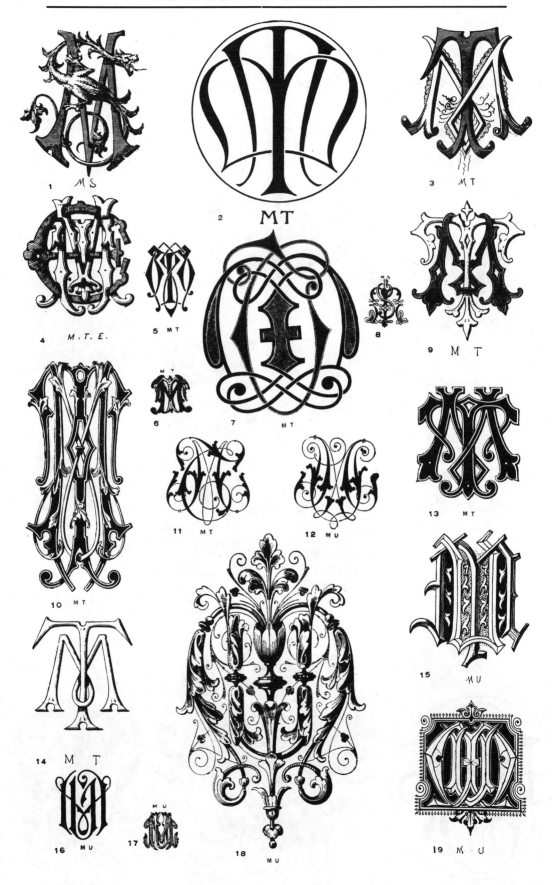

1   M S

2   M T

3   M T

4   M . T . E .

5   M T

6   M T

7   M T

8   M S

9   M   T

10   M T

11   M T

12   M U

13   M T

14   M   T

15   M U

16   M U

17   M U

18   M U

19   M U

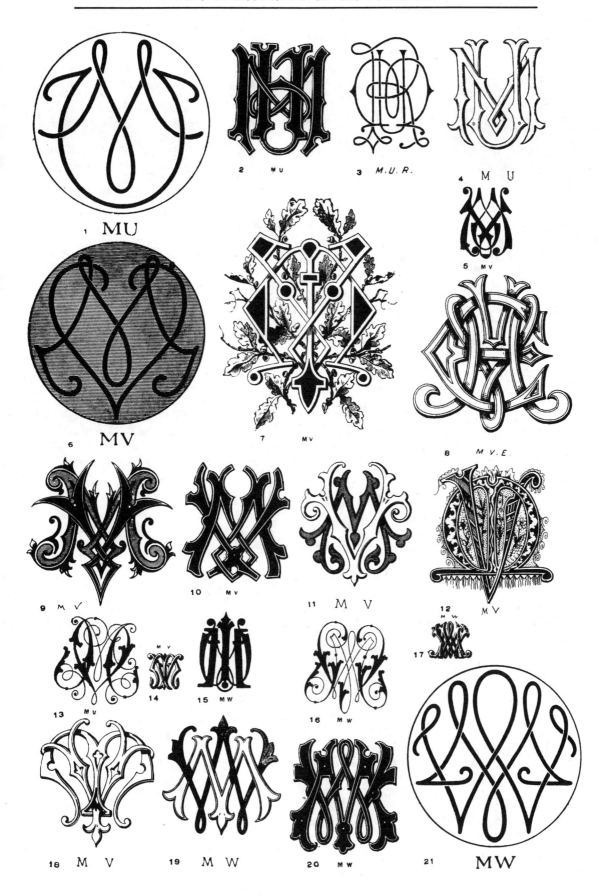

1 MU

2 M U

3 M.U.R.

4 M U

5 M V

6 MV

7 M V

8 M V . E .

9 M V

10 M V

11 M V

12 M V

13 M V

14 M V

15 M W

16 M W

17 M W

18 M V

19 M W

20 M W

21 MW

1   M W

2   M X

3   M X

4   M Y

5   M X

6   M X

7   M X

8   M W

9   M Y

10   M Z

11   M Y

12   M Y

13   M Z

14   M Z

15

16   M Z

17   M Y

18   M Z

19   M X

20   M Z

1   Marguerite.

2

3 Marguerite

6 MARIE

4 MARIA

5   Maria.

7   MARIE

8   Maria.

1 MARIE.

2 Martha.

3 Martin.

4 MARY.

5 MARY

6 MAUD.

7 MARY Y.

8 MAY

9 Max

10 MATHILDE.

Cnne de Prince
et Prince Souverain

Cnne de Prince
du Saint-Empire

1   N&M

2   N&O

3   N&Cͦ

4   N&Cͦ

5   Natalia.

6

7   NORA.

8   NETTIE.

9   NELLY.

1 NE

2 ND

3 NE

4 N.E.D.H

5 NF

6 NF

7 NF

8 NESA.

9 NG

10 NG

11 NH

12 NFY

13 NH

14 NG

15 NG

16 NF

17 N.H.M.

18 NGB.

1　NH

2　NH

3　NI

4　NL

5　NJ

6　NM

7　NJ

8　NK

9　N.J.P

10　NK

11　NL

12　NK.

13　NJ

14　NL

15　NM

16　NJ

17　N.H.M.B.

18　NK

1 NL

2 NM

3 N.M.E.Q.

4 NN

5 NM.

6 NN

7 NN

8 NN

9 NN

10 N N

11 NN

12 NN

13 NN

14 NMN

15 NNA

16 NN

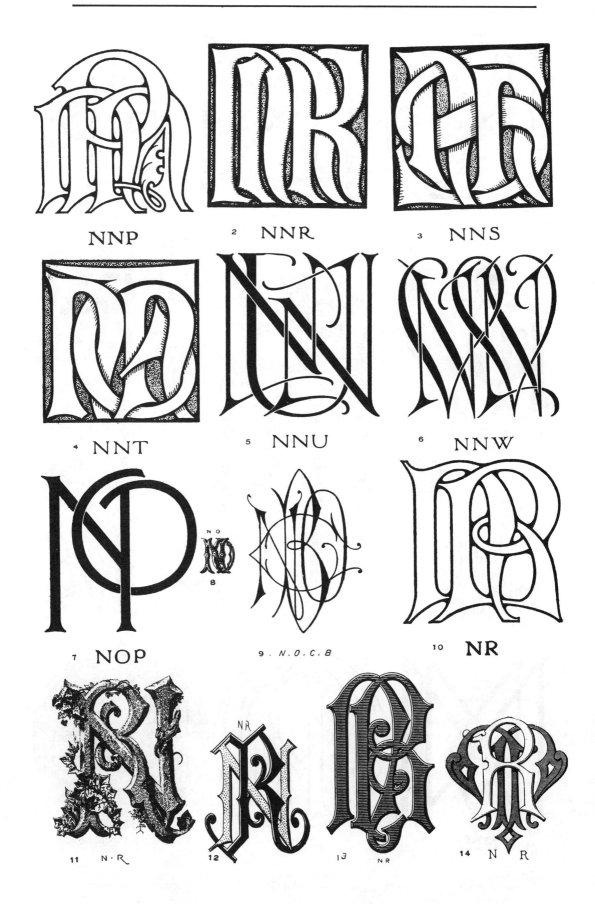

NNP

2 NNR

3 NNS

4 NNT

5 NNU

6 NNW

7 NOP

9 . N.O.C.B

10 NR

8 N O

11 N·R

12 NR

13 NR

14 N R

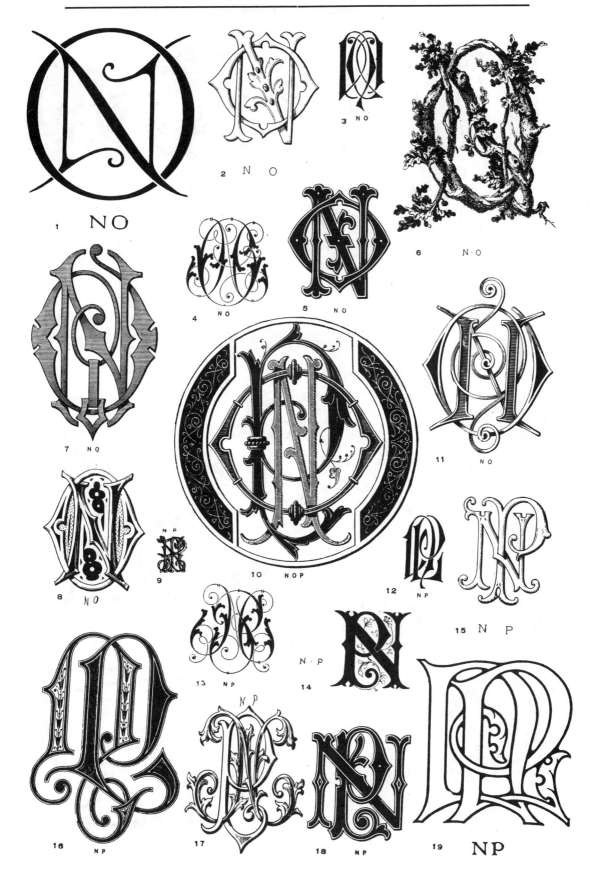

1   NO

2   N O

3   NO

6   N·O

4   NO

5   NO

7   NQ

8   NO

9

10   NOP

11   NO

12   NP

13   NP

14

15   N P

16   NP

17

18   NP

19   NP

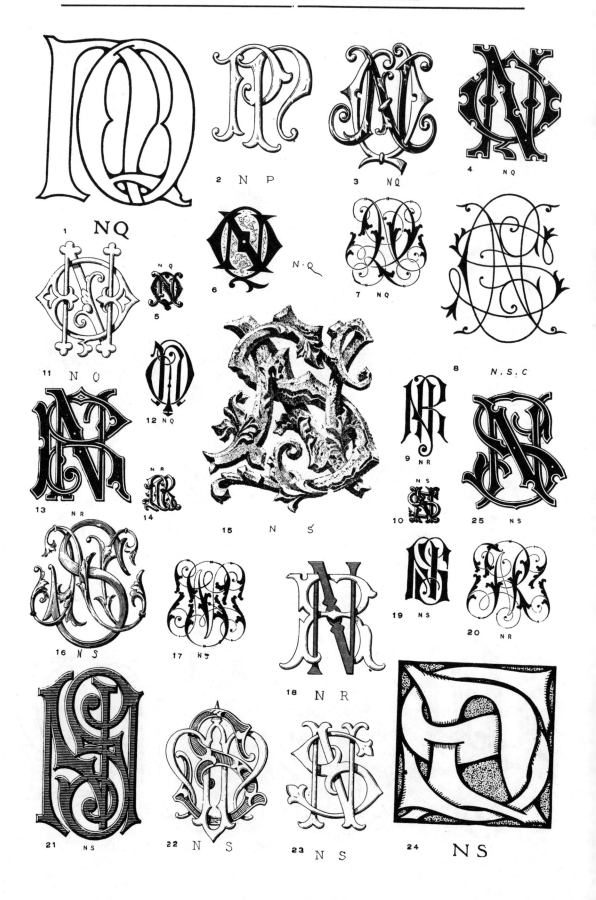

1   NQ

2   N P

3   NQ

4   NQ

5

6   N.Q.

7   NQ

8   N.S.C

9   NR

10   NS

11   N O

12   NQ

13   NR

14   NR

15   N S

16   N S

17   NS

18   N R

19   NS

20   NR

21   NS

22   N S

23   N S

24   N S

25   NS

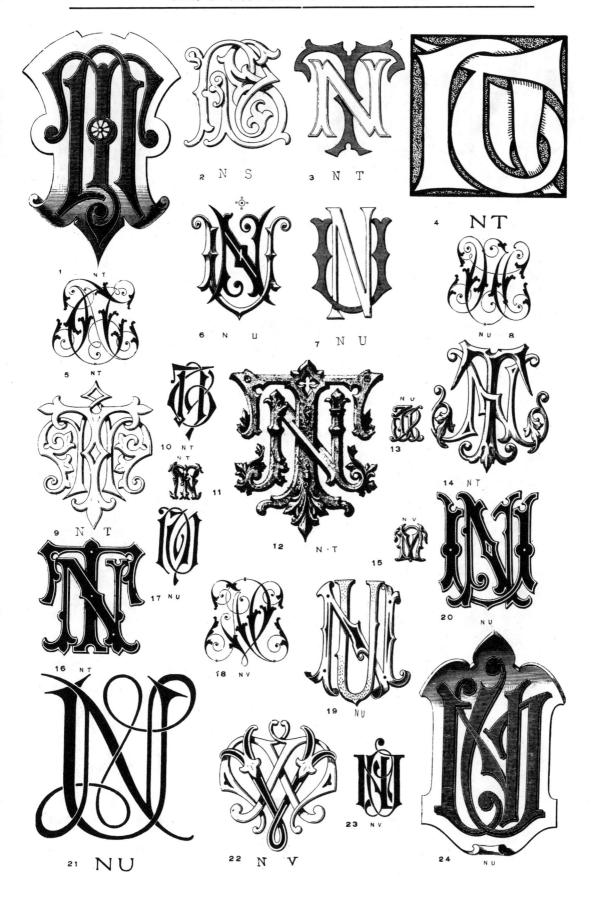

1 N T
2 N S
3 N T
4 NT
5 N T
6 N U
7 NU
8 NU
9 N T
10 N T
11 N T
12 N · T
13 N U
14 NT
15 N V
16 NT
17 NU
18 NV
19 NU
20 NU
21 NU
22 N V
23 N V
24 NU

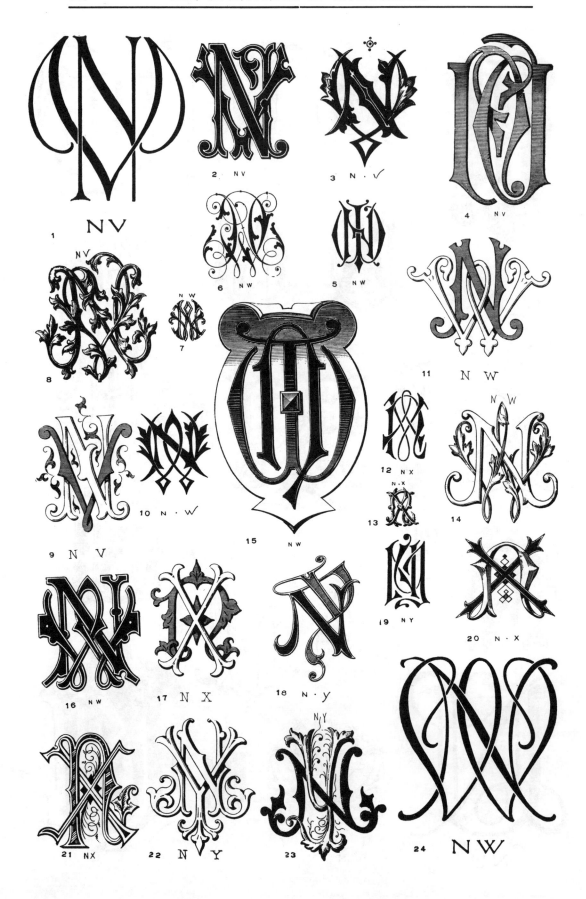

1   NV

2   NV

3   N·V

4   NV

6   NW

5   NW

8

7   NW

11   N W

9   N V

10   N·W

12   NX

13   N·X

14

15   NW

16   NW

17   NX

18   N·y

19   NY

20   N·X

21   NX

22   NY

23

24   NW

1 NX

2 O.B.B.

3 NY

4 NY

5 NZ

6 N Z

7 OB

8 N Z

9 OAS

10 NY

11 NZ

12 NZ

13 NZ

14 OC

15 OB

16 NZ

17 N Z

18 NZ

19 O.C.G.

20 OC

21 OB

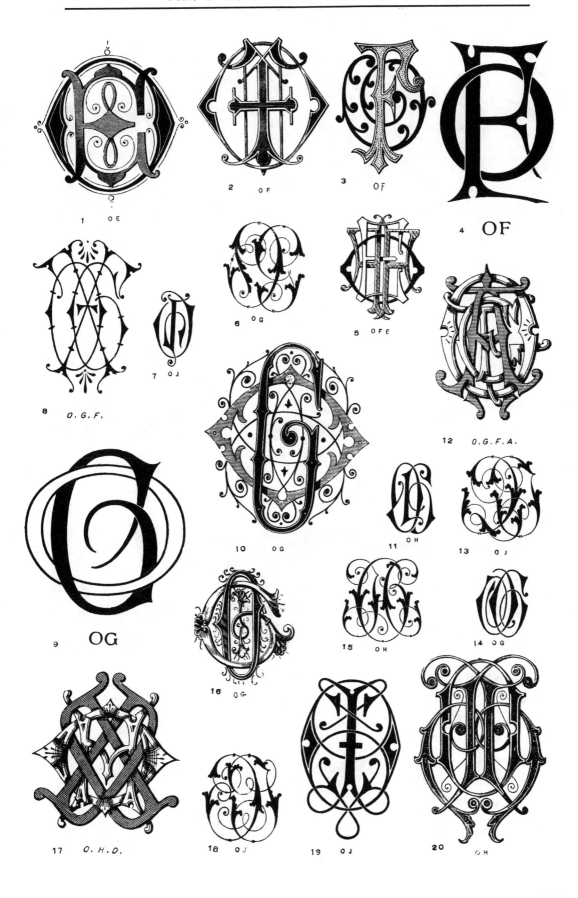

1   O E

2   O F

3   O F

4   O F

5   O F E

6   O G

7   O J

8   O. G. F.

9   O G

10   O G

11   O H

12   O. G. F. A.

13   O J

14   O G

15   O H

16   O G

17   O. H. D.

18   O J

19   O J

20   O H

OK

2   OK

3   OM

5   OL

4   OL

7   OK

6   OK

8   O. la K.

12   OL

9   O.M.O

10 ON

11   ON

13   OM

15   OM

16   O.M.P.

14   OM

17   ON

18   O. N'. H. K.

1   ON

2   OO

3   OO

4   OL

5   OO

6   OO

7   OO

8   OO

9   OO

10   OO

11   OO

12   OO

13   OOA

14   OO

15   OO

16   OOC

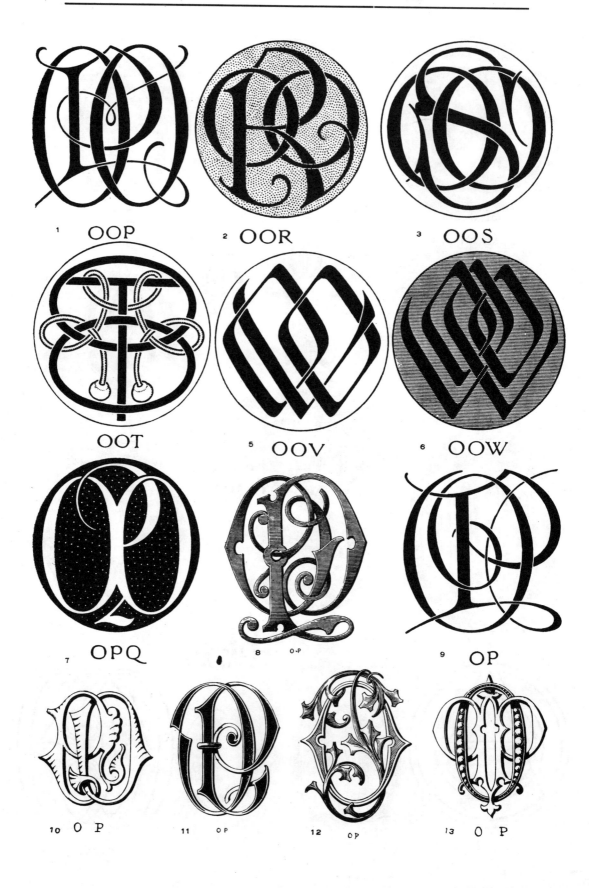

1 OOP

2 OOR

3 OOS

OOT

5 OOV

6 OOW

7 OPQ

8 O·P

9 OP

10 O P

11 O P

12 O P

13 O P

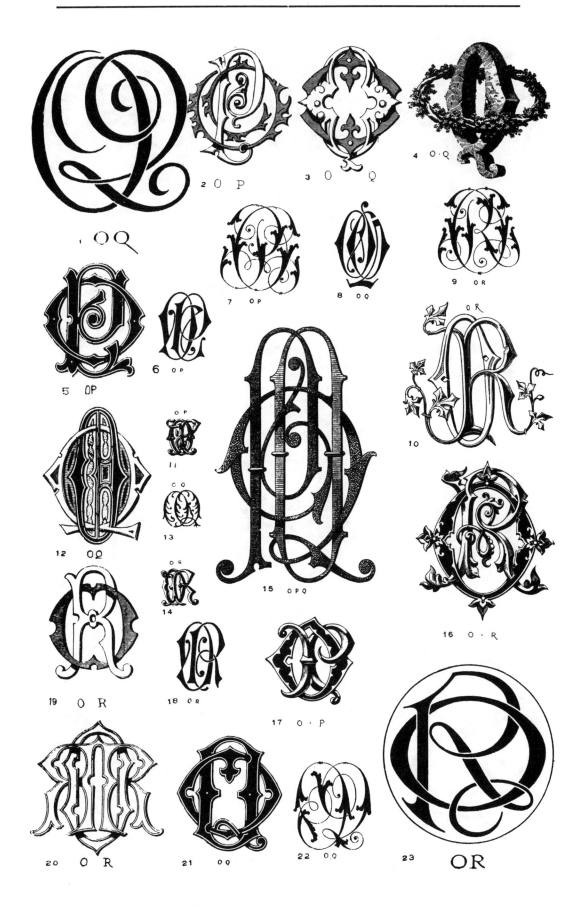

1 O Q

2 O P

3 O Q

4 O·Q

5 OP

6 OP

7 OP

8 OQ

9 OR

10

11 OP

12 OQ

13 OQ

14 OR

15 OPQ

16 O·R

17 O·P

18 OR

19 O R

20 O R

21 OQ

22 OQ

23 OR

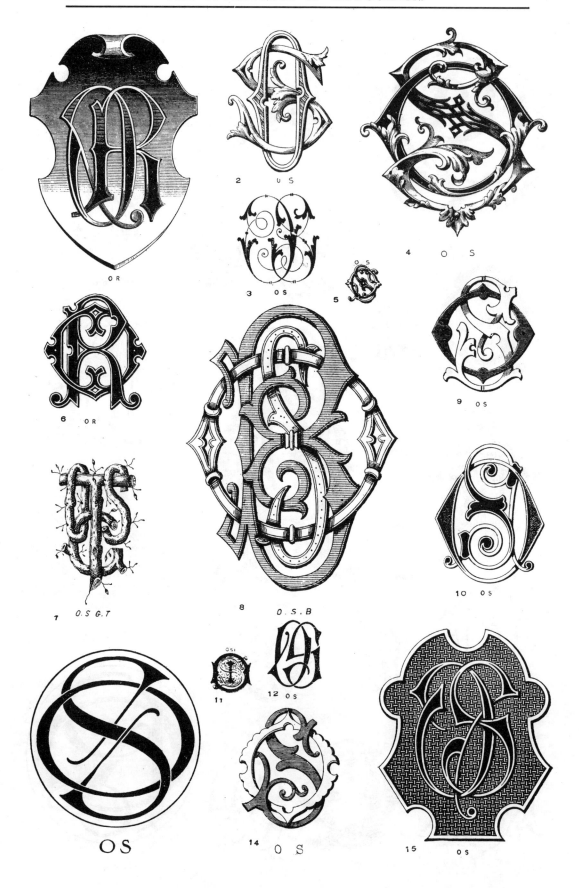

OR

2   U S

4   O S

3   O S

5   O S

6   OR

9   OS

7   O.S.G.T

8   O.S.B

10   OS

OSI

11

12   OS

OS

14   O S

15   OS

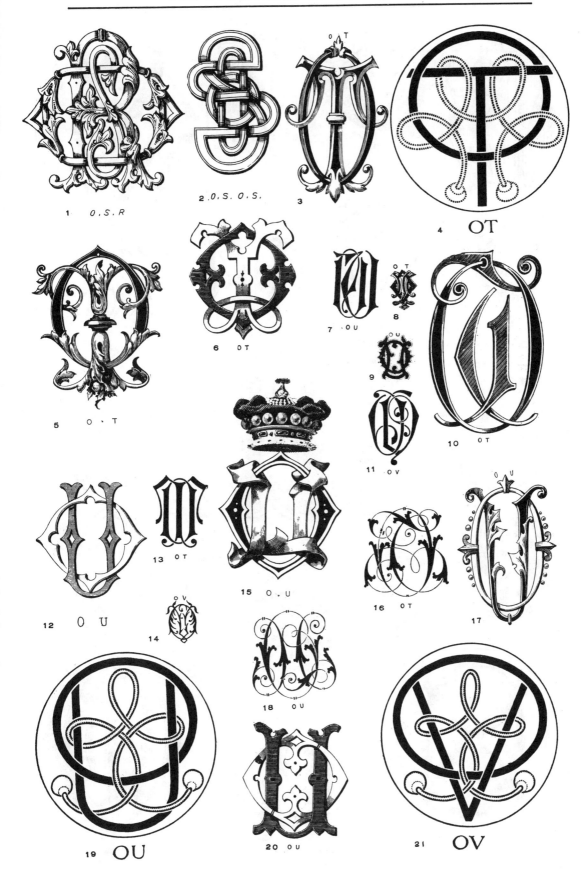

1   O.S.R

2 .O.S. O.S.

3

4   OT

5   O.T

6   OT

7 .OU

8   OT

9 OU

10   OT

11 OV

12 OU

13 OT

14

15 O.U

16 OT

17

18 OU

19 OU

20 OU

21 OV

1 O V

2 O V

3 O V

4

5 O . V

6 O V

7 OWH

8 O V

9 O W

10 O U

11 O W

13 O . W

14 OW

15 O X

16 O X

17 O X

18 O W

19 OX

20 O W

21 O W

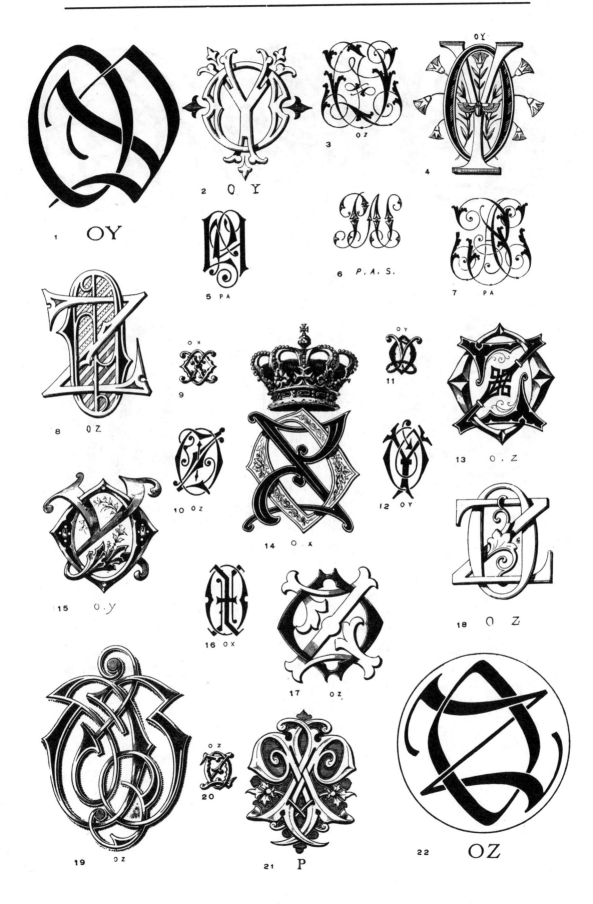

1 OY

2 O Y

3 OZ

4 OY

5 PA

6 P.A.S.

7 PA

8 OZ

9 OX

10 OZ

11 OY

12 OY

13 O.Z

14 O.X

15 O.Y

16 OX

17 OZ

18 OZ

19 OZ

20 OZ

21 P

22 OZ

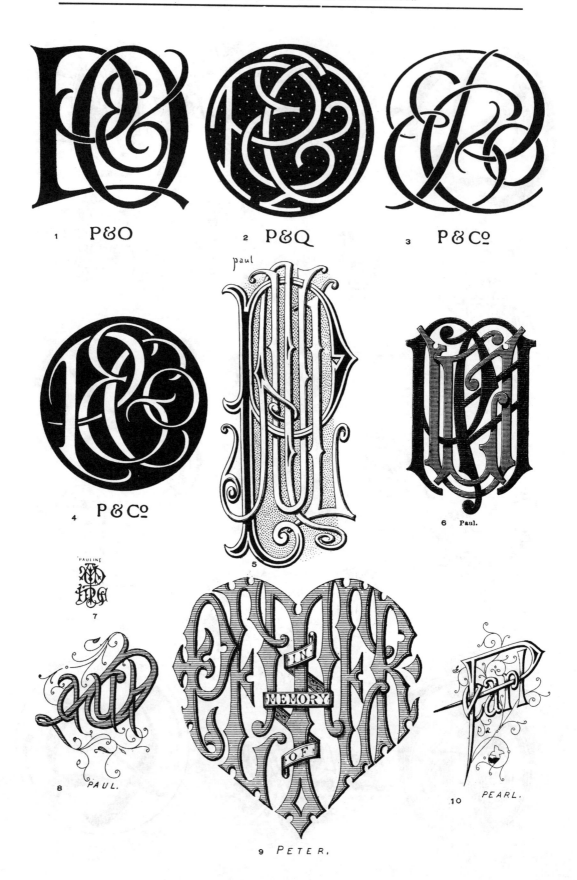

1 P&O

2 P&Q

3 P&Cº

4 P&Cº

paul

5

6 Paul.

PAULINE
7

8 PAUL.

9 PETER.

IN MEMORY OF

10 PEARL.

1   P B

2   P C A

3   PA

4   P D

5   P

6   P D

7   P D C

8   P A

9   P A

10   P D

11   P.B.S.

12   P B

13   P C

14   P C R

15   PB

16   P B

17   P C

18   P C

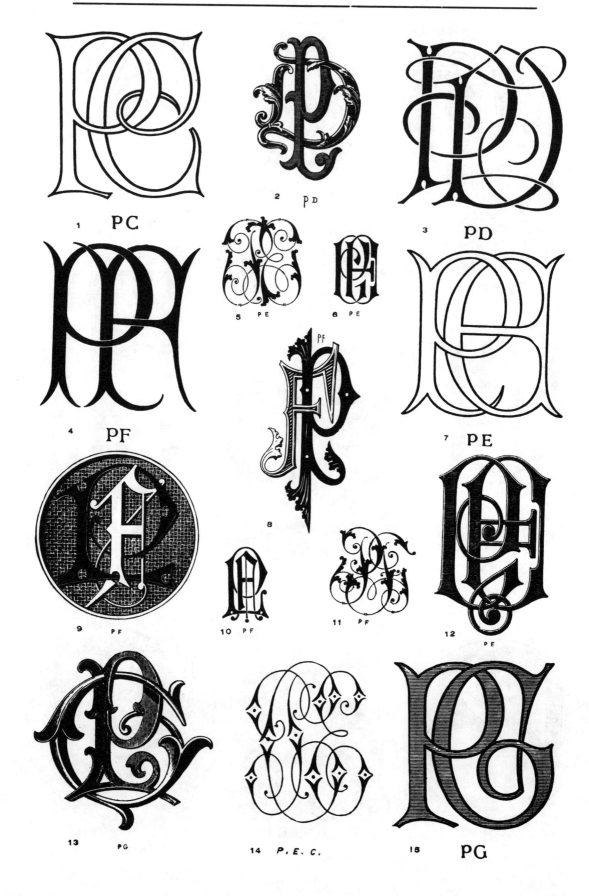

1   PC

2   P D

3   PD

4   PF

5   P E

6   PE

7   PE

8

9   PF

10   PF

11   PF

12   PE

13   PG

14   *P.E.C.*

15   PG

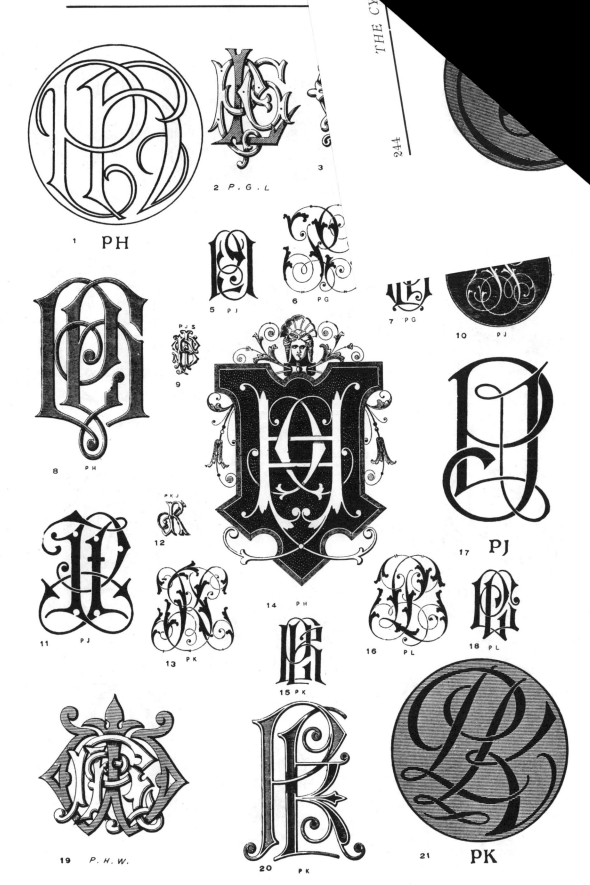

1 PH

2 P.G.L

3

5 PJ

6 PG

7 PG

10 PJ

9 PJS

8 PH

12 PKJ

14 PH

17 PJ

11 PJ

13 PK

15 PK

16 PL

18 PL

19 P.H.W.

20 PK

21 PK

1   PL

2   PK

3   PL

4   P.J.B

5   P.L.G.

6   PN

7   PM

8   PM

9   PN

10   PM

11   PM

12   PN

13   PM

14   PO

15   PP

16   PN

17   PP

18   PP

19   PO

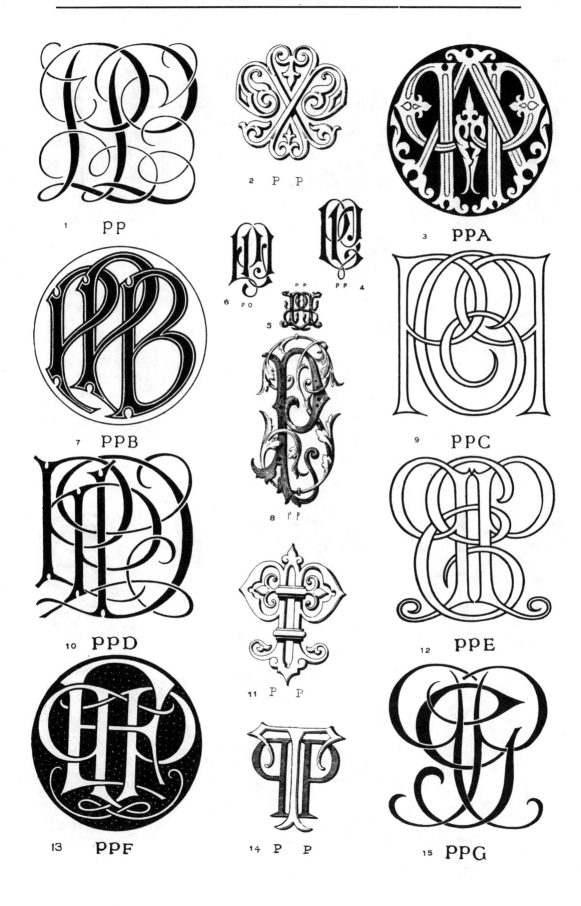

1 PP

2 P P

3 PPA

4 PP

5

6 PO

7 PPB

8 P P

9 PPC

10 PPD

11 P P

12 PPE

13 PPF

14 P P

15 PPG

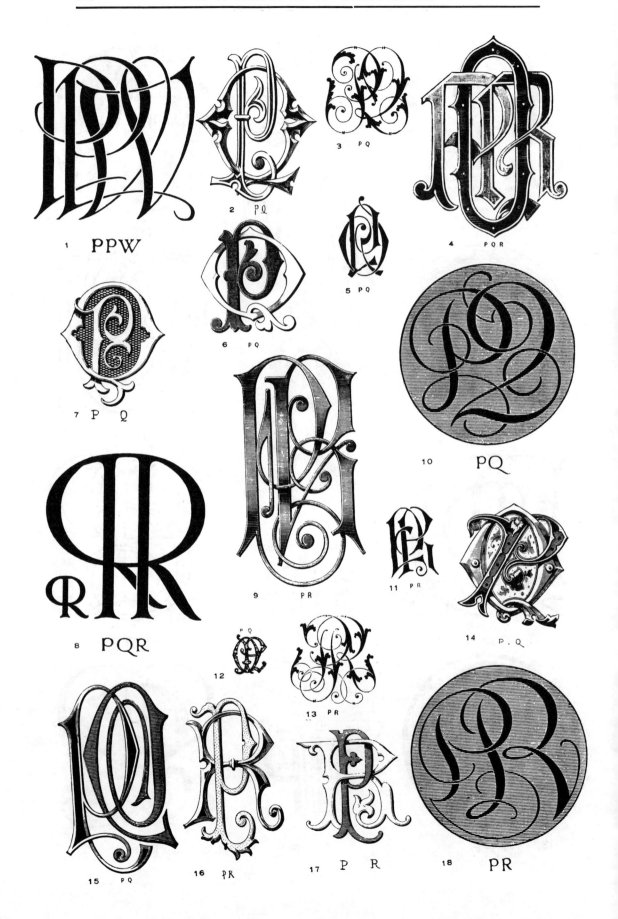

1 PPW

2 PQ

3 PQ

4 PQR

5 PQ

6 PQ

7 P Q

8 PQR

9 PR

10 PQ

11 PR

12 PQ

13 PR

14 P Q

15 PQ

16 PR

17 P R

18 PR

1 PRR

2 PR

3 P.R

4 PR

5 P S

6 PS

7 PS

8 PS

9 PS

10 PS

11 PS

12 PT

13 PS

14 PSS

15 PT

16 PT

17 PT

18 P S

19 P.S

20 P S

21 PT

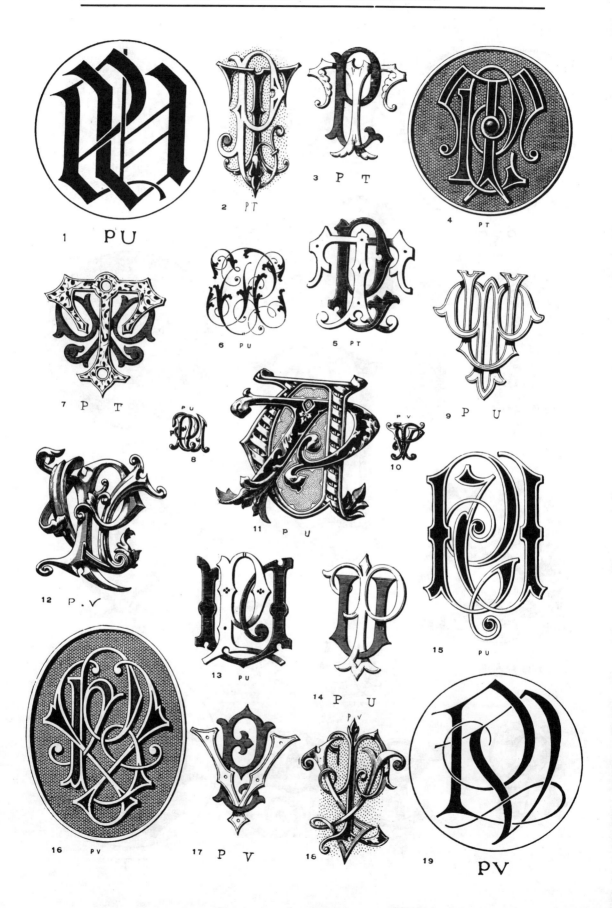

1   P U

2   P T

3   P T

4   P T

5   P T

6   P U

7   P T

8   P U

9   P U

10   P V

11   P U

12   P. V

13   P U

14   P U

15   P U

16   P V

17   P V

18   P V

19   P V

1 P W

2 P W

3 P X

4 P · W

5 P W

6 P X

7 P V

8 P U

9 P V

10 P W

11 P V

12 P · X

13 P W

14 P X

15 P W

16 P Y

17 P Y

18 P X

19 P W

20 P W

21 P · X

22 PX

1   PY

2   PZ

3   PY

4   PZ

5   PZ

6   P·y

7   PZ

8   PZ

9   QA

10   PZ

11   PZ

12   PY

13   QA

14   PZ

15   PZ

16   QA

17   PZ

18   Q

19   PZ

1   QA

2   Q B

3

4   Q C

5   Q D

6   Q C

7   QB

8   Q B

9   Q E

10   Q D.

11   Q . E . R . V . B .

12   Q E

13   Q E

14   Q F

15   Q D

16   QE

17

18   . Q F

19   QF

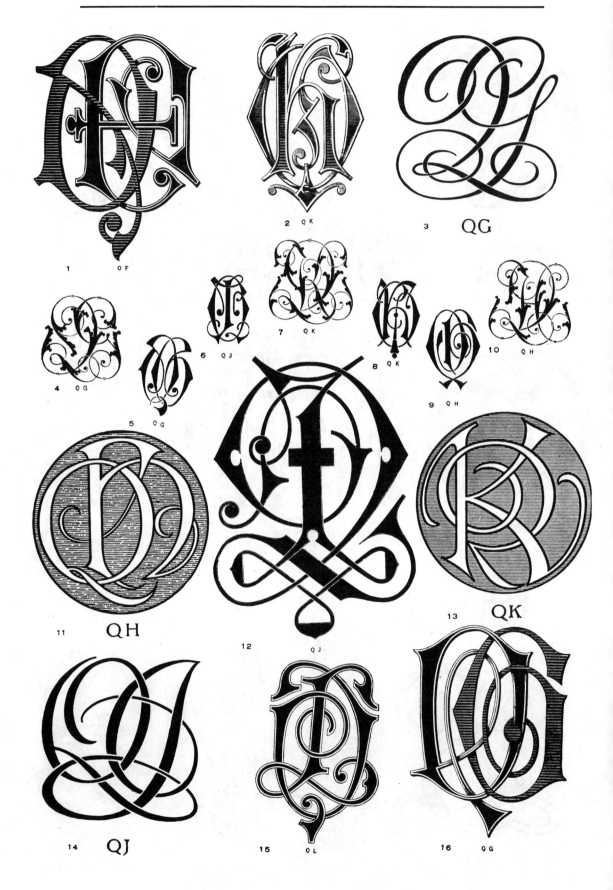

1   O F

2   Q K

3   QG

4   Q G

5   Q G

6   Q J

7   Q K

8   Q K

9   Q H

10   Q H

11   QH

12   Q J

13   QK

14   QJ

15   Q L

16   Q G

1   QL

2   QL

3   QM

4   QM

5   QL

6   QM

7   QL

8   QM

9   QO

10 QN

11 QO

12 QN

13 QN

14 QO

15 QN

1   Q P

2   Q Q

3

4   Q P

5   Q Q

6   Q Q

7   Q P

8   Q P

9   Q R

10   Q Q

11   Q R

12   Q R

13   Q R

14   Q Q

15   Q R

16   Q R

QQ

18   Q Q

19   Q Q

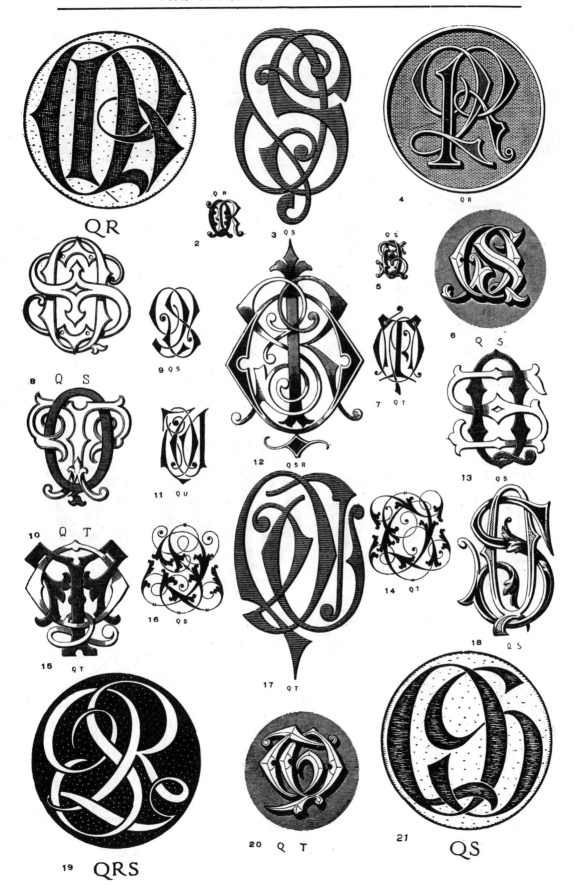

QR

2 QR

3 QS

4 QR

5 QS

6 QS

8 QS

9 QS

7 QT

10 QT

11 QU

12 QSR

13 QS

15 QT

16 QS

14 QT

17 QT

18 QS

19 QRS

20 QT

21 QS

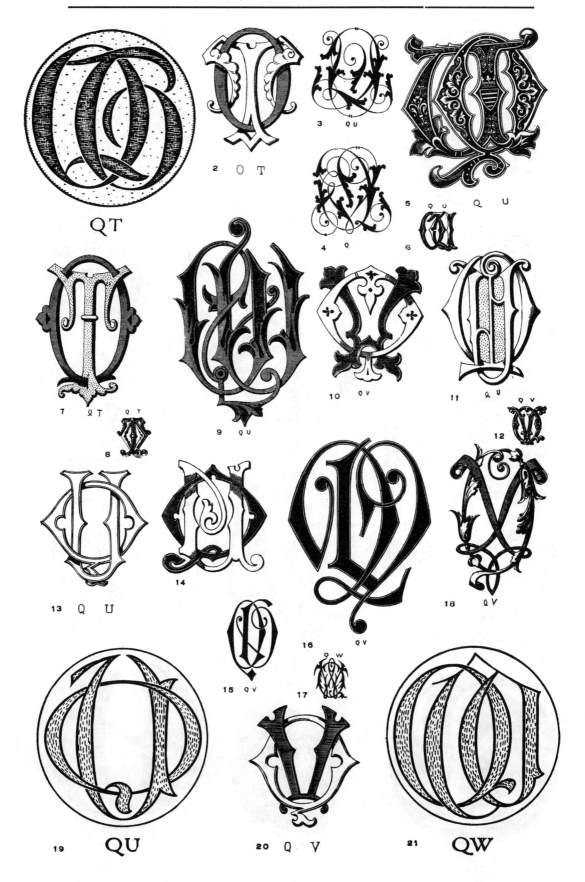

QT

2 O T

3 Q U

5 Q U   Q U

4 Q

6

7 Q T   Q T

8

9 Q U

10 Q V

11 Q U   Q V

12

13 Q U

14

16 Q V

18 Q V

15 Q V   17 Q W

19 QU

20 Q V

21 QW

1 Q · W

2 Q   W

3 Q W

4 Q W

5 Q   X

6 Q · X

7 O W

8 Q Z

9 QX

10 Q W

11 Q Y

12 O W

13 Q · Y

14 Q X

15 Q Y

16 Q Z

17 Q Z

18 Q   Y

19 QY

20 Q Y

21 Q X

22 Q · Z

23 O Y

1 Q X

2 Q X

3 QZ

4 QZ

5 QZ

6 RA

7 R.A & J.H

8 RA

9 RA

10 R

11 RA

12 RA

13 R.A.H.

14 RB

16 RB

17 RB

18 RC

19 R.C.S.

1   RC

2   RC

3   RC

4   RD

5   RD

6   RD

7   R.C.M.

8   RE

9   RE

10   R.D.W.

11   RD

12   RCH

13   RE

14   R.E.H.Q.

15   RC

1   RE

2   RE

3   RF

4   RFP

5   RF

6   RFTJ

7

8   RG

9   RF

10   RG

11   RG

12   RF

13   R.G.N.

14   RG

15   RH

16   RH

17   RH

18   RH

19   RH

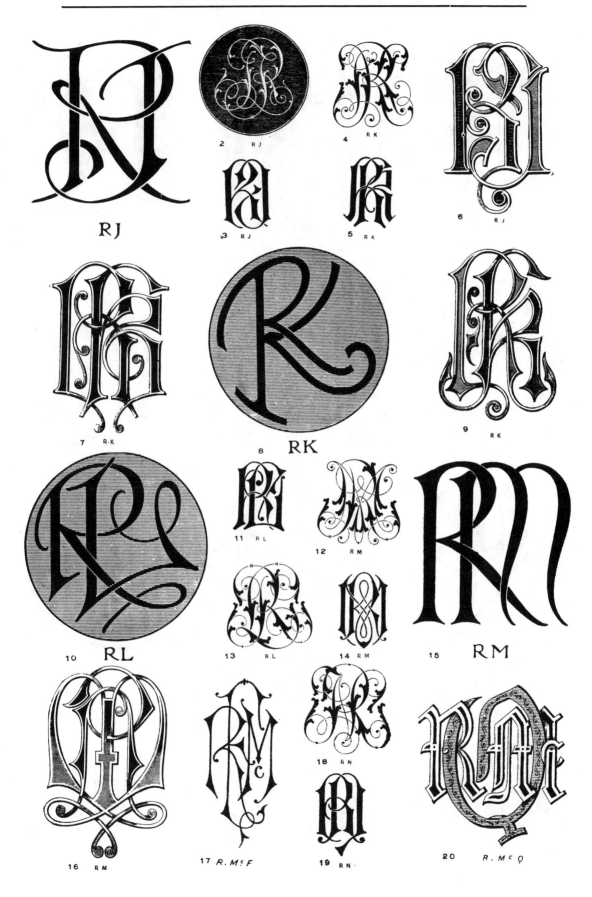

RJ

2   RJ

4   RK

3   RJ

5   RK

6   RJ

7   R·K

8   RK

9   RK

10   RL

11   RL

12   RM

13   RL

14   RM

15   RM

16   RM

17   R. McF

18   RN

19   RN

20   R. McQ

RN

2 RN

3 RO

4 RC

5 RO

6 RO

7 RP

8 RP

9 RP

10 RP

11 RQ

12 RQ

13 R R

14 RO

15 R R

16 R R

17

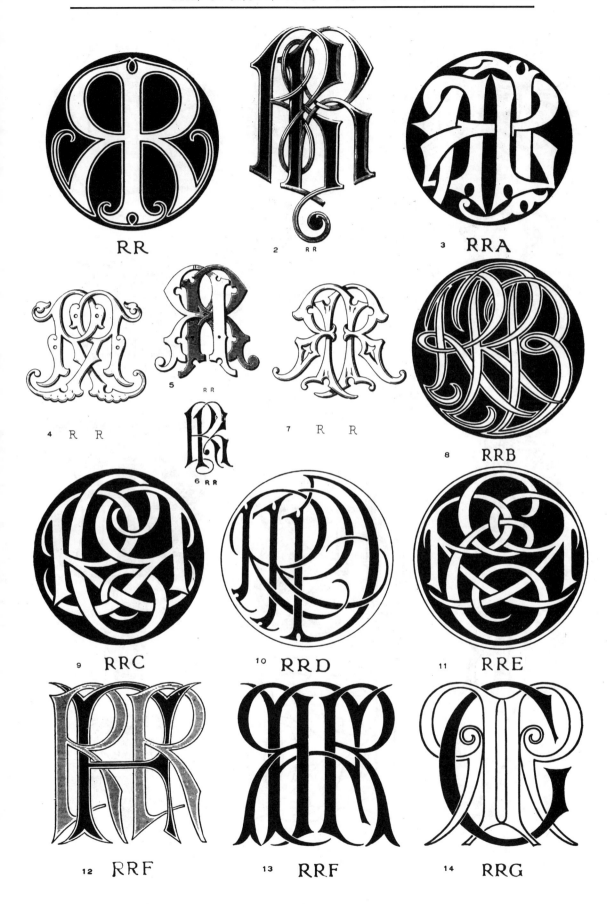

RR

2 RR

3 RRA

4 R R

5 RR

6 RR

7 R R

8 RRB

9 RRC

10 RRD

11 RRE

12 RRF

13 RRF

14 RRG

1   R S
2   R S
3   R S
4   RS
5   R S
6   R S
7   R S
8   R S
9
10 R S
11 R · S
12 R S M
13 R S T
14 RST
15 R T
16 R T
17 RT
18
19 R T
20 R   T

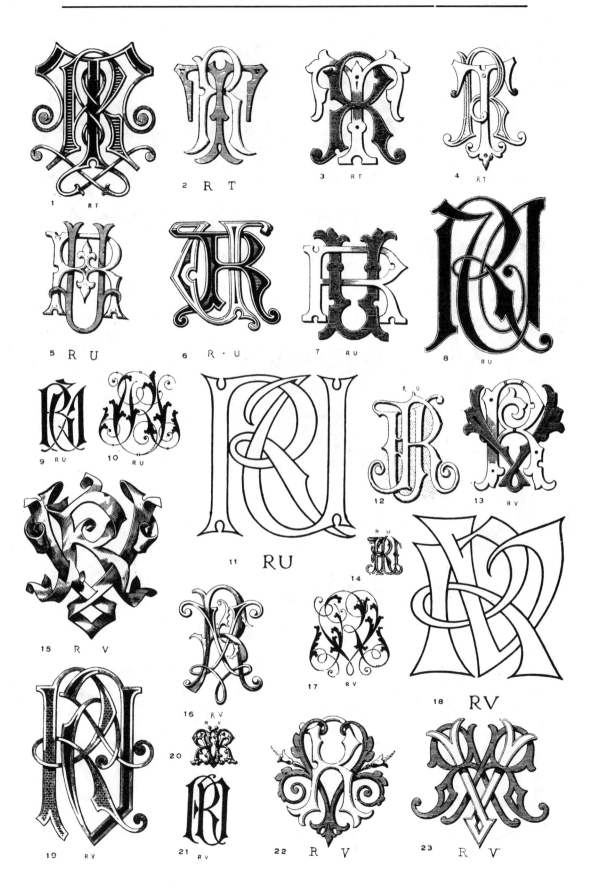

1 RT

2 RT

3 RT

4 RT

5 RU

6 R·U

7 RU

8 RU

9 RU

10 RU

11 RU

12 RU

13 RV

14 RU

15 RV

16 RV

17 RV

18 RV

19 RV

20 RV

21 RV

22 RV

23 RV

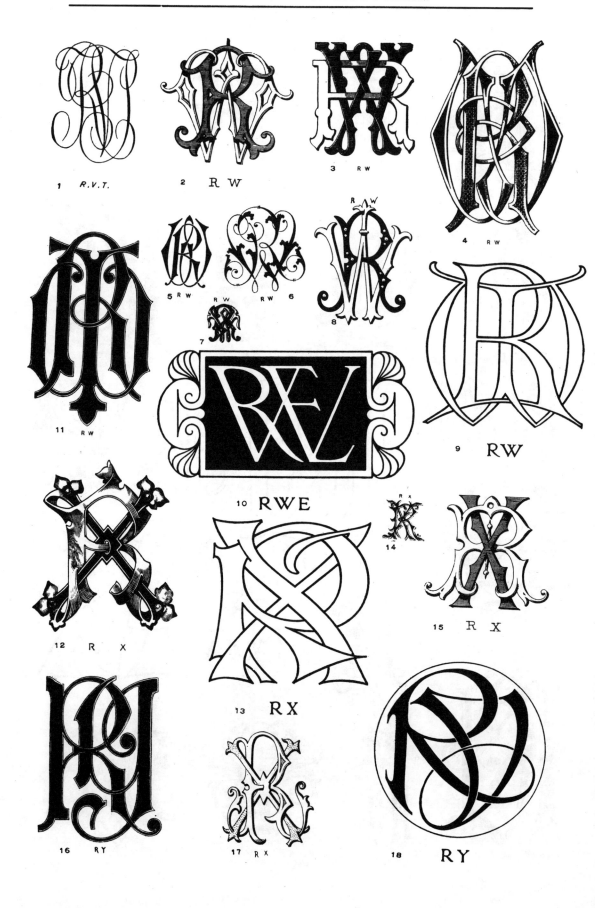

1 *R.V.T.*

2 R W

3 R W

4 R W

5 R W

6 R W

7

8 R W

9 R W

10 RWE

11 R W

12 R X

13 R X

14 R X

15 R X

16 R Y

17 R X

18 RY

1 R Y

2 R Y

3

4

5 Z

6 RZ

7 RY

8 RZ

9 RZ

10 R.Z

11 RZ

12 R Z

13 RZ

14 RZ

1

2 SA

3 SAB

4 SA

5 S.A.D.

6 SAR

7 S

8 SA

9 S.A.G.

10 S.A.H.

11 SA

12 S   B

13 SAR

14 SB

15 SB

16 S.A.P.

20

17 SB

18 S.B.G.C.

19 S.B.S.I.

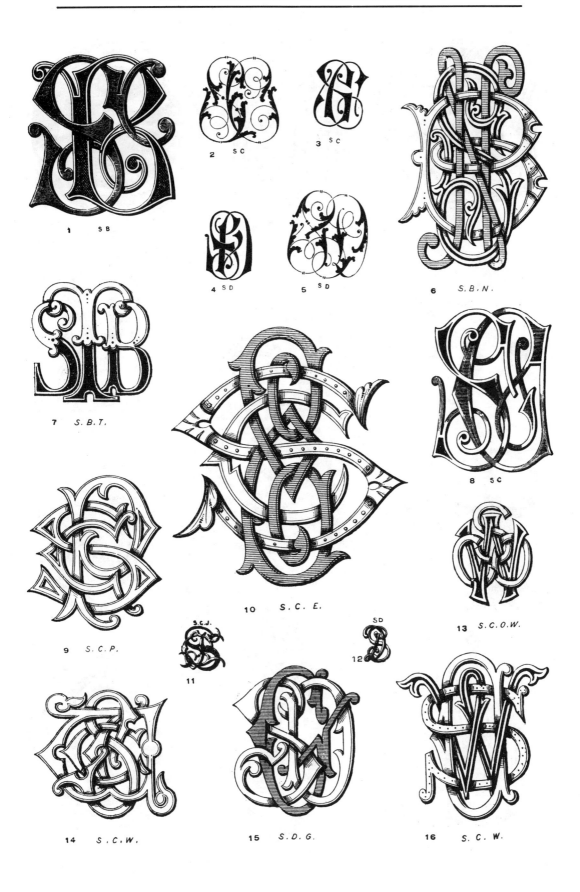

1 S B

2 S C

3 S C

4 S D

5 S D

6 S.B.N.

7 S.B.T.

8 S C

9 S.C.P.

10 S.C.E.

11 S.C.J.

12 S D

13 S.C.O.W.

14 S.C.W.

15 S.D.G.

16 S.C.W.

1   SD

2   *S . E . L*

3   SE

4 SE

5   SF

6   SE

7   SF

8   *S . G . A .*

9 SF

10   SG

11   SG

12   SG

13   SC

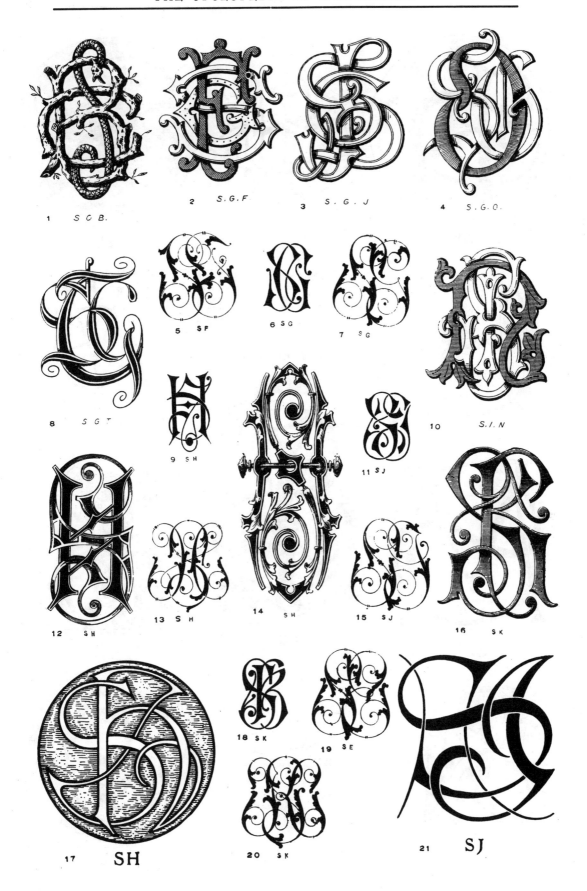

1 S C B.

2 S. G. F

3 S. G. J

4 S. G. O.

5 SF

6 SG

7 SG

8 S G T

9 SH

10 S. I. N

11 SJ

12 SH

13 S H

14 SH

15 SJ

16 SK

17 SH

18 SK

19 SE

20 SK

21 SJ

1, SK

2 S. L. A.

3 SL

6 SL

5 SL

4 SL

S. MᶜT.

8 SM

9 SJ

10 SM

11 S. M. L.

12 S. M. Y.

13 SN

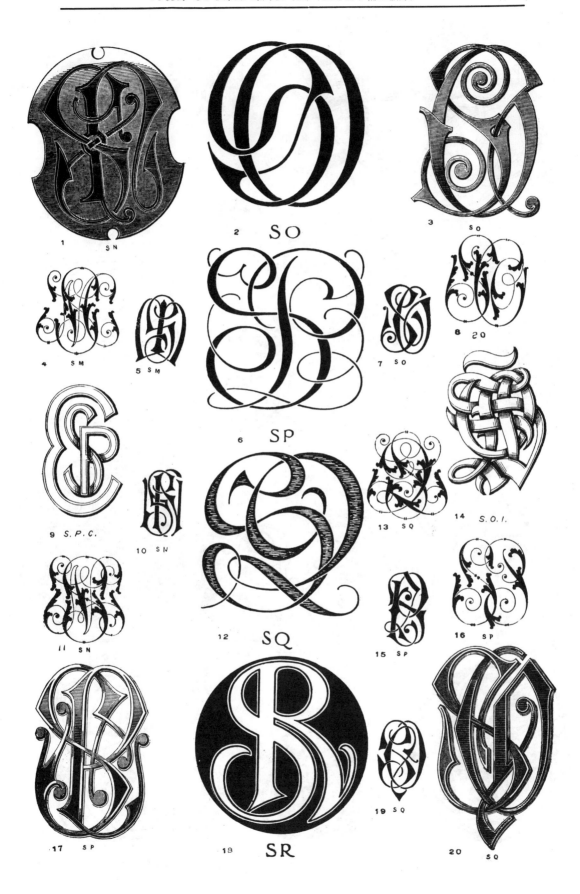

1   SN

2   SO

3   SO

4   SM

5 SM

6   SP

7   SO

8 20

9 S.P.C.

10 SN

11   SN

12   SQ

13 SQ

14   S.O.I.

15   SP

16   SP

17   SP

18   SR

19 SQ

20   SQ

1   SR

2   SR

3   SR

4   SS

5   6

7 SS   8 SS   9 SR

10   S S

11   S S

12   SS

13   SS

14   SSA

15   S S

16   S S

17   SSB

18   SSC

19   S. S. D.

20   SSD

1 SST

2 SSV

3 St. A

4 St N.

5 ST

6 ST

7 St P.

8 ST

9 S T

10 ST

11 STU

12 St G.

13 S T

14 STU

15 S. T

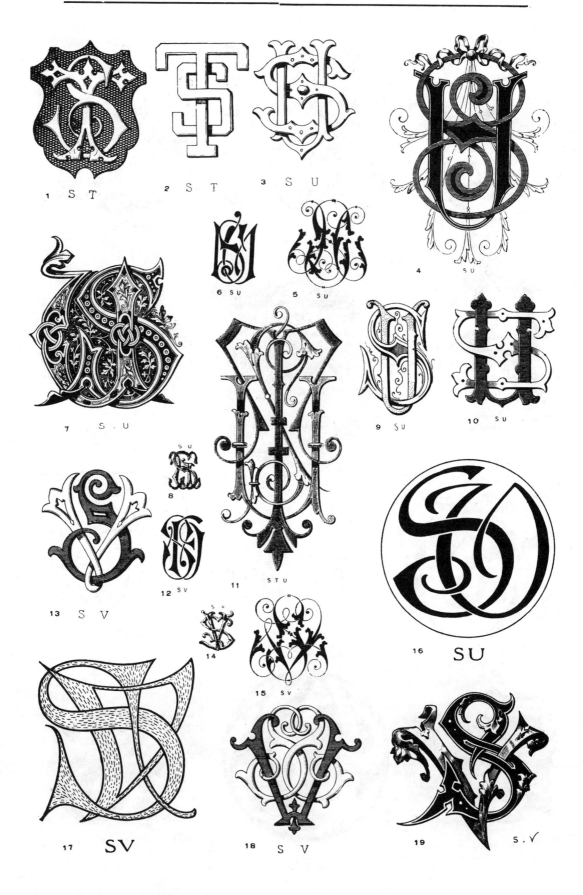

1 ST

2 ST

3 SU

4 SU

5 SU

6 SU

7 S . U

8 SU

9 SU

10 SU

11 STU

12 SV

13 S V

14 SV

15 SV

16 SU

17 SV

18 S V

19 S . V

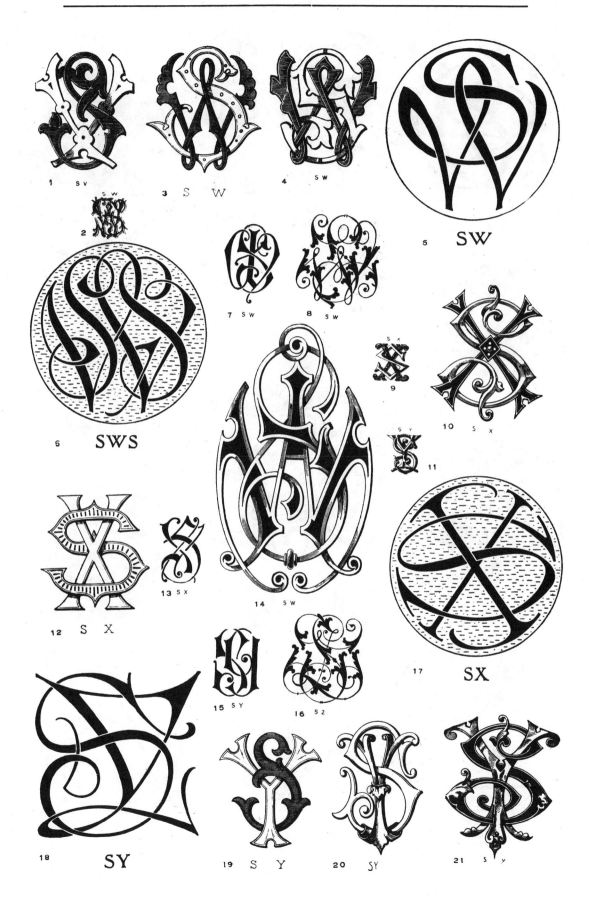

1 S V

2 SW

3 S W

4 S W

5 SW

6 SWS

7 SW

8 SW

9 S X

10 S X

11 S Y

12 S X

13 S X

14 S W

15 S Y

16 S Z

17 SX

18 SY

19 S Y

20 SY

21 S Y

1 SYS

2 S z

3 S Z

4 S Z

5 T A

6 S Z

7 S Y

8 T

9 T.A.N.

10 T A

11 T.A.D.

12 T A

13 T B

14 T B

15 SZ

16 T.A.T.

17 TA

1   STEPHEN.

2   SOPHIE

3   S . Y & C?

4   COURONNE ROSTRALE — ROME ANTIQUE

SOPHIE

5   SARAH.

6   SEMPER

7   COURONNE DE FER DES ANCIENS ROIS LOMBARDS.

SUZANNE

8   Souvenir.

9   SUSAN.

10   S&T

1   TB

2   3   T.B.A.   4

5   TC

6 T B   7   T C   8   T C

9   T. C. F.

10   T. C. K.

11   T. C. C.

12   T. C. J.

13   T D

14   TD

15   T D.L.

16   T C

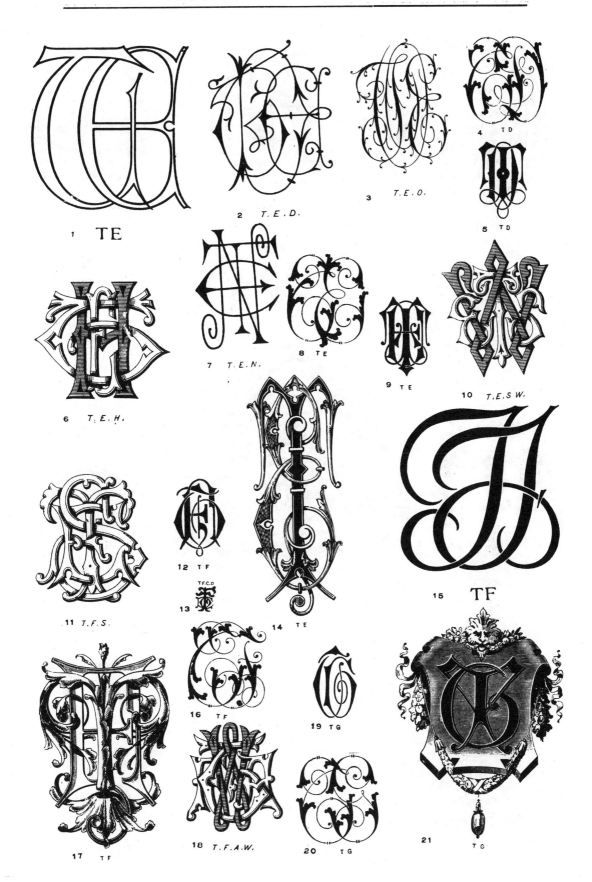

1   TE

2   *T. E. D.*

3   *T. E. O.*

4   TD

5   TD

6   *T. E. H.*

7   *T. E. N.*

8   TE

9   TE

10   *T. E. S. W.*

11   *T. F. S.*

12   TF

13

14   TE

15   TF

16   TF

17   TF

18   *T. F. A. W.*

19   TG

20   TG

21   TG

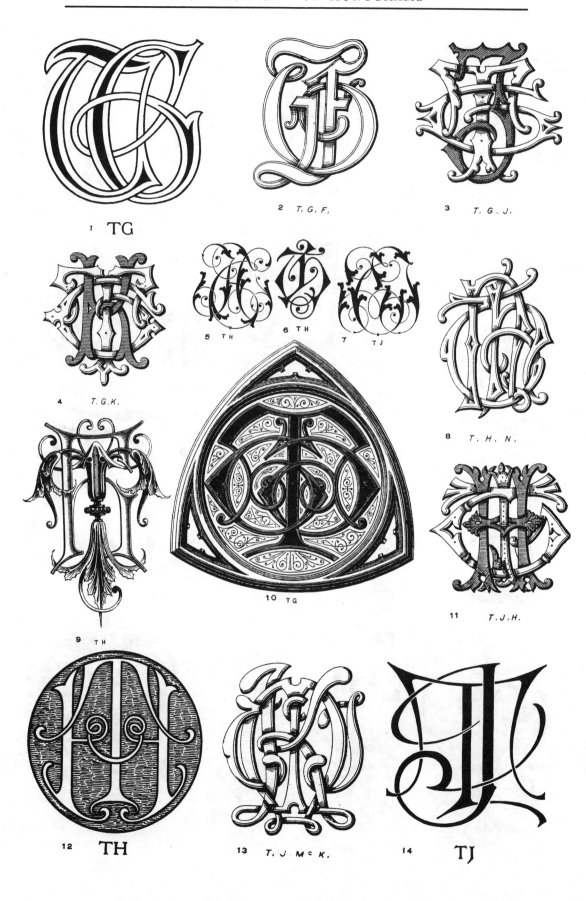

1   TG

2   T.G.F.

3   T.G.J.

4   T.G.K.

5 TH

6 TH

7   TJ

8   T.H.N.

9 TH

10 TG

11   T.J.H.

12   TH

13   T.J.McK.

14   TJ

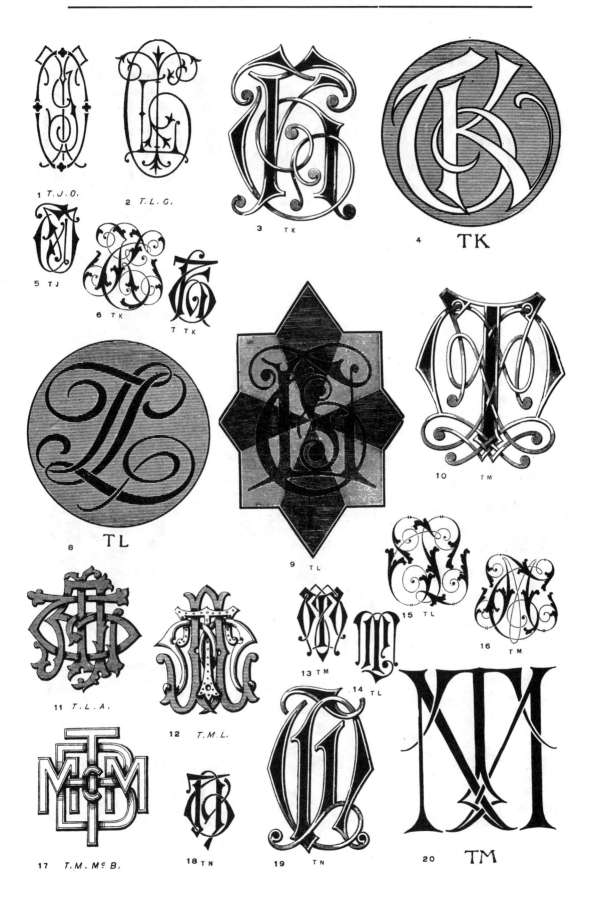

1 T.J.O.
2 T.L.G.
3 TK
4 TK
5 TJ
6 TK
7 TK
8 TL
9 TL
10 TM
11 T.L.A.
12 T.M.L.
13 TM
14 TL
15 TL
16 TM
17 T.M.McB.
18 TN
19 TN
20 TM

1   TN

2   *T.O.N.*

3   TO

4   TO

5   *T.O.Z.*

6   TP

7   TQ

8   TO

9   TR

10   TP

11   *T.R.E.*

12   TP

13   TQ

14   TQ

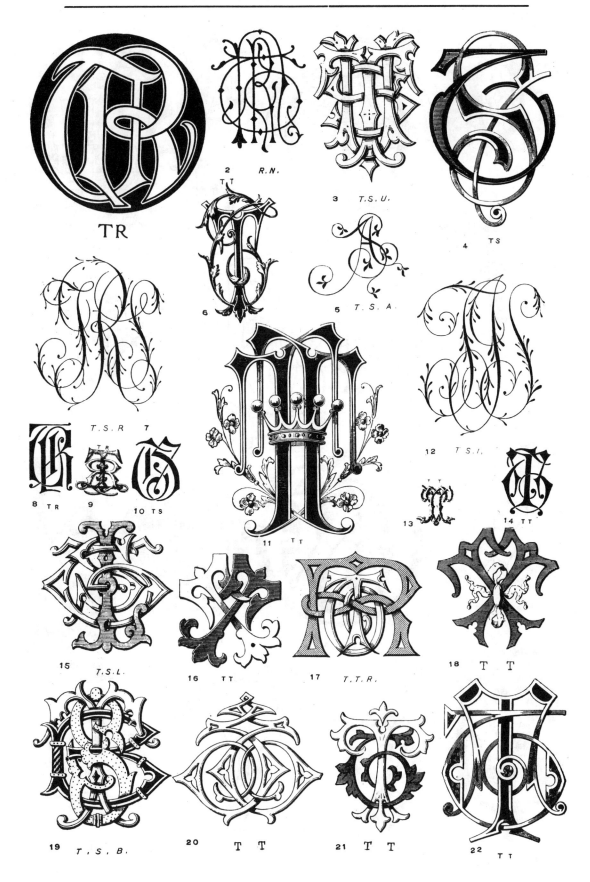

TR

2   R.N.

3   T.S.U.

4   TS

6

5   T.S.A.

T.S.R 7

8 TR   9   10 TS

11   T T

12   T.S.I.

13

14 T T

15   T.S.L.

16   T T

17   T.T.R.

18   T   T

19   T.S.B.

20   T T

21   T T

22   T T

1   T U

2   TU

3   T U A

4   T U

5   T U

6   T U

7   T U H R.

8   TUV

9   T V

10   T. U. S.

11   TUV

12   T V W.

13   T U

14   T V

15   T V

16   T U

17   T V

18   TV

19   T V

1 TW

2 T W

3 T W

4 T W

5 T W

6 T X

7

T X

8 T V

9 T Z

10 T V

11 T Y

12 T X

13 T W

14 TX

15 TY

16 TY

17 T W

18 T X

19 T X

1 T.Y.W.

2 T Y

3

4 T y

5 TZ

6 T Z

7 T Z

8 TOM

9 T Z

10 T & A.H.

11 T Z

12 Theodore

13 TIMOTHY.

14 T Y

15 T Z

16 TOM.

17 THOMAS.

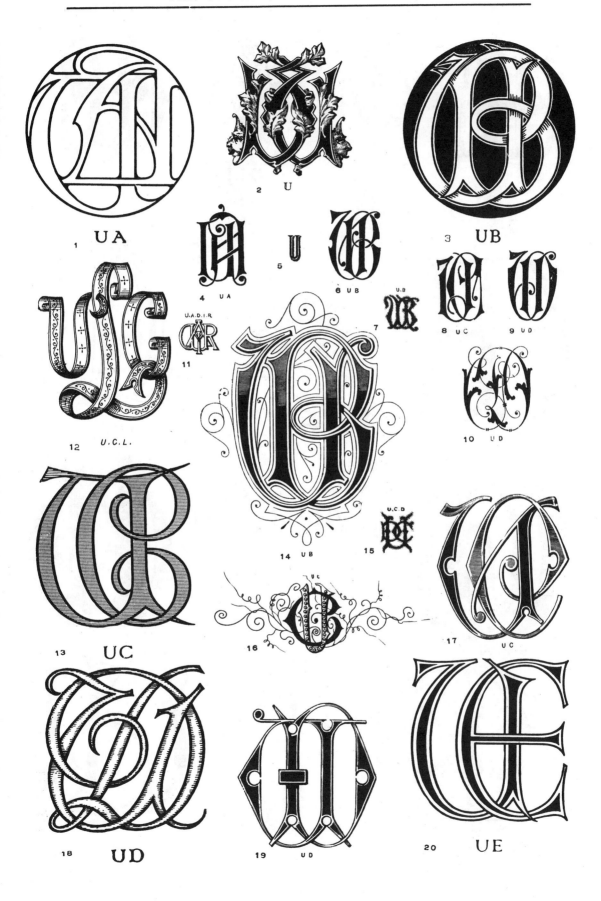

1 UA

2 U

3 UB

4 UA

5 U

6 UB

7 UB

8 UC

9 UD

10 UD

11 U.A.D.I.R.

12 U.C.L.

13 UC

14 UB

15 U.C.D.

16 UC

17 UC

18 UD

19 UD

20 UE

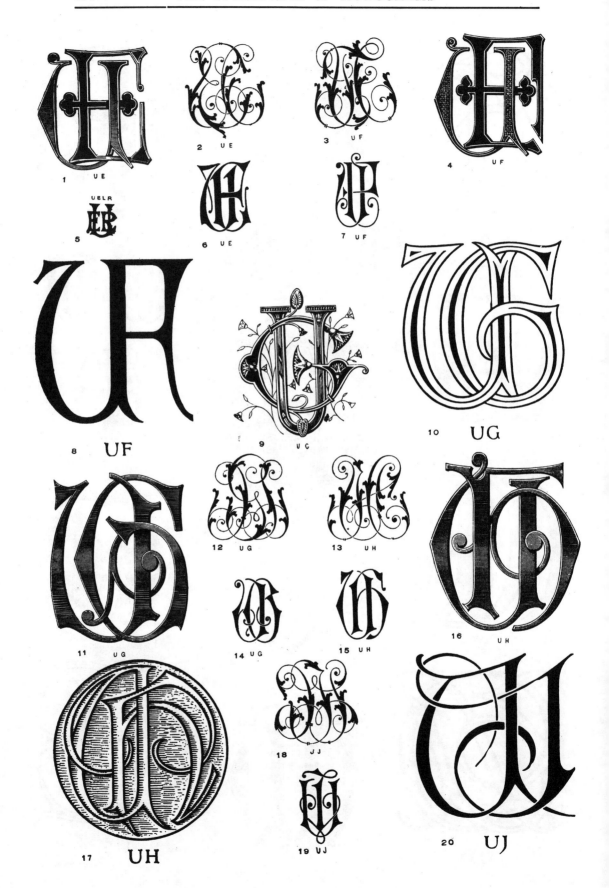

1 U E

2 U E

3 U F

4 U F

5 UELR

6 U E

7 U F

8 UF

9 U C

10 UG

11 U G

12 U G

13 U H

14 U G

15 U H

16 U H

17 UH

18 J J

19 UJ

20 UJ

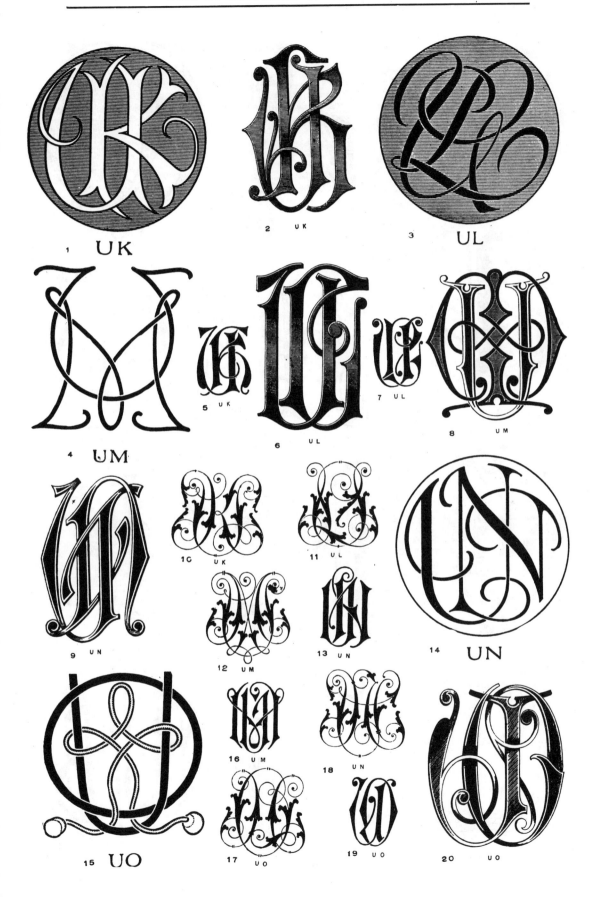

1 UK

2 UK

3 UL

4 UM

5 UK

6 UL

7 UL

8 UM

9 UN

10 UK

11 UL

12 UM

13 UN

14 UN

15 UO

16 UM

17 UO

18 UN

19 UO

20 UO

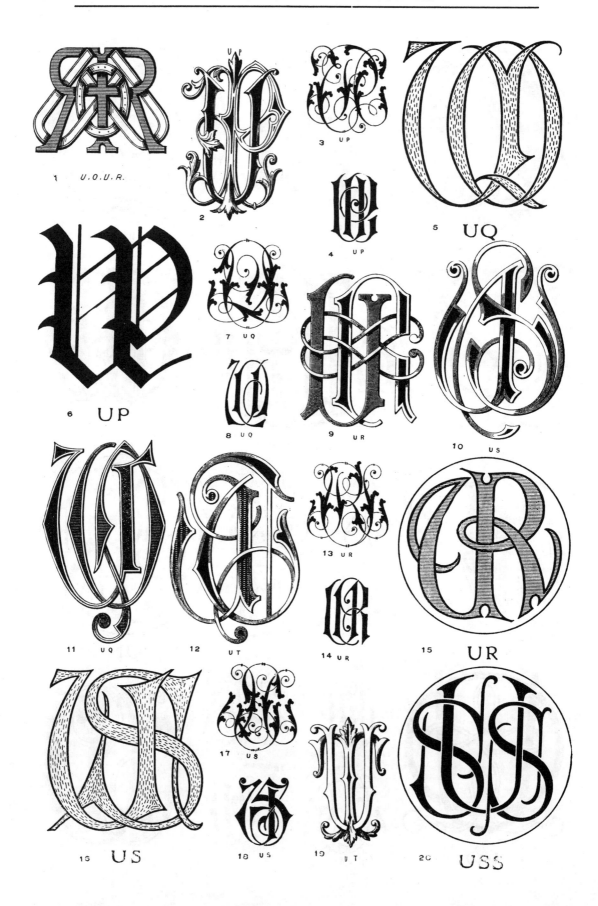

1 U.O.U.R.

2

3 UP

4 UP

5 UQ

6 UP

7 UQ

8 UQ

9 UR

10 US

11 UQ

12 UT

13 UR

14 UR

15 UR

16 US

17 US

18 US

19 UT

20 USS

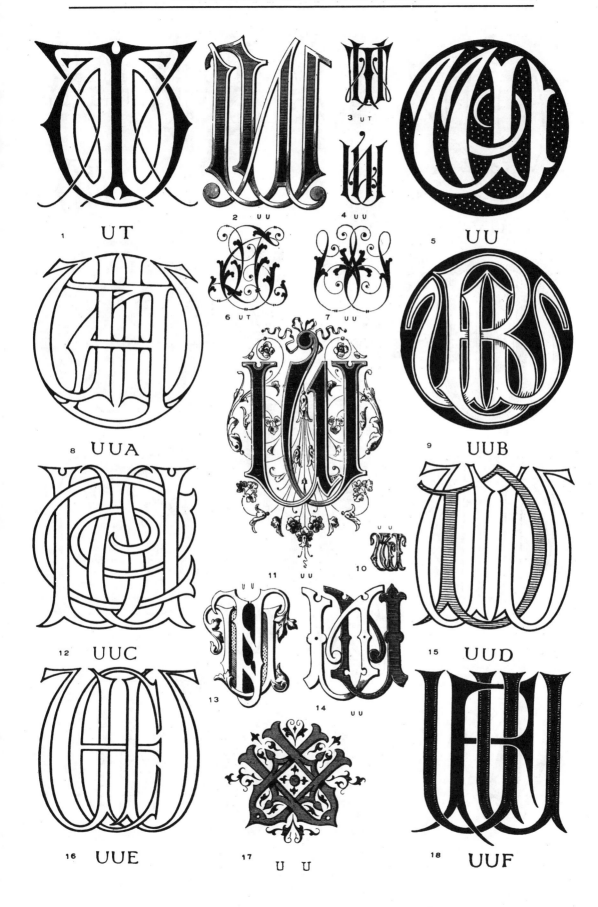

1 UT

2 UU

3 UT

4 UU

5 UU

6 UT

7 UU

8 UUA

9 UUB

10 UU

11 UU

12 UUC

13

14 UU

15 UUD

16 UUE

17 U U

18 UUF

1 UV

2 UV

3 UV

4 UV

5 UV

6 UV

8 UV

9 UV

10 UVW

11 UVW

12 UVW

13 UW

14 UW

15 UW

16 UW

17 UW

18 UW

19 UW

20 UW

1 U X

2 U X

3 U X

4 U X

5 U Y

6 U · Y

7 U X

8 UY

9 U Y

10 U Z

11 U Z

12 U Z

13 U Z

14 UZ

15 U Y

16 U Z

17 U Z

18 U Z

19 U Z

1   VA

2   VA

3   VA

4   VB

7   VB

5 VB

6

9   VC

8   VC

12   VD

13   VD

10   VC

11 ' VB

14   VD

16   VE

15   VE

17   VE

18   VD

19   VC

1 VF

2 VFR

3 V.G.P.

4 VG

5 VG

6 VF

7 VF

8 VG

9 VG

10 V.G.A

11 VF

12 VH

13 VHR

14 VJ

15 VJ

16 VH

17 VK

18 VJ

19 VK

20 VK

21 VK

22 VK

1   VL

2   VL

3   VM

4   VM

6   VL

5   VM

7   V.O

9

8   V.M.A.

10   V.M.L

13   VN

11   VN

12   VN

15   VO

16   VO

14

17   VM

18   V.O.C.

19   VN

1   VO

2   V P

3   V Q

4   V P

5   V Q

6   VP

7   V Q

8   V R

9   V S

10

11   V T

12   V T

13   V P

14   VR

15   V T

16   V U

17   VS

18   VT

19   V V

20   VU

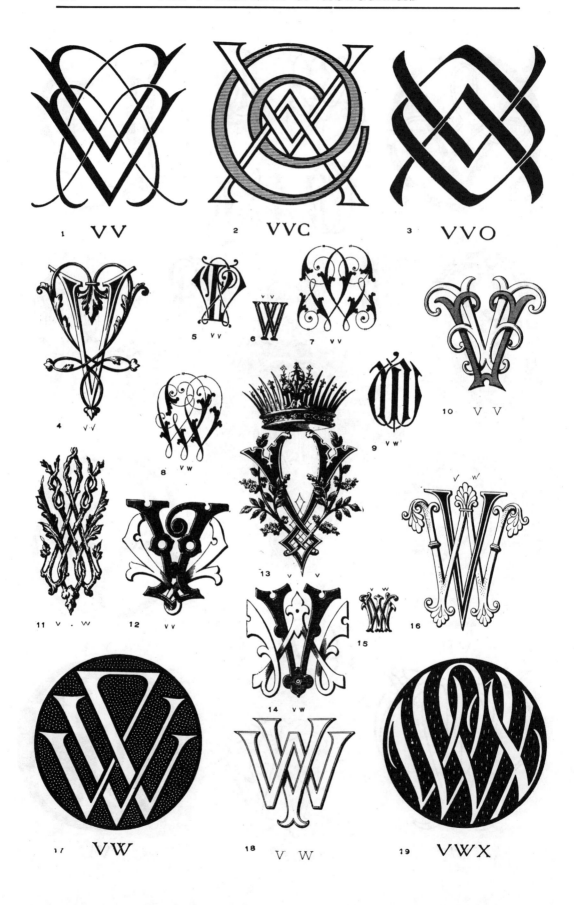

1   VV

2   VVC

3   VVO

4   v v

5   v v

6   vv

7   v v

8   v w

9   v w

10   V V

11   v . w

12   v v

13   v . v

14   v w

15   v w

16   v w

17   VW

18   V W

19   VWX

1 V W X

2 V X

3 VX

4 V X

5 V X

6

7 V Y

8 VY

9 V X

10 V Z

11 V Z

12 V Z

13 V U

14 V Y

15 V Z

16 V Y

17 V Y

18 V Z

19 V Z

20 VZ

WA

4

5   W. A. C

6   WWA

7   WA

8   W. A. P.

9   WB

10   W. B. S.

11   WAM

12   WAT

13

WC

14   WB

15   W.A.S.

16   WB

17   WC

18   WC

19   WCE

20   WC

21   W.A.W.

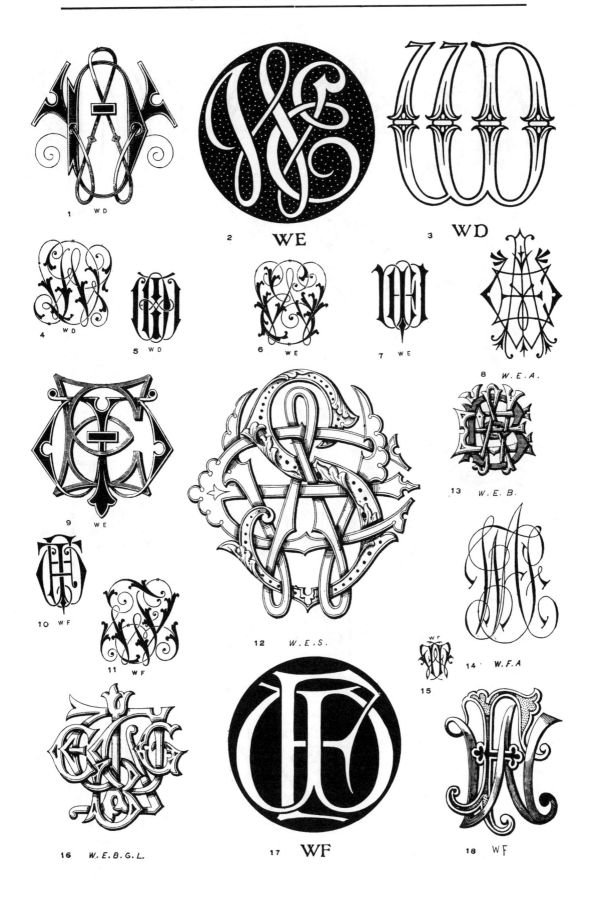

1 WD

2 WE

3 WD

4 WD

5 WD

6 WE

7 WE

8 W.E.A.

9 WE

10 WF

11 WF

12 W.E.S.

13 W.E.B.

14 W.F.A

15

16 W.E.B.G.L.

17 WF

18 WF

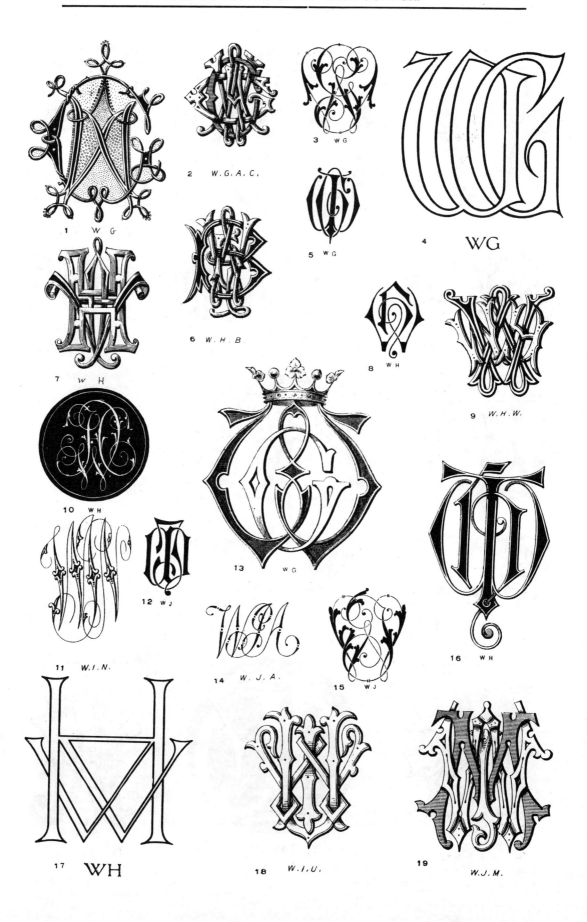

1   W G

2   W. G. A. C.

3   W G

4   WG

5   W G

6   W. H. B.

7   W H

8   W H

9   W. H. W.

10   W H

11   W. I. N.

12   W J

13   W G

14   W. J. A.

15   W J

16   W H

17   WH

18   W. I. U.

19   W. J. M.

1 WJ

2 WL

3 WK

4 WK

5 WK

6

7 WK

8 WL

9 WM

10

11 WM

12 WL

13 WL

14 WM

15 W.M.P.

16 WM

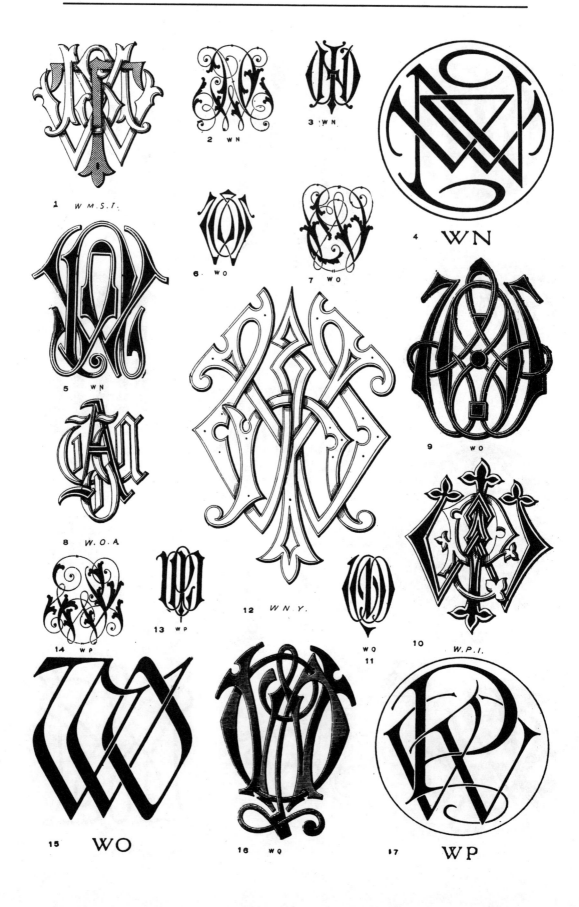

1   W M . S . T .

2   W N

3   W N

4   WN

5   W N

6   W O

7   W O

8   W . O . A

9   W O

10   W . P . I .

11   W Q

12   W N Y .

13   W P

14   W P

15   WO

16   W Q

17   WP

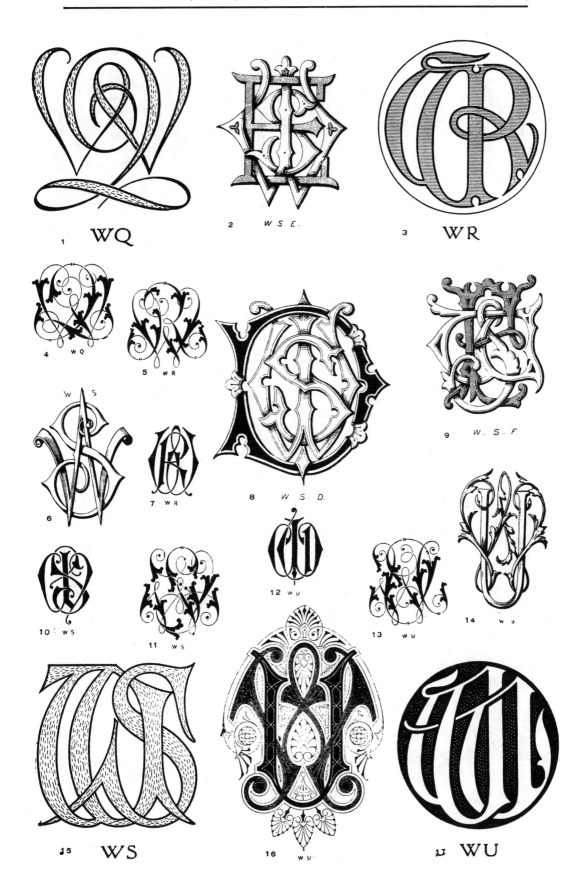

1 WQ

2 W S E.

3 WR

4 WQ

5 WR

6

7 WR

8 W S D.

9 W. S. F

10 WS

11 WS

12 WU

13 WU

14 WU

15 WS

16 WU

17 WU

1 WT

2 W. T. M

3 WT

4 W T G

5 WT

6 WT

7 WV

8 W T

9 WW

10 WV

11 W. W

12 WV

13 WW

15 W W

16 W W

17 WV

17 WTW

1

2 WW

3 ww

4 W.W.M.

5 WWB

6 WWC

7 WWD

8 ww

9 WWE

10 WWF

11 WWG

12 WWH

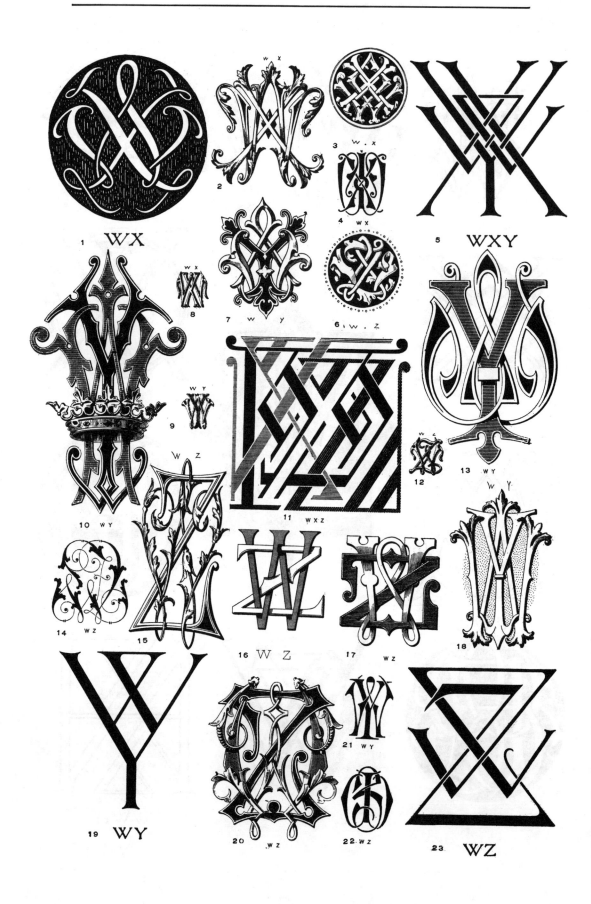

1 WX

2

3 W . X

4 WX

5 WXY

6 ｜w . z

7 w . y

8 w x

9 w y

10 WY

11 WXZ

12 w z

13 WY

14 w z

15

16 W Z

17 w z

18

19 WY

20 .W Z

21 WY

22 WZ

23 WZ

1   X A
2   X
3 X A   4   5 X B   6 X B
7 X C   8 X D
9 X E   10   11 X C   12   13 X D
14   X F   15 X F   16 X G   17 X H   18   X E
19   X G   20   X H   21   X G

1   XI

2   X J

3   X K

4   X K

5   X L

6   XIRILLA

7   X M

8   X L

9   X M

10 X N

11   X N

12   X O

13   X O

14   X P

15   X P

16   XPC

17   X P

18   XPC

XPC

2 XPS

3 XQ

4 XO

5 XR

6 XR

7

8 XU

10

11 XS

9 XV

12 XV

13 XU

14 XT

15 XV

16 X W

17 XW

18 X X

19 XX

20 XW

1　X W

2　XX

3

4　XX

5　XY

6　X　X

7　X. X. X.

8　XX

9　X Z

10　XZ

11　X X

12　XY

13　XZ

14　XZ

15　XY

16

17　x　y

18　XY

19　XZ

20　XYZ

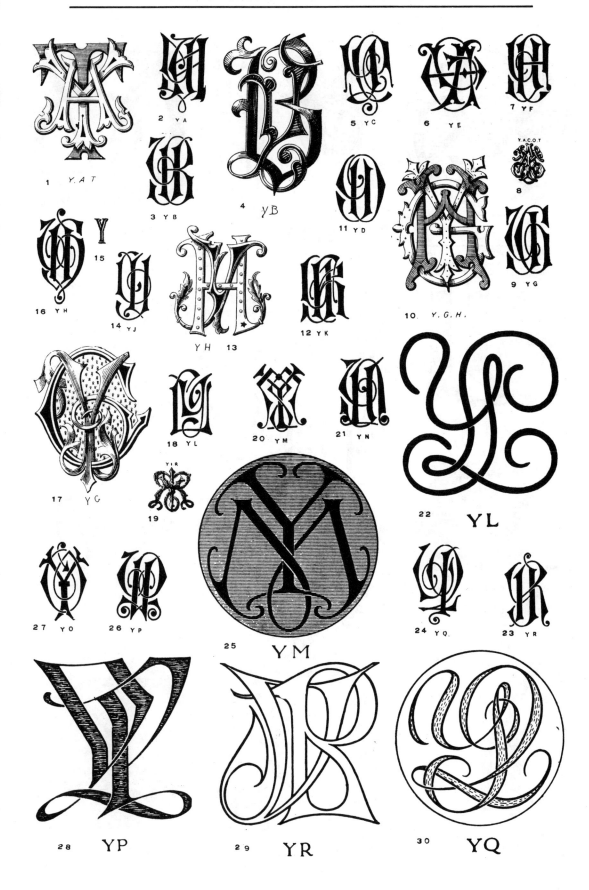

1 Y. A T

2 Y A

3 Y B

4 Y B

5 Y C

6 Y E

7 Y F

8 Y.A.C.O.T

9 Y G

10 Y. G. H.

11 Y D

12 Y K

13 Y H

14 Y J

15

16 Y H

17 Y C

18 Y L

19 Y R

20 Y M

21 Y N

22 Y L

23 Y R

24 Y Q

25 Y M

26 Y P

27 Y O

28 Y P

29 Y R

30 Y Q

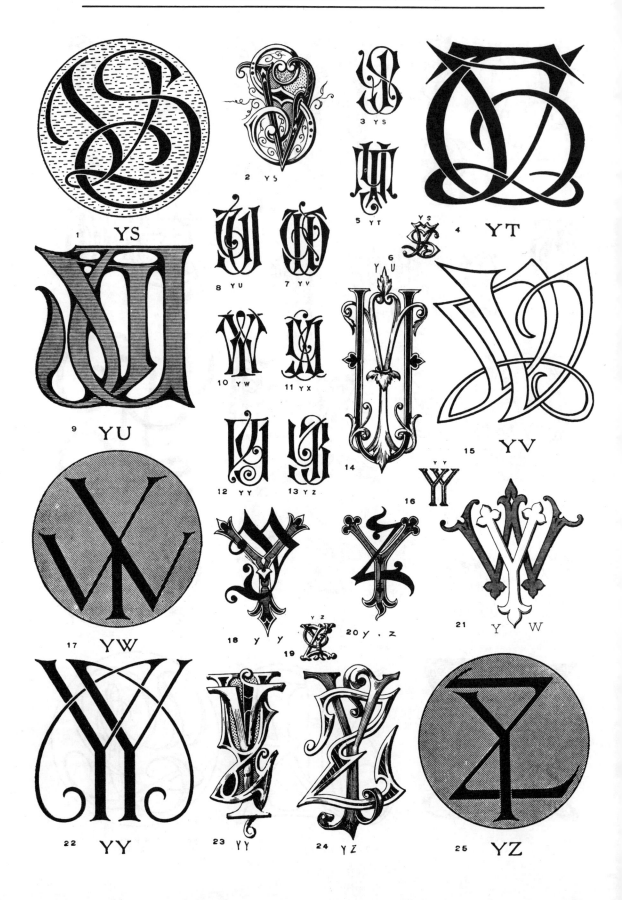

1 YS

2 YS

3 YS

4 YT

5 YT

8 YU

7 YV

6 YS

9 YU

10 YW

11 YX

14 YU

15 YV

12 YY

13 YZ

16 YY

17 YW

18 YY

19 YZ

20 Y.Z

21 YW

22 YY

23 YY

24 YZ

25 YZ

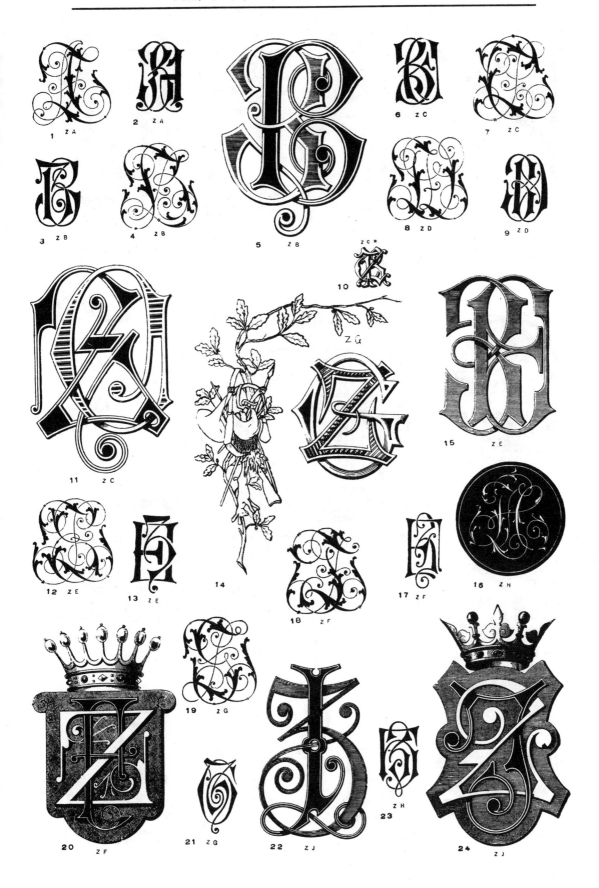

1 Z A
2 Z A
3 Z B
4 Z B
5 Z B
6 Z C
7 Z C
8 Z D
9 Z D
10 Z C R
11 Z C
Z G
15 Z E
12 Z E
13 Z E
14
16 Z H
17 Z F
18 Z F
19 Z G
20 Z F
21 Z G
22 Z J
23 Z H
24 Z J

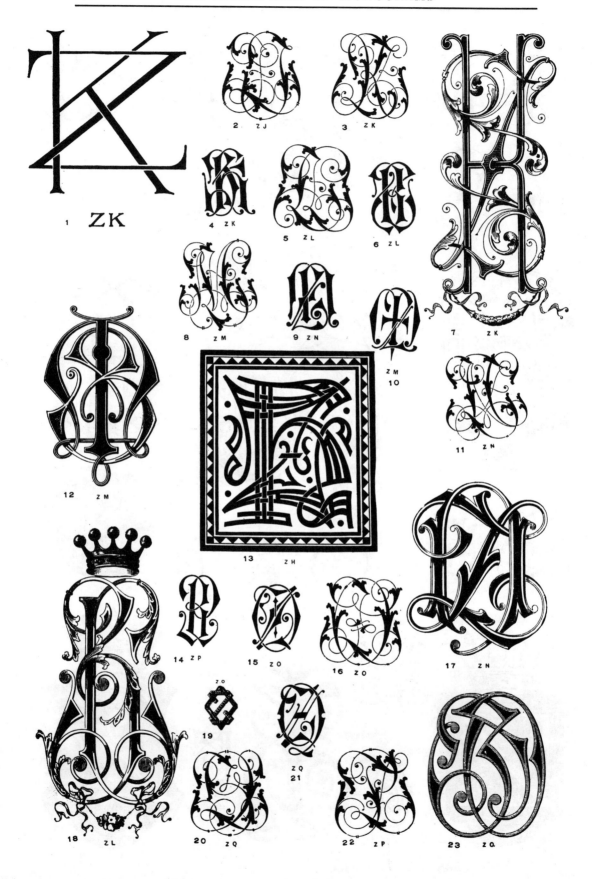

1 ZK

2 ZJ

3 ZK

4 ZK

5 ZL

6 ZL

7 ZK

8 ZM

9 ZN

10 ZM

11 ZN

12 ZM

13 ZH

14 ZP

15 ZO

16 ZO

17 ZN

18 ZL

19 ZO

20 ZQ

21 ZQ

22 ZP

23 ZQ

1 Z V

2 Z W

3 Z Y

4 Z W

5 Z . Z

6 Z W

7 Z X

8 Z Z

9 ZZ

10 Z . Z

11 Z Z

12 Z Z

13 Z Z

14 Z Z

15 Z Z

1   Z Q
2   Z R
3   Z R
4   Z S
5   Z R
6   Z S
7   Z S
8   Z S
9   Z T
10   Z P
11   Z T
12   Z U
13   Z U
14   Z T
15   Z T
16   Z V
17   Z U E
18   Z V
19   Z U

PART III.

Shields ❧ ❧
Coats of Arms
Crests ❧ ❧
Emblems ❧ ❧
Badges ❧ ❧
Decorations ❧
Crowns ❧ ❧
Escutcheons ❧

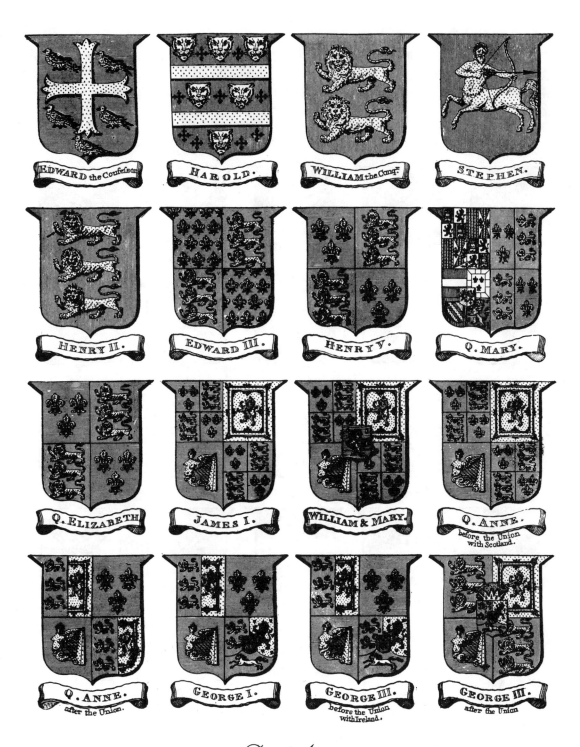

Royal Arms.

Canterbury   York   London   Durham

Winchester   St. Asaph   Bangor   Bath & Wells   Bristol

Carlisle   Chester   Chichester   St. Davids   Ely

Exeter   Gloucester   Hereford   Lichfield   Lincoln

Landaff   Norwich   Oxford   Peterborough   Rochester

Salisbury   Worcester   Calcutta   Quebec   Sodor & Man

Episcopal Sees

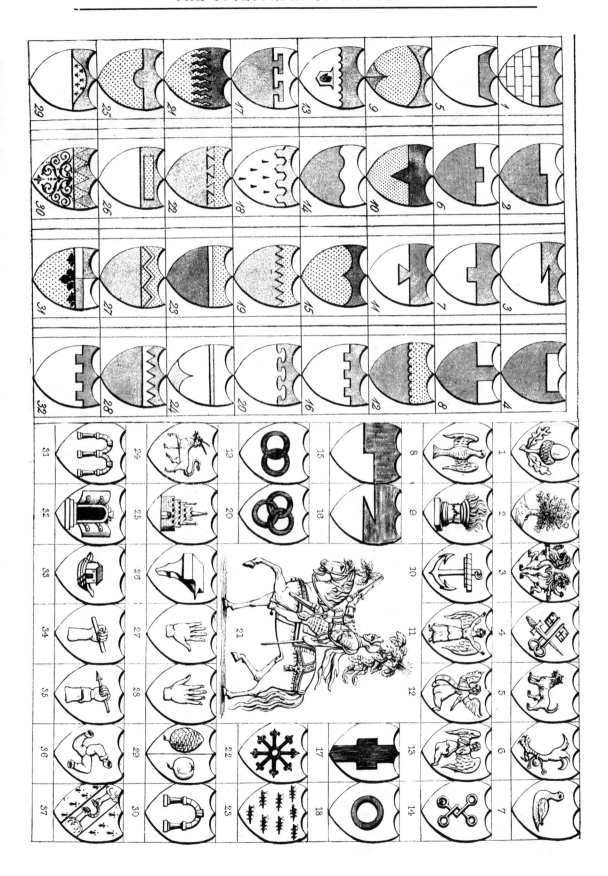

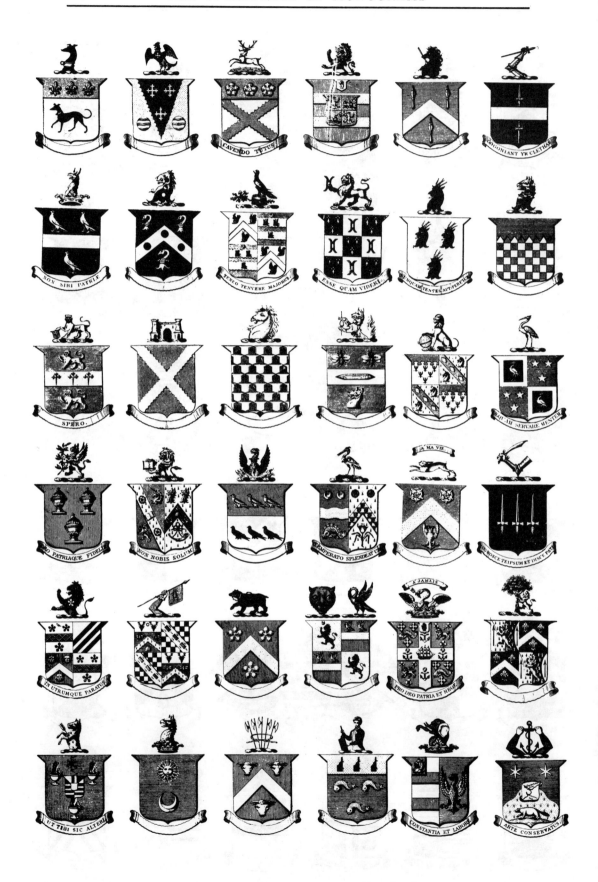

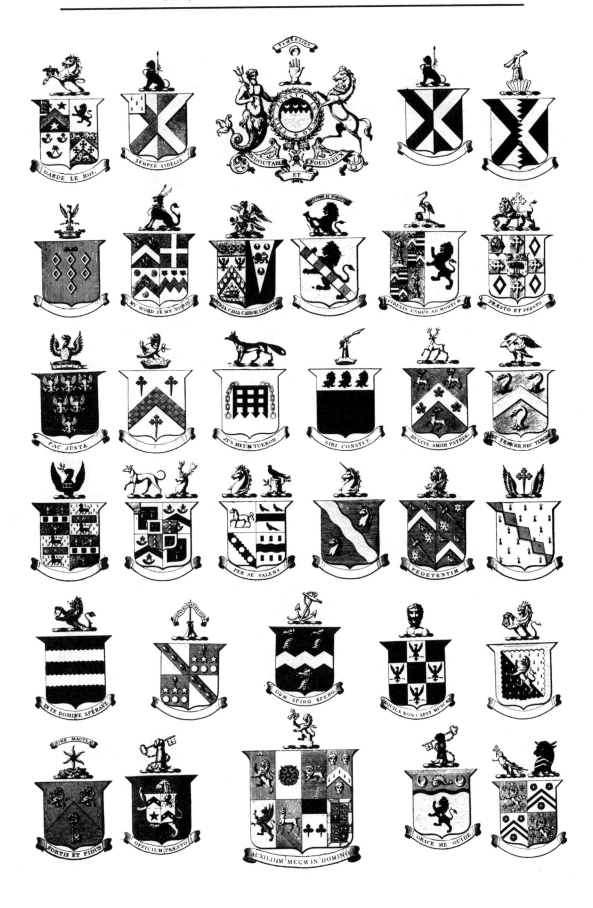

ORDER of St. PATRICK

Golden Angel or St. George.

Golden Angel or St. George.

Chase.

Star Chase.

Ullum

Goog

Brician.

Collar. Chase.

ORDER of the THISTLE.

St. Januarius. Naples.

Star

St. Januarius.

The Badge.

The Jewel.

St. Anne. Russia.

2. Thistle of Bourbon.

St. Ferdinand

Dragon overthrown.

Concord, Prussia.

Badge, Legion of Honor

Badge, Legion of Honor

Star. Legion of Honor

Crown. Bavaria.

Isabel, the Catholic, Spain

Crown. Bavaria.

Double Crescent, or Ship & Escallop-shell.

Isabel, the Catholic, Spain.

Generosity Prussia

St. Anthony Hainault

Maria Theresa, Austria

St. Stephen, Aust.ª

St. Stephen, Aust.ª

Maria Theresa Aust.ª

St. Stephen, Austria.

Two Sicilies.

St. Stephen, Tuscany

Seraphim, Sweden.

Two Sicilies

St. Stephen, Tuscany.

Templars.

St. James, France.

Seraphim.

Order of Bath.

Collar

Helmet or Iron Casque.

Charles III

St. Anne, Russia.

Badge.

Holy Phial, France.

Collar, Charles III.

Charles III. Knights Pensioners.

Charles III. Grand Cross.

St. George, Rome.

Crescent, Turkey.

Crescent, Turkey.
Reverse of Badge.

Crescent, Turkey.
Medal.

Amaranta.

Order of Danebrog.

1
Badge, Grand Cross

Collar

4
Badge, Second Class

Badge, Third Class.

Star

Badge, Fourth Class.

Teutonic

Teutonic Order

Teutonic

St. Andrew, Russia.

Tower & Sword

Bear.

Tower & Sword

Vasa.

Black Eagle, Prussia.

Collar.

St Elizabeth

Elizabeth Thérèse.

Alcantara.

Badge.
Star.

SUUM CUIQUE.

St Blaise & the Virgin.

St Blaise or St Bass.

St Alexander Newski.

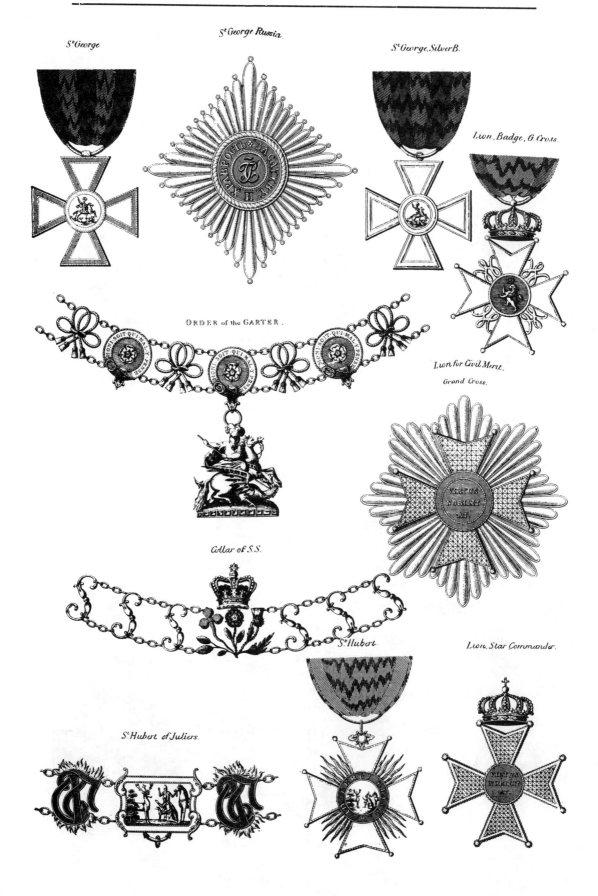

St George

St George Russia.

St George, Silver B.

Lion, Badge, G. Cross.

ORDER of the GARTER.

Lion for Civil Merit.

Grand Cross.

Collar of S.S.

St Hubert.

Lion, Star Commander.

St Hubert of Juliers.

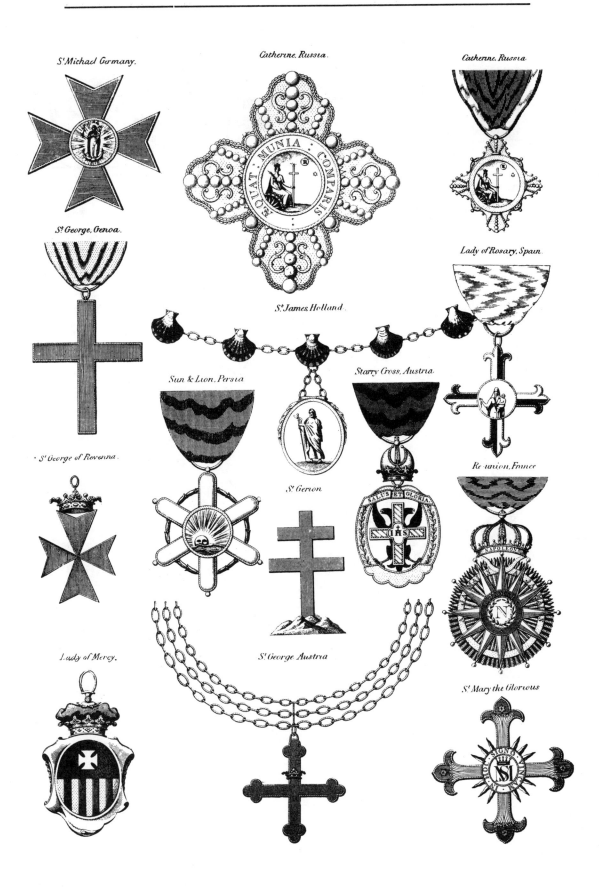

St Michael Germany.

Catherine, Russia.

Catherine, Russia.

St George, Genoa.

Lady of Rosary, Spain.

St James, Holland.

Sun & Lion, Persia.

Starry Cross, Austria.

St George of Ravenna.

Re-union, France

St Gerion.

Lady of Mercy.

St George Austria.

St Mary the Glorious

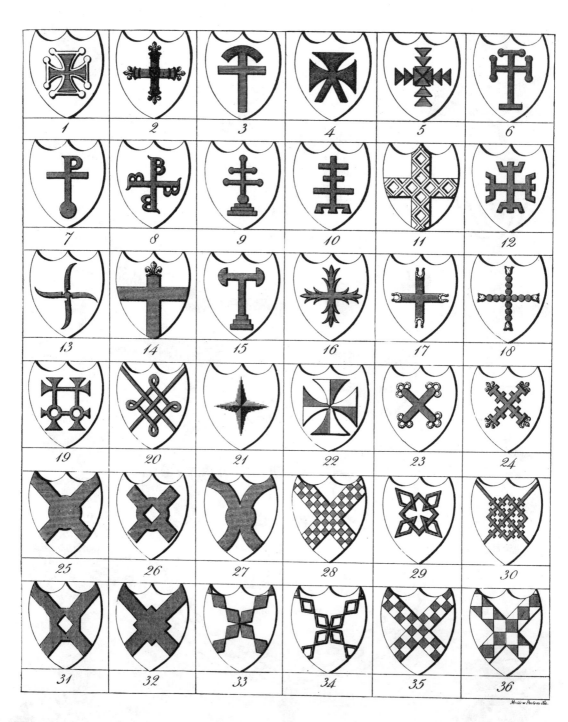

Crosses

CROWNS OF GERMANY AND AUSTRIA

Royal crown of Bohemia I.

Coronet of Austrian archduke II.

Royal crown of Bohemia II.

Imperial crown of Austria.

The iron crown I.

Royal crown of Hungary I

Crown of the holy roman german empire.

The iron crown II.

Ancient crown.

Coronet of the heir apparent of Germany.

Prince's coronet.

Modern royal crown.

Royal crown of Hannover.

Coronet of count's bearing the title „Erlaucht"

Coronet of Austrian archduke I.

Prince's coronet.

Crown of the German Empress.

Modern coronet of Knights and nobleman.

Royal crown of Hungary II.

Modern coronet of a count.

Coronet of an Elector.

Present royal crown of Prussia.

Ancient coronet of a count.

Ancient Baron's coronet.

Modern Baron's coronet.

Coronet of a count.

New Imperial crown of Germany.

CROWNS OF THE NAPOLEONIC DYNASTY

Herzogskrone.
La couronne de Duc.
Ducal coronet.

Napoleonische Kaiserkrone.
La couronne imperiale des Napoléonides.
Imperial crown of the Napoleonic dynasty.

Marquiskrone.
La couronne de Marquis.
Coronet of a Marquis.

Königskrone der Bourbonen. II.
La couronne royale des Bourbons. II.
Royal coronet of the house of Bourbon. II.

Krone der Prinzen vom Geblüt (Orleans).
La couronne des Princes du sang (Orleans).
Coronet of Princes of blood royal
(house of Orleans).

Königskrone Louis Philipp (Orleans).
La couronne royale Louis Philipp (Orléans).
Royal crown of Louis Philipp (house of Orleans).

Bannerherr.
Banneret.
Baronet's coronet

Krone des Dauphin (Kronprinz der Bourbonen).
La couronne du Dauphin (prince royale des Bourbons)
Coronet of the Dauphin (house of Orleans).

Freiherrnkrone.
La couronne de Baron.
Baron's coronet.

Krone des Kronprinzen (Herzog v. Orleans).
La couronne du Prince royale (Duc de Orléans).
Coronet of the heir apparent (Duke of Orleans).

Ritter.
Chevalier.
Knight.

Königskrone der Bourbonen. I.
La couronne royal des Bourbons. I.
Royal crown of the house of Bourbon. I.

Coronet of royal Princes
(house of Bourbon).

Krone des Vidame.
La couronne du Vidame.
Coronet of a Vidame.

Zepter der
Napoleoniden.
Sceptre des
Napoléonides.
Scepter of the
Napoleonic
dynasty.

Coronet of Princes of blood royal
(house of Bourbon).

Alte Marquiskrone.
La couronne ancienne de Marquis.
Ancient coronet of a Marquis.

Grafenkrone.
La couronne de comte.
Count's coronet.

Die Hand der
Gerechtigkeit.
Main de
justice.
Judicial
Sceptre.

Zepter der Bourbonen.
Sceptre des Bourbons.
Sceptre of the house of Bourbon.

Zepter der Orleans.
Sceptre des Orleans.
Scepter of the house of Orleans.

Krone des Vicomte.
La couronne du Vicomte.
Viscount's coronet.

CROWNS OF THE NETHERLANDS

Freiherrnkrone.
Couronne de baron.
Baron's coronet.

Krone der Ritter.
Couronne de chevalier.
Knight's coronet.

Marquiskrone.
Couronne de marquis.
Coronet of a marquis.

Krone des Vicomte (Burggrafen.).
Couronne de vicomte (Burgrave).
Viscount's (Burgrave's) coronet.

Adelskrone.
Couronne de gentilhomme.
Nobleman's coronet.

Spanien. — Espagne. — Spain.

Grafenkrone.
Conronne de comte.
Count's coronet.

Königskrone.
Couronne royal.
Royal crown.

Fürstenkrone.

Grafenkrone.
Couronne de comte.
Count's coronet.

Marquiskrone.
Couronne de marquis.
Coronet of a marquis.

Freiherrnkrone.
Couronne de baron.
Baron's coronet.

Alte Herzogskrone.
Couronne ancienne de duc.
Ancient ducal coronet.

Herzogkrone.
Couronne de duc.
Ducal coronet.

Krone der Ritter.
Couronne de chevalier.
Knight's coronet.

Portugal. — Portugal. — Portugal.

Königskrone.
Couronne royale.
Royal crown.

Marquiskrone.
Couronne de marquis.
Coronet of a marquis.

Fürstenkrone.
Couronne des princes.
Coronet of a prince.

Viscount's coronet.

Freiherrnkrone.
Couronne de baron.
Baron's coronet.

Krone der Ritter.
Couronne de chevalier.
Knight's coronet.

CROWNS OF IMPERIAL RUSSIA

Krone von Kasan.
Couronne de Kassan.
Crown of Kassan.

Krone der Kaiserin.
Couronne de l'Impératrice.
Empress' crown.

Krone von Astrachan.
Couronne d'Astrakhan.
Crown of Astrachan.

Krone der Erlauchten Fürsten.
Couronne des princes de l'Empire.
Coronet of imperial Princes.

Freiherrnkrone.
Couronne de baron.
Baron's coronet.

Krone der Durchlauchten Fürsten.
Couronne des princes ayant le titre d'altesse.
Coronet of Princes addressed as "your Highness"

Krone des Hauses Romanow.
Couronne de la Maison des Romanows.
Coronet of the house of Romanoff.

Krone des Kaisers.
Couronne de l'Empereur.
Imperial crown.

Krone von Krusinien.
Couronne de Krusinie.
Coronet of Grusinia.

Krone von Taurien.
Couronne de la Tauride.
Crown of Taurida.

Grafenkrone.
Couronne de comte.
Count's coronet.

Krone von Kiew.
Couronne de Kiew.
Crown of Kiew

Krone von Polen.
Couronne de Pologne.
Crown of Poland.

Krone von Finnland.
Couronne de Finlande.
Crown of Finland.

Krone von Sibirien.
Couronne de Sibérie.
Crown of Siberia.

CROWNS OF ITALY

Herzogskrone.
La couronne de Duc.
Ducal coronet.

Königskrone.
La couronne royal.
Royal crown.

Krone des Marchese.
La couronne de Marquis.
Coronet of a Marquis.

Grafenkrone.
La couronne de comte.
Count's coronet.

Patricierkrone.
La couronne du patricien.
Coronet of a patrician.

Erbritterkrone.
La couronne du Chevalier
héréditaire.
Coronet of a hereditary Knight.

Krone der Edelleute.
La couronne des nobles.
Nobleman's coronet.

Fürstenkrone.
La couronne de prince.
Princes coronet.

Freiherrnkrone.
La couronne de baron.
Baron's coronet.

Krone der Visconte.
La couronne de Vicomte.
Coronet of a Viscount.

England. — Angleterre. — England.

Königliche Krone. I.
Couronne royale. I.
Royal crown. I.

Krone des Prinzen von Wales (Kronprinz).
Couronne du prince de Galles (prince royal).
Coronet of the Prince of Wales.

Königliche Krone. II.
Couronne royale. II.
Royal crown. II.

Prinzessinkrone.
Couronne des princesses
Princess' coronet.

Krone der königlichen Neffen.
Couronne de neveux royaux.
Coronet of the royal nephews.

Prinzenkrone.
Couronne des princes.
Princes' coronet.

Herzogskrone.
Couronne de duc.
Ducal coronet.

Marquiskrone.
Couronne de marquis.
Coronet of a marquis.

Freiherrnkrone.
Couronne de baron.
Baronet's coronet.

Grafenkrone.
Couronne de comte.
Earl's coronet.

Viscountkrone.
Couronne de vicomte.
Viscount's coronet.

CROWNS OF SWEDEN - NORWAY

Prinzessinkrone.
Couronne des princesses.
Princess' coronet.

Königskrone.
Couronne royale.
Royal crown.

Kronprinz- und Prinzenkrone.
Couronne du prince royal et des princes.
Coronet of the Heir apparent and other princes.

Adelskrone.
Couronne de noble.
Nobleman's coronet.

Freiherrnkrone.
Couronne de baron.
Baron's coronet.

Alte Grafenkrone.
Couronne ancienne de comte.
Ancient count's coronet.

Grafenkrone.
Couronne de comte.
Count's coronet.

CROWNS OF BELGIUM

Freiherrnkrone.
Couronne de baron.
Baron's coronet.

Königskrone.
Couronne royal.
Royal crown.

Grafenkrone.
Couronne de comte.
Count's coronet.

Fürstenkrone.
Couronne des princes.
Prince's coronet.

Adelskrone.
Couronne de gentilhomme.
Nobleman's coronet.

Freiherrnkrone.
Couronne de baron.
Baron's coronet.

Fürsten- und Herzogskrone.
Couronne des princes et des ducs.
Prince's and Ducal coronet.

Grafenkrone.
Couronne de comte.
Count's coronet.

CROWNS OF THE NETHERLANDS

Herzogskrone.
Couronne de duc.
Ducal coronet.

Königskrone.
Couronne royale.
Royal crown.

Fürstenkrone.
Couronne des princes.
Prince's coronet.

VARIOUS CROWNS

Krone des Herzogthums Zara und Ragusa.
Couronne ducale de Zara et de Raguse.
Crown of the Duchies of Zara and Ragusa.

Krone der Herrschaft Cattaro.
Couronne de la Seigneurie de Cattaro.
Crown of the domain of Cattaro.

Königliche Krone von Dalmatien.
Couronne royale de Dalmatie.
Royal crown of Dalmatia.

China, Japan etc.
Chine, Japon etc.
China, Japan etc.

Persien.
Perse.
Persia.

Türkei.
Turquie.
Turkey.

Schiffskrone.
Couronne navale ou rostrale.
Naval or rostral crown.

Pallisadenkrone.
Couronne vallaire.
Corona vallaris.

Mauerkrone.
Couronne murale.
Mural crown.

Dogenmütze.
Bonnet de doge.
Cap of a doge.

Kaiserkrone von Brasilien.
Couronne imperiale du Brésil.
Imperial crown of Brazil.

Krone von Montenegro und der Donau-Fürstenthümer.
Couronne de Montenegro et des Principautes Danubiennes.
Crown of Montenegro and Danubian Principalities.

I.
I—III. Weibliche Attribute.
I—III. Attributs féminins.
I—III. Female attributes.

II.

III.

Geistlichkeit. — Clergé. — Ecclesiastical.

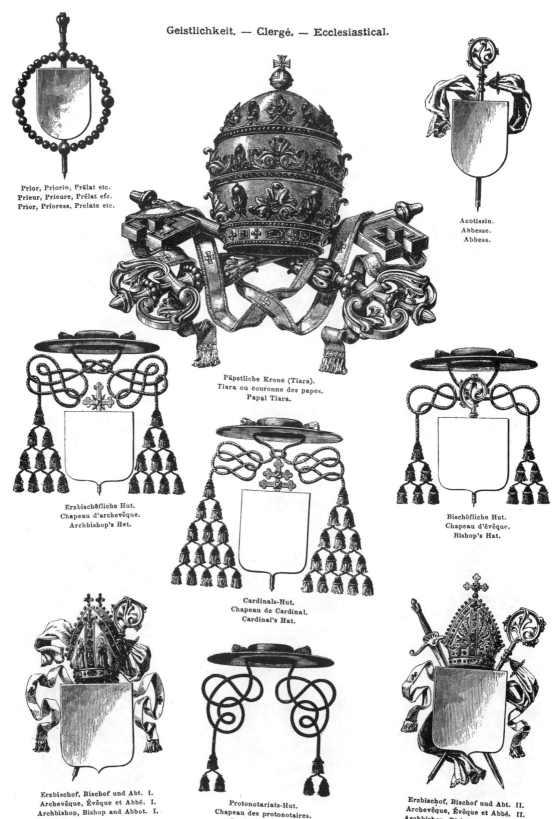

Prior, Priorin, Prälat etc.
Prieur, Prieure, Prélat etc.
Prior, Prioress, Prelate etc.

Päpstliche Krone (Tiara).
Tiara ou couronne des papes.
Papal Tiara.

Aebtissin.
Abbesse.
Abbess.

Erzbischöfliche Hut.
Chapeau d'archevêque.
Archbishop's Hat.

Cardinals-Hut.
Chapeau de Cardinal.
Cardinal's Hat.

Bischöfliche Hut.
Chapeau d'évêque.
Bishop's Hat.

Erzbischof, Bischof und Abt. I.
Archevêque, Évêque et Abbé. I.
Archbishop, Bishop and Abbot. I.

Protonotariats-Hut.
Chapeau des protonotaires.
Protonotary's Hat.

Erzbischof, Bischof und Abt. II.
Archevêque, Évêque et Abbé. II.
Archbishop, Bishop and Abbot. II.

1 HELMET OF EMPERORS AND KINGS.   2 DUKES AND PRINCES.   3 MARQUIS.
4 COUNTS AND VICOUNTS.   5 BARONS.   6 CHEVALIERS.   7 GENTLEMEN.

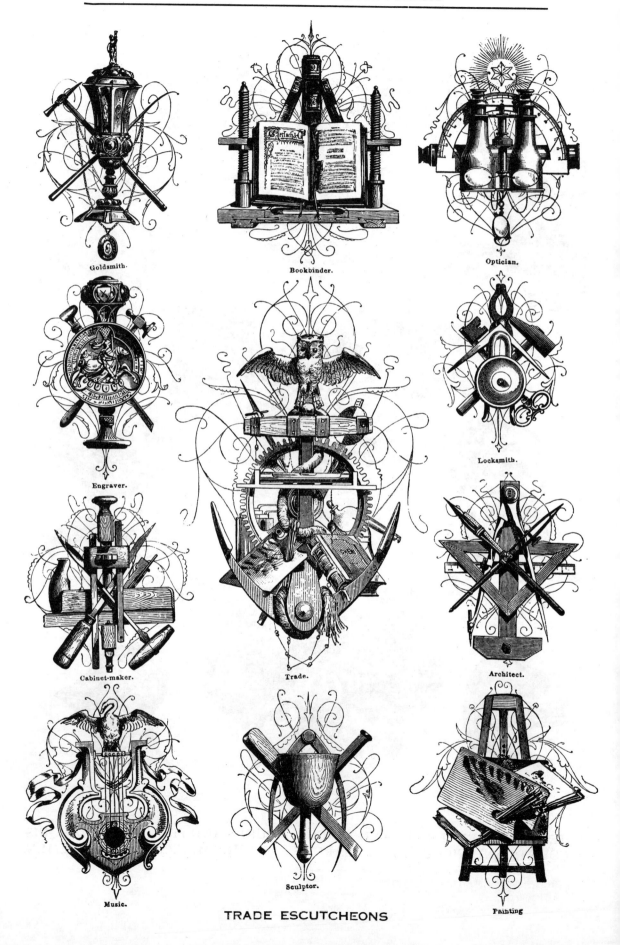

Goldsmith.

Bookbinder.

Optician.

Engraver.

Locksmith.

Cabinet-maker.

Trade.

Architect.

Music.

Sculptor.

Painting

TRADE ESCUTCHEONS

PART IV.

Types and Forms
— For —
Refined Engraving
And Printing ❧ ❧

MODERN REFINED ENGRAVING AND PRINTING.

The types, monograms, crests, coats-of-arms and ornamental designs in this volume will naturally have a special interest to engravers, printers, stationers and to retail merchants taking commissions for fine engraving or printing.

Its service to members of these trades being a special concern of this volume, some suggestions as to how to achieve the best results may be of interest.

The important essentials in successful printing, either copper plate or type, are correctness as to style, a fine quality of paper, perfect engraving or type, artistic printing and neatness of package. There is little excuse for anything but the best work, the only real item of increased cost, as be-

The appropriate style of engraved lettering or type is indicated by the smaller sizes of the series appearing on the pages entitled ''Types for Cards and Announcements.''

The quality of the cardboard should always be of the best. The weight or thickness is largely a matter of personal taste, though the present tendency is toward the thinner boards known as the ''two-ply.'' These are on sale in the correct sizes packed in attractive boxes.

Mourning Cards.—The width of black band varies according to relationship. For a widow's card a band of about one-third inch during first year of widowhood, diminishing about one-sixteenth

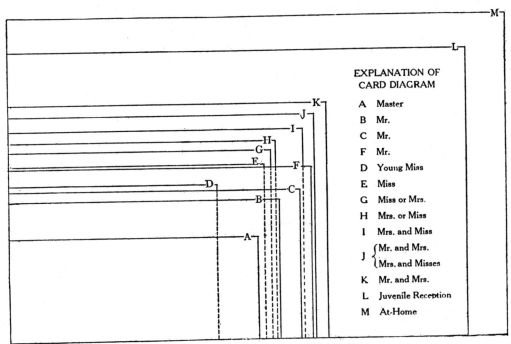

EXPLANATION OF
CARD DIAGRAM

A Master
B Mr.
C Mr.
F Mr.
D Young Miss
E Miss
G Miss or Mrs.
H Mrs. or Miss
I Mrs. and Miss
J { Mr. and Mrs.
{ Mrs. and Misses
K Mr. and Mrs.
L Juvenile Reception
M At-Home

DIAGRAM OF CORRECT SIZES OF CARDS

tween inferior and superior results, being in the paper, and this at the most is comparatively a small percentage of the total cost.

CORRECT STYLE.

Cards.—The diagram above will indicate the accepted sizes for society printing, ladies' cards being, it will be observed, nearly square, while gentlemen's are oblong:

The correct wording of cards, according to an accepted authority, is as follows, the sizes in each case being indicated by numbers referring to the Diagram.

inch each six months thereafter. On a widower's card one-quarter inch is the widest, diminishing gradually from time to time. For other relations, the band is not so wide. Envelopes are made to match, when required.

Mrs. John James Brown	
Fridays	Ninety Church Street

At home between 3:00 and 6:00 o'clock to receive calls, meaning Friday of every week; or it may be limited to "First Fridays" (of the month), "Fridays until April," "First and Third Fridays," etc. Sizes H, I.

> Mrs. John James Brown
> Ninety Church Street

The address may be omitted, but it is usually printed. Spell out the street number and numbered streets when practicable. Sizes G, H, I.

> Miss Brown

An elder or only daughter does not print her Christian name, and, while residing with her mother, omits her address. Size E, G, H.

> Mrs. John James Brown
> Miss Sarah Brown
> Fridays   Ninety Church Street

On first entering society a young lady does not use a calling card of her own. Her name is printed below that of her mother, with or without the "At-Home" day. If she calls alone a pencil line is run through the mother's name. Size I.

> Mrs. John James Brown
> The Misses Brown
> Ninety Church Street

When two daughters enter society in the same season this form is used. Even after the daughters have calling cards of their own, this or the form above it is used for calling together or for days at home. Sizes, I, J.

> Miss Mary Brown

The younger daughters use their full names. Sizes E, G, H.

> The Misses Brown

For calling together. Sizes G, H.

> Mr. and Mrs. John Brown
> Ninety Church Street

For sending with wedding gifts, for joint regrets, and returning first calls after marriage. Use of separate cards is better form. Sizes J, K.

> Mr. John James Brown

It is not usual to put the home address on a married gentleman's card or that of a gentleman residing with his parents. Sizes B, C.

> Mr. Robert Brown
> York Athletic Club

For bachelor whose address is at his club. Sizes B, C.

> Mr. Justice Arthur Brown

For a judge of a supreme court, or "Mr. Justice Brown." Sizes B, C.

> Mr. Robert Brown
> Lieutenant, Sixth Cavalry
> United States Army

For military or naval officer below rank of captain. Instead of designating regiment, "United States Army" is equally correct. Sizes B, C.

> Rear Admiral Thomas Brown
> United States Navy

For general officer. Sizes B, C.

> Colonel William Brown
> Sixth Cavalry, United States Army

For regimental officer. Sizes B, C.

> Harold Brown, M. D.
> Hours: 8-10 a. m.
>   3-5 p. m.   70 Broadway

Physician's professional card; or "Dr. Harold Brown." Size F.

For all correct social purposes the use of the plain titles Mr., Mrs., Miss, and Master, is imperative. Exceptions are: for clergymen, who use Rev. or Reverend, or, if a doctor of divinity, the Rev. is discarded for D. D. following the name, without Mr.; for naval and military officers of the rank of captain or higher, Captain, General, etc.; for judges of supreme courts, Mr. Justice; for physicians, Dr. or M. D., without Mr., Mrs., or Miss. Ladies do not use the titles of their husbands.

> [Punch Holes Here]
> John Walter Brown
> April the Tenth
>
> One Thousand Nine Hundred and Seven
> Mr. and Mrs. Charles Lewis Brown
> Ninety Church Street
> Marywell

Announcement of birth. The cards are punched and the smaller attached with a white satin bow.

> Mr. and Mrs. John James Brown
> Request the Pleasure of
> [Blank Line]
> Company at Dinner
> on
> at   O'Clock
> Ninety Church Street

For dinners, names and dates to be written in. A correct size of card is 5⅝x3⅜ inches

---

> Mrs. John James Brown
> The Misses Brown
> Tuesdays
> October Third and Tenth
> Bridge   Ninety Church Street

Another form of At-Home card The name of entertainment (if any) will vary. A correct size is 5⅜x3⅜ inches.

> Miss Sarah and Master Thomas Brown
> Hope to Have the Pleasure of
> [Name here]
> Company on Thursday Afternoon
> the Tenth of April
> at Five O'Clock
> Dancing Ninety Church Street

For a juvenile party. The card being addressed to the parents, the child's name is written on invitation. A correct size of card is 4⅞x3 inches.

> Mrs. John James Brown
> and Miss Brown
> Will be at Home
> On Monday, the Sixteenth of September
> From Four Until Six O'Clock
> at Ninety Prospect Street

At-Home card, sometimes called tea card, because tea is served. For this form 5⅜x3⅜ inches is a correct size.

> To Meet
> Mr. Justice and Mrs. Brown
> Mr. and Mrs. John James Brown
> Request the Pleasure of Your Company
> on Tuesday, the Tenth of October
> From Four Until Seven O'Clock
> Ninety Church Street

At-Home card. For this form a correct size is 5⅜x3⅜ inches.

> Mrs. John James Brown
> Will be at Home
> On Wednesday, the Seventeeth of August
> From Four Until Seven O'Clock
> Garden Party Harrytown

Garden party card; or "Mr. and Mrs. John James Brown," or "Mrs. John James Brown and the Misses Brown," or the name of hostess with a house guest or other friend. A correct size for this form is 5⅜x3⅜ inches.

For garden parties out of town, train cards are enclosed with the invitations, in the same form and size as printed on another page.

> Mr. and Mrs. John James Brown
> Request the Pleasure of
> [Blank line]
> Company on Tuesday, the Fourteenth of July
> From Four Until Seven O'Clock
> Garden Party Harrytown

Another form of card for garden party. A correct size is 5⅜x3⅜ inches.

INVITATIONS AND ANNOUNCEMENTS (SOCIETY).

Paper Stock.—A special kind of paper is made for society printing. It is sold under various names by different manufacturers. The size is 21x33, and the preferred weights are 70-lb. for the announcements and the inner envelopes, and 60-lb. for the outer envelopes. It is sold in packages of 240 sheets; or in "wedding cabinets" containing 50 or 100 folded sheets of various cut sizes, with inner and outer envelopes; or in sets of three "wedding boxes," containing 100 sheets with inner and outer envelopes, each in a separate box.

FORMS OF INVITATIONS AND ANNOUNCEMENTS.

The following forms and arrangements of lines are correct and under the forms correct sizes are given. Sizes may vary according to lettering. All cards should have envelopes matching in size, but not any outer envelopes. Card is required, as a general rule, for all daylight functions and paper for evening occasions. When paper is used both inner and outer envelopes are required. Sizes of lines should be uniform, with the exception of disconnected address lines and the designation of entertainment, which should be smaller. The rule is to avoid capitals wherever possible. Lines for writing on are not used, except on admission cards.

> To Meet
> Mr. Justice and Mrs. Brown
> Mr. and Mrs. John James Brown
> Request the Pleasure of
> Company at Dinner
> on the Evening of Monday,
> the Fourth of June
> at Eight O'Clock
> Ninety Church Street

For a formal dinner, with or without names of guests in whose honor the dinner may be given. Correct sizes of paper (folded) are 6 7-16x5⅛ and 6⅝x5¾ inches.

> Mr. Robert Brown
> Requests the Pleasure of
> [Blank Line]
> Company on the Evening of Friday,
> the First of June
> at Eight O'Clock
> at The Crescent Assembly Rooms,
> Thirty-nine Willow Avenue
> Music

Bachelor's reception. For this form correct sizes of paper (folded) are 6 7-16x5¾ and 7¼x5¾ inches.

The Hackensack Assembly Dances
Season of 1910-11
December the First and Twentieth
January the Eighth and
February the Eleventh
From Nine Until Two O'Clock
Rispolli's
Patronesses
[Here Follows List in Two Columns in
Smaller Letters]
Subscription $12.00, payable before November 16th to Mrs. John Brown, Treasurer, Eighty Delaware Street

For subscription dances. A correct size of paper (folded) is 7⅞x6 inches. When the list of patronesses is very long, it may be printed on the third page.

The Pleasure of
[Name Here]
Company Is Requested
at the Twentieth Regiment Ball
at Assembly Hall
on the Evening of Tuesday,
the Seventeenth of April
at Ten O'Clock
R. S. V. P.
John Robinson, Adjutant
The Armory, Willow Avenue

For a ball. Correct sizes of paper (folded) are 6⅝x5¾ and 7¼x5¾ inches.

The Lowland Golf Club
Requests the Honor of Your Company
at the Club Ball
to Be Given at the Lowland Field Club
On Tuesday Evening,
September the Second
at Nine O'Clock
R. S. V. P.
The Secretary

Another correct form for a ball. Correct sizes of paper (folded) are 6⅝x5¾ and 7¼x5¾ inches.

Mr. and Mrs. John James Brown
Request the Pleasure of
[Blank line]
Company at a Musicale
on the Evening of Monday,
the Eighth of April
at Half After Nine O'Clock
Mozart Orchestra   Ninety Church Street

Musicale reception at residence; or, to avoid writing name, "request the pleasure of your company | at a musicale," etc. For this form correct sizes of paper (folded) are 6 7-16x5⅛ and 6⅝x5¾ inches.

The Pleasure of
[Blank Line]
Company Is Requested
at a Dinner to Be Given in Honor of
John James Brown
District Attorney of Gnome County
on the Evening of Friday,
the Second of April
One Thousand Nine Hundred and Ten
at Half After Seven O'Clock
at Delmonico's
Robert Smith   Reverend Joseph Jones
Justice Robinson Colonel Chas. Fearey
[And Other Names of Committee]
R. S. V. P.
Charles X. Jones, Secretary
Seventy Munn Avenue

For large public banquet, usually made imposing in appearance with large lettering. Correct sizes of paper (folded) are 10⅛x7⅞ and 9⅝x7¼ inches.

You Are Cordially Invited to the
Charity Ball
to Be Given at Rispolli's
on Wednesday, the Seventeenth of February
One Thousand Nine Hundred and Ten
at Half After Eight O'Clock
Proceeds to Be Given to the Orphan Asylum
Patrons and Patronesses
Mr. and Mrs. John Brown Mrs. Thomas Smith
Mr. Justice Brown   Admiral William Brown
Kindly send reply on or before
February the Second
to Mr. Robert Brown
Ninety Church Street
Miss Sarah Brown
Mr. Thomas Smith
Committee

For subscription ball. Lettering usually larger than for private invitations. If the list of patrons and patronesses is very long it may be printed on third page. A correct size of paper (folded) is 8½x6⅜ inches.

Mr. and Mrs. John James Brown
Miss Brown
Miss Sarah Brown
Request the Pleasure of Your Company
on the Evening of Wednesday,
the Seventeeth of April
at Ten O'Clock
Cotillon   Ninety Church Street

For a dancing party, or "cotillion," which is the English form of the French word "cotillon." Correct sizes of paper (folded) are 6⅝x5¾ and 7¼x5¾ inches.

Dinner Tendered to
John James Brown
on Friday, the Second Day of April
One Thousand Nine Hundred and Ten
at Delmonico's
Admit

Card to admit to large banquet A correct size
is 4⅞x3 inches. (L)

The Club of Printing Craftsmen
of the City of New York
Cordially Invites You to Be Present
at a Banquet
in Honor of the One Hundred and Seventh
Anniversary of the Club
on Saturday, the Seventeenth of December
Two Thousand and Nine
Cafe de l'Opera
Broadway and Forty-second Street
at Eight O'Clock
R. S. V. P.
Evan Quadrat   Follows de Copy
Secretary   President
. 270

Name
    Table No.
                [Perforate Here]
Admit Mr.   270
            Anniversary Banquet
    The Club of Printing Craftsmen
            Cafe de l'Opera
    Saturday, the Seventh of June
            at Eight O'Clock
Present This Card at Door of Banquet Room

For a club dinner. A correct size of paper
(folded) 8½x6¾ inches. Admission ticket to club
dinner. A correct size of card is 6x3½ inches.

Mr. and Mrs. John James Brown
and The Misses Brown
Request the Pleasure of Your Company
on the Evening of Monday, the Third of June
at Half After Eight O'Clock
at Hoyle's
Two Hundred and Sixty May Street
                        Kindly Send Reply to
Dancing   Ninety Church Street

Reception in public hall; or "R. s. v. p. Ninety
Church Street." For this form correct sizes of
paper (folded) are 6 7-16x5⅛ and 6⅝x5¾ and
7¼x5¾ inches.

Wedding Stationery.—Each invitation printed
on paper has its own envelope, matching in size and
stock. The whole set is enclosed in an outer envelope of the same stock. When a single invitation or announcement is sent out, printed on

paper, both inner and outer envelopes are required.

Mr. and Mrs. John James Brown
Request the Honor of Your Presence at the
Marriage of Their Daughter
Sarah
to
Mr. Thomas Smith
on the Afternoon of Thursday,
the Sixth of March
at Four O'Clock
at the First Methodist Church
Marywell

For church ceremony; "request the honor" is
used, while for ceremony at residence "request the
pleasure" is the correct form, as printed below.
Other correct forms are printed below. Correct
sizes (folded) are 6 7-16x5⅛, 6⅝x5¾, 7¼x5¾
inches. The two larger sizes are preferred for invitations.

Mr. and Mrs. John James Brown
Request the Pleasure of
[Blank Line]
Presence at the Marriage of Their Daughter
Sarah
to
Mr. Thomas Smith
on the Evening of Friday,
the First of May
at Four O'Clock
at Ninety Church Street
Marywell

Another correct and, at present, more fashionable
form of invitation to a wedding ceremony.

The Pleasure of Your Company Is Requested
at the Marriage of
Miss Lillian Kilgour
to
Mr. Robert Thomas
On the Afternoon of Friday,
the First of May
at a Quarter After Four O'Clock
at the Residence of
Mr. and Mrs. William Smith
Twelve Canon Avenue
Rome

For wedding ceremony in residence of friends of
the bride.

Reception
From Eight Until Ten O'Clock
at The Magnolias
Marywell

For reception card after church ceremony, to be

enclosed with the invitation. A correct size is 5x3 inches.

Another form of reception card reads "Mr. and Mrs. John James Brown | request the pleasure of | [blank line] | company on Friday, the sixth of October | at half after four o'clock | at Ninety Church Street." Correct size for this form is 5⅝x3⅜ inches.

```
Please Present This Card
at the First Methodist Church
on Thursday, the Sixth of March
```

For admission card, to be enclosed with church invitation. A correct size for this form is 3½x 1⅞ inches. Another form is "Please present this card at the Church," in one line, a correct size for which is 4 3-16x2¼ inches. An extreme form has the guests' name written at top of card, followed by, "will please present this card | at the First Methodist Church | Marywell | on Thursday, the sixth of March." For such a card a correct size is 4⅜x2¾ inches.

```
A Special Car Will Leave
Pennsylvania Station for Marywell
at 3:20 P. M.
Returning, Leaves Marywell at 6:10 P. M.
Please Present This Card at the Train.
Train Leaves Pennsylvania Station
for Marywell at 3:20 P. M.
Returning, Leaves Marywell
for Philadelphia at 6:10 P. M.
```

For train cards, to be enclosed with the invitation. A correct size for these two forms is 4½x2¾ inches. Lines are centered. Train cards may require very full directions, and size will vary accordingly, up to 5⅝x3⅜ inches. In cases where a special car is provided, the name of guest is sometimes written on card, after the directions, and followed by the words, "will please present this card at the station door and to the conductors." Another form ends, "Please present this card instead of a ticket to the gatemen and conductors." The phrase "carriages will convey the guests to the house and return them to the train" is sometimes added after the train information.

```
Will be at Home
Wednesday, the Tenth of April
at Seventy-five Gutenburg Avenue
Marywell
```

For At-Home card, to be enclosed with the invitation; or "on the afternoons of Tuesdays | the tenth and seventeenth of April | at," etc. Correct sizes are 5¾x2¾ and 5⅝x3⅜ inches.

```
Ceremony at Half After Six O'clock
```

For card for wedding at residence, to accompany the invitation to reception, part of the guests only being invited to the ceremony; or "marriage ceremony at," etc., in which case use two lines, "Marriage" being the first. A correct size is 4 5-32x2⅝ inches.

```
Mr. and Mrs. John James Brown
Request the Pleasure of Your Presence
at the Wedding Reception of Their Daughter
Sarah
and
Mr. Thomas Smith
On the Evening of Thursday,
March the Sixth, at Seven O'clock
at Ninety Church Street
Marywell
```

For reception after wedding at residence. Correct sizes of paper (folded) are 6 7-16x5⅛, 6⅝x5¾, 7¼x5¾ inches.

```
Owing to the Death of Mrs. Brown's
Sister, Mr. and Mrs. John James Brown
Beg to Recall the Cards Issued for the
Wedding Reception of Their Daughter
Sarah.
```

For recall of invitations. A correct size of black-bordered card is 4⅞x3⅛ inches.

```
Mr. and Mrs. John James Brown
Have the Honor of Announcing
the Marriage of Their Daughter
Sarah
to
Mr. Thomas Smith
on Thursday, the Seventh of March
One Thousand Nine Hundred and Ten
at the First Methodist Church
in Marywell
```

For announcement of wedding; if at residence, substitute the address for name of church; or either may be omitted properly. Another correct form has the name written in, and reads, "have the honor of announcing to [here write name] the marriage," etc., as above. Correct sizes of paper (folded) are 6 7-16x5⅛, 6⅝x5¾, 7¼x5¾ inches.

```
Mr. and Mrs. Thomas Smith
Will be at Home    Seventy Gutenberg Ave.
After Seventh of April    Marywell
```

For At-Home card, to be enclosed with wedding announcement. A correct size is 5⅝x3⅜ inches.

```
Mr. Thomas Smith
and
Miss Sarah Brown
Have the Honor
of Announcing Their Marriage
on Friday, the Eighth of March
One Thousand Nine Hundred and Ten
```

For a wedding announcement; private ceremony, when the bride has no near relatives; the name of church may be added. A correct size of paper (folded) is 6 7-16x5⅛ inches.

Mr. Thomas Smith
Miss Sarah Brown
Married
On Monday, the First of March
One Thousand Nine Hundred and Ten
at the First Methodist Church
Marywell

Another correct form of announcement; name of church may be omitted. A correct size of paper (folded) is 6 7-16x5⅛ inches.

1900—1910
Mr. and Mrs. Thomas Smith
Request the Pleasure of Your Company
at the
Tenth Anniversary of Their Marriage
on the Evening of Monday, the Fifth of July
From Half After Eight Until Eleven O'Clock
at Seventy Gutenberg Avenue
Marywell

For a wedding anniversary. Another form reads "1900—1910 | Mr. and Mrs. Thomas Smith | will be at home | on the evening of Monday, the fifth of July" | etc., as above. Correct sizes of paper (folded) are 6 7-16x5⅛ and 6⅝x5¾ inches.

Mr. and Mrs. John James Brown
Request the Pleasure of Your Company
at the Christening of Their Son
on Thursday Afternoon, the Third of July
at Four O'Clock
Ninety Church Street

For a christening. A correct size is 5⅜x3⅜ inches (M). If in the evening, this form should be printed on paper, a correct size for which (folded) is 6 7-16x5⅛ inches.

1900   B.S.   1910
[Monogram or Initials Here]
Mr. and Mrs. Thomas Smith
Will be at Home
on the Evening of Monday
the Fifth of July
From Half After Eight Until Eleven O'Clock
at Seventy Gutenberg Avenue
Marywell

For a wedding anniversary. Correct sizes of paper (folded) are 6 7-16x5⅛ and 6⅝x5¾ inches.

DEATH AND ACKNOWLEDGMENTS OF CONDOLENCES.

These forms are much used, as relieving the bereaved from the painful task of writing individual acknowledgements.

The Family of the Late
John James Brown
Gratefully Acknowledge Your Kind
Expression of Sympathy

For acknowledgment of condolences; the address may be added in the right hand lower corner, but usually is not. A corerct size of card is 4⅞x3⅛ inches, with quarter-inch (No. 4) black border, and envelopes to match.

It Is With Great Sorrow
That We Announce the Death of
Mr. John Smith
President of This Company
Which Occurred at Harryton, Alaska
on Sunday, the Third of August
One Thousand Nine Hundred and Ten
Smithson Company, Ltd.
Robert Roy Smith
Thirty Faust Avenue   Secretary

For announcement of demise. A correct size of paper (folded) is 6⅝x5¾ inches, with 5-32-inch (No. 2) black border, and envelopes to match.

Business Announcements.—The forms of announcement of a business which caters to a select patronage are more effective the closer they conform to the stationery and printing used by its customers in their social affairs. The same papers and types should be used.

Robinson & Co.
Jewelers
Invite Your Inspection of Their
Beautiful Collection of
Clocks, Bronzes and Porcelains
at Their New Showrooms
Three Seventy-One Gnome Avenue
One Block From Post Office
Pearyton·

A correct form of announcement for tailors, milliners, hairdressers, modistes, etc. A correct size is 6⅝x5¾ inches, with one envelope to match.

The various forms in this chapter are by an eminent authority, Mr. Henry Lewis Bullen, and are republished from a brochure issued by the American Type Founders Company, designed to promote the use of letter-press printing in place of engraving for society cards and announcements. The type fonts of the company illustrated on the following pages will indicate how well adapted for society printing are these beautiful type faces.

Explanatory.

As the technical printing terms employed in the pages following may not be generally understood, a few definitions may not be superfluous:

Point.—Indicating the **size** of the type, there being 72 points in space of one inch.

Price Indices.—The number of **As** or **as** indicates the number in a font or set of the alphabet, the number of all the other letters being in a fixed and uniform proportion.

The **prices** are given in order that comparisons may be made with the cost of copperplate engraving, the prices being subject to a varying discount of 10 to 30 per cent to the trade.

Cheltenham Old Style for Fine Circular Work

24 Point   6 A $1 85   12 a $1 65 $3 50

MODERN FASHIONS
Original American Quality

18 Point   10 A $1 65   21 a $1 60 $3 25

ELECTRIC JOB PRINTING
Handsome Cheltenham Character

14 Point   15 A $1 50   30 a $1 50 $3 00

SEVENTH ANNUAL EXHIBITION
Lovers of Art are invited to visit the rooms of the Raphael Artists Club on Mora Street

12 Point   18 A $1 40   38 a $1 35 $2 75

GUTENBERG, ROYCROFT & CHAUCER
Standard and classic publications are obtainable from this well-known firm which has aimed to satiate $3

11 Point   20 A $1 40   42 a $1 35 $2 75

AMERICAN TYPE FOUNDERS COMPANY
ARBITER OF FASHIONS FOR
Printers and largest purveyor of printing office requisites in the world. It carries in stock everything which enters into the equipment of a modern printery, from tweezers

10 Point   21 A $1 15   42 a $1 35 $2 50

READING IS MADE REAL PLEASURE IF THE
CHELTENHAM OLDSTYLE TYPE IS
The means used to convey the favorite author's impressions or thoughts to the mind of the reader because of its legibility which enables him to concentrate his thoughts on the subject

8 Point   24 A $1 15   48 a $1 10 $2 25

THE CHELTENHAM OLDSTYLE BIDS FAIR TO RIVAL IN POPULARITY THE JUSTLY FAMOUS

Jenson Oldstyle, the extended and continued use of which is marvelous; but this is not surprising when we consider the wide sphere of usefulness which it possesses by reason of its adaptability to either book or job work

6 Point   24 A $1 00   48 a $1 00 $2 00

DESIGNATE THE LINES OF PRINTING FOR WHICH THE JENSON OLDSTYLE IS ADAPTED AND YOU HAVE NAMED

The classes of work for which the Cheltenham type is available. And yet it is an entirely different letter, as much so as the Jenson Oldstyle is from the De Vinne. Cheltenham is a book and job letter, as well as a roman and display. There are extremely few such letters

---

Strip Rule

NO.	BODY	PER FOOT
1336	6 Point	30
1338	8 Point	40
13310	10 Point	50
13312	12 Point	60
1343	3 Point	15
1344	4 Point	20
1346	6 Point	30
1348	8 Point	40
13410	10 Point	50
13412	12 Point	60
13418	18 Point	90
1356	6 Point	30
1358	8 Point	40
13510	10 Point	50
13512	12 Point	60
13518	18 Point	90
1326	6 Point	30
1328	8 Point	40
13210	10 Point	50
13212	12 Point	60
18212	12 Point	72

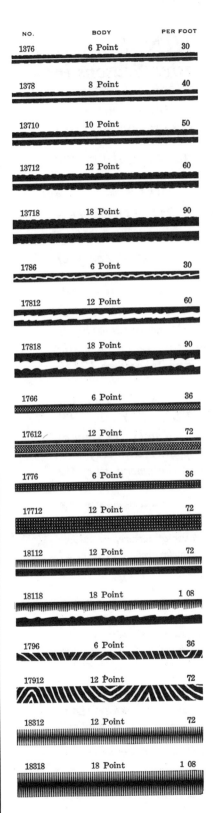

NO.	BODY	PER FOOT
1376	6 Point	30
1378	8 Point	40
13710	10 Point	50
13712	12 Point	60
13718	18 Point	90
1786	6 Point	30
17812	12 Point	60
17818	18 Point	90
1766	6 Point	36
17612	12 Point	72
1776	6 Point	36
17712	12 Point	72
18112	12 Point	72
18118	18 Point	1 08
1796	6 Point	36
17912	12 Point	72
18312	12 Point	72
18318	18 Point	1 08

Cheltenham Italic
For Fine Circular Work

24 Point   7 A $1 90   12 a $1 60 $3 50

MODEST BUILDER
Noted American Quality

18 Point   11 A $1 70   21 a $1 55 $3 25

ELECTRIC JOB PRINTER
Handsome Cheltenham Character

14 Point   15 A $1 55   28 a $1 45 $3 00

REGULAR ANNUAL SHOWING
Lovers of Art are invited to visit the rooms
of the Raphael Artists Club at Roylstone

12 Point   17 A $1 45   36 a $1 30 $2 75

GUTENBERG, ROYCROFT & CHAUCER
Standard and classic publications are obtainable of
this well-known firm which has aimed to satiate $3

11 Point   21 A $1 45   42 a $1 30 $2 75

AMERICAN TYPE FOUNDERS COMPANY
ARBITER OF FASHIONS FOR

Printers and largest purveyor of printing office requisites
in the world. It carries in stock everything which enters
into the equipment of a modern printery, from tweezers

10 Point   20 A $1 30   46 a $1 20 $2 50

READING MADE REAL PLEASURE WHEN
CHELTENHAM ITALIC IS USED
The means used to convey the favorite author's impressions
or thoughts to the mind of the reader because of its legibility
which enables him to concentrate his thoughts on the subject

8 Point   23 A $1 15   46 a $1 10 $2 25

THE CHELTENHAM ITALIC ALREADY RIVALS FOR
POPULARITY THE JUSTLY FAMOUS

Jenson Italic, the extended and continued use of which is marvelous;
but this is not surprising when we consider the wide sphere of usefulness
which it possesses by reason of its adaptability to either book or job work

6 Point   22 A $1 00   46 a $1 00 $2 00

DESIGNATE THE LINES OF PRINTING FOR WHICH JENSON
ITALIC IS ADAPTED AND YOU HAVE NAMED

The class of work for which the Cheltenham Italic is available. And yet is an entirely
different letter, as much so as Jenson Oldstyle is from the De Vinne. Cheltenham
Italic is a book and job letter, as well as text and display. There are few such letters

Grasset and Grasset Italic for Circular Work

18 Point   10 A $1 60   21 a $1 65 $3 25

CLOTHING FOR
The Easter Season is

18 Point   10 A $1 65   20 a $1 60 $3 25

CLOTHINGS FOR
The Easter Seasons in

Point   12 A $1 50   23 a $1 50 $3 00

ANCIENT RECORD
In the beautiful Cities of

16 Point   11 A $1 55   23 a $1 45 $3 00

ANCIENT RECORD
In the beautiful City of the

14 Point   14 A $1 45   29 a $1 55 $3 00

NATIVE HEADGEARS
Imagine an immense hood
of crown silk falling to the

14 Point   14 A $1 55   28 a $1 45 $3 00

NATIVE HEADGEARS
Imagine an immense hood of
black silk falling to the feet

12 Point   16 A $1 35   32 a $1 40 $2 75

GRECIAN TOWNS AND
Malta boasts many remarkable
attractions for the enthusiastic
explorer. In its western 12345

12 Point   15 A $1 35   34 a $1 40 $2 75

GRECIAN TOWNS AND
Malta boasts many remarkable
attractions for the enthusiastic
explorer. For its western 12345

11 Point   18 A $1 35   39 a $1 40 $2 75

BEAUTIFUL CITY OF THE
Philippines. Manila, the Capital
of the Philippines, was very well
chosen, for no site among all the

11 Point   18 A $1 40   37 a $1 35 $2 75

DELIGHTFUL CITY OF THE
Philippines. Manila, the Capital
of the Philippines, was very well
chosen, for no site among all of the

10 Point   19 A $1 20   40 a $1 30 $2 50

FLOWERS THAT BLOOM IN
To the true lover of nature, no outdoor days are ever melancholy And
of all the year, the glorious days of

10 Point   20 A $1 30   40 a $1 20 $2 50

THE FLOWERS THAT BLOOM
To the true lover of nature, no outdoor
days are ever melancholy. And of all
the year, the glorious days of summer are

9 Point   22 A $1 25   44 a $1 25 $2 50

THE EASTERN MATTINGS ARE
The conditions governing the selection
of mattings include the inspection of the
straw itself, for on the straw depends all

9 Point   24 A $1 30   48 a $1 20 $2 50

THE EASTERN MATTINGS ARE
The conditions governing the selection of the
mattings include inspection of the straw itself
for on the straw depends the life of the matting

8 Point   22 A $1 10   45 a $1 15 $2 25

WRITERS SACRIFICE ORIGINALITY
Human nature is complex, it is many-sided,
even self-contradictory to any but the most
penetrative views ; and so slender are the

8 Point   23 A $1 10   46 a $1 15 $2 25

WRITERS SACRIFICING ORIGINALITY
Human nature is complex, it is many-sided, it
is even self-contradictory to any but the most
penetrative view ; and so slender are the lines

6 Point   24 A $0 95   50 a $1 05 $2 00

FOREIGNERS DELIGHT AT GREAT LAKES
Nothing so touches the imagination of the foreigner
who visits the United States, especially if he be a ship
loving German or Britain, as the Great Lakes. I shall

6 Point   25 A $1 00   50 a $1 00 $2 00

FOREIGNERS DELIGHT AT GREAT LAKES
Nothing so touches the imagination of the foreigner who
visits the United States, especially if he be a ship loving
German or Britain, as the Great Lakes. I shall not soon

Types for Cards and Announcements.

The smaller sizes of these letters (from 12 point to 24 point) are admirably adapted for cards, while the larger sizes produce exceptionally handsome society and business announcements. The list prices for the type (subject to varying market discounts of from 10 to 30 per cent) are given as indicating the cost per font to the printer.

Tiffany Upright

12 Point   10 A $1 30   48 a $2 20 $3 50
Matrimonial Questions Rapidly Solved

14 Point   9 A $1 40   44 a $2 35 $3 75
Delightful Strains of Sacred Music

18 Point   9 A $1 80   35 a $2 70 $4 50
Handsome Orange Blossom

24 Point No. 2   7 A $2 20   26 a $2 80 $5 00
Three Musical Concerts

24 Point No. 1   6 A $2 15   21 a $2 85 $5 00
Thursday the Seventh

30 Point   5 A $2 35   18 a $3 15 $5 50
Fourth Exhibition

36 Point   4 A $3 00   14 a $3 50 $3 50
Grand Carnival

48 Point   3 A $3 50   10 a $4 00 $7 50
Right Day

Tiffany Text

8 Point   14 A $0 95   40 a $1 30 $2 25
Especially Designed to Vie with the Engravers

10 Point   11 A $1 05   34 a $1 45 $2 50
Very Neat for Wedding Invitations

12 Point   11 A $1 20   31 a $1 55 $2 75
Clear and Pleasing Appearance

14 Point   9 A $1 25   28 a $1 75 $3 00
Remarkable Characteristic

18 Point   6 A $1 40   18 a $1 85 $3 25
Beautiful Stationery

24 Point   4 A $1 60   11 a $2 05 $3 65
Neat Conception

Tiffany Shaded

14 Point   12 A $2 00   40 a $2 40 $4 40
Millionaires Ridicule Constitutions

18 Point   10 A $2 50   32 a $2 90 $5 40
Hinsdalle Nearing Throne

24 Point No. 2   8 A $2 55   25 a $2 95 $5 50
Anticipating Dangerous

24 Point No. 1   6 A $2 45   22 a $3 05 $5 50
Reciprocates Hourly

30 Point   5 A $2 40   18 a $3 20 $5 60
Tuneful Revivals

36 Point   4 A $2 80   15 a $3 70 $6 50
Recent Model

48 Point   3 A $3 70   12 a $4 40 $8 10
Bright Girl

Tiffany Slope

12 Point   9 A $1 20   32 a $2 30 $3 50
Fragrant Roses and Tropical Plants

14 Point   8 A $1 30   27 a $2 45 $3 75
This Picturesque Mountain Scene

18 Point   7 A $1 50   23 a $3 00 $4 50
Handsome Color Designs

24 Point No. 2   5 A $1 65   19 a $3 35 $5 00
Sumptuous Reception

24 Point No. 1   5 A $1 80   16 a $3 20 $5 00
Members Honored

Types for Cards and Announcements.

The meaning of the "point" and of the numbered letters with prices are given on another page.

Engravers Old English Open

8 Point   16 A $1 00   48 a $1 25 $2 25
Bashful Youth Courting Vivacious Maid

10 Point   14 A $1 10   44 a $1 40 $2 50
Inspiring Oration Recently Heard

12 Point   13 A $1 25   37 a $1 50 $2 75
Refreshing Afternoon Siesta

14 Point   10 A $1 25   33 a $1 75 $3 00
Pleasing Musical Concert

18 Point   8 A $1 40   22 a $1 85 $3 25
Harmonious Colors

Engravers Old English

6 Point   16 A $0 85   50 a $1 15 $2 00
Eighteenth Annual Chrysanthemum Exhibition

8 Point   16 A $1 00   48 a $1 25 $2 25
Curious Bronze Images from the Orient

10 Point   14 A $1 10   44 a $1 40 $2 50
Wonderful Operatic Performances

12 Point   13 A $1 25   37 a $1 50 $2 75
Political Schemes Frustrated

14 Point   10 A $1 25   33 a $1 75 $3 00
Delightful Ornamentation

18 Point   8 A $1 40   22 a $1 85 $3 25
American Diplomats

Cloister Black

6 Point   17 A $0 95   55 a $1 05 $2 00
Serious International Questions Recently Settled

8 Point   16 A $1 05   52 a $1 20 $2 25
Admiring Throngs Constantly Gesticulating

10 Point   14 A $1 20   42 a $1 30 $2 50
Conservative Members Welcomed

12 Point   12 A $1 30   36 a $1 45 $2 75
Shorthand Writers Mentioned

14 Point   10 A $1 40   32 a $1 60 $3 00
Unsophisticated Damsels

18 Point   8 A $1 60   22 a $1 70 $3 30
Handsome Raiment

Lining Royal Script

12 Point No. 551   9 A $1 40   36 a $2 65 $4 05
American Designs Lead World

18 Point No. 551   7 A $1 85   21 a $2 95 $4 80
Better Result Obtained

24 Point No. 552   6 A $2 35   18 a $3 10 $5 45
Mountains Highest

24 Point No. 551   6 A $2 35   18 a $3 25 $5 60
Demand Printers

30 Point No. 552   4 A $2 35   12 a $3 40 $5 75
Denying Quoter

Lining Steelplate Script

12 Point No. 550   8 A $1 25   32 a $2 75 $4 00
Diplomatic Presiding Officers

24 Point No. 552   6 A $2 25   18 a $2 75 $5 00
Bright German Student

24 Point No. 551   6 A $2 25   18 a $3 25 $5 50
Rare English Laces

30 Point No. 551   4 A $2 05   12 a $3 45 $5 50
Original Designs

Bond Script

12 Point   8 A $1 15   30 a $2 60 $3 75
Pleasant Childhood Memories

18 Point   7 A $1 85   20 a $2 99 $4 75
Winsome Maids Rejoice

24 Point   6 A $2 15   18 a $3 60 $5 75
Romantic Parisian

36 Point   4 A $2 85   10 a $3 90 $6 75
Finest Orator

Types for Cards and Announcements.

The term "point" and the numbered letters with prices are defined on another page.

HEAVY COPPERPLATE GOTHIC CONDENSED

6 Point No. 11   42 A $1 00
THE AMERICAN ASSOCIATION OF FOREIGN REPRESENTATIVES

6 Point No. 12   37 A $1 00
SECOND ANNUAL RECEPTION OF THE CLIFTON SOCIAL

6 Point No. 13   31 A $1 00
SERIOUS DIPLOMATIC OBSTACLES OVERCOME

6 Point No. 14   27 A $1 00
REFRESHING WINDS FROM THE OCEAN

12 Point No. 15   29 A $1 50
DELIGHTFUL FLOWER GARDENS

12 Point No. 16   25 A $1 50
DETERMINED CONTRACTOR

12 Point No. 17   21 A $1 50
ORNAMENTS REJECTED

12 Point No. 18   18 A $1 50
GOLDEN MEMORIES

LIGHT COPPERPLATE GOTHIC CONDENSED

6 Point No. 31   42 A $1 00
THE AMERICAN ASSOCIATION OF FOREIGN REPRESENTATIVES

6 Point No. 32   37 A $1 00
SECOND ANNUAL RECEPTION OF THE CLIFTON SOCIAL

6 Point No. 33   31 A $1 00
SERIOUS DIPLOMATIC OBSTACLES OVERCOME

6 Point No. 34   27 A $1 00
REFRESHING WINDS FROM THE OCEAN

12 Point No. 35   29 A $1 50
DELIGHTFUL FLOWER GARDENS

12 Point No. 36   26 A $1 50
DETERMINED CONTRACTOR

12 Point No. 37   22 A $1 50
ORNAMENTS REJECTED

12 Point No. 38   18 A $1 50
GOLDEN MEMORIES

ENGRAVERS BOLD FOR CIRCULAR WORK

18 Point No. 2   7 A $2 00
THIS OLD STATE IS NOTHING

12 Point No. 3   10 A $1 50
TYPES WERE NEVER MADE ANY BETTER

12 Point No. 1   17 A $1 50
WHEN YOU BUY THIS DIGNIFIED FACE YOU ARE DOING CREDIT TO YOUR FINE JUDGMENT

6 Point No. 4   20 A $1 00
NEVER SACRIFICE THE RESULTS BY LACK OF HAVING SUFFICIENT MATERIAL OR THE PROPER KIND YOU WILL AVOID MANY A DELAY AND REALIZE A BETTER PROFIT

6 Point No. 2   30 A $1 00
KEEP UP WITH THE MARCH OF PROGRESSION IN TYPE STYLES WHICH ARE BEING PRODUCED FOR YOUR BENEFIT AND DO NOT LET YOUR BUSINESS GO TO A MORE ENTERPRISING PRINTER WHILST YOU ARE SOUNDLY SLEEPING BY THE ROADSIDE

18 Point No. 1   8 A $2 00
AMERICAN TYPES ARE CAST BEST

12 Point No. 2   12 A $1 50
PAY IN TRIBUTE WHAT YOU HAVE NEGLECTED AND

6 Point No. 5   16 A $1 00
ENGRAVERS BOLD USED ON ANNOUNCEMENTS HAS THE ARTISTIC APPEARANCE OF HAND ENGRAVED WORK AT ONCE RECOGNIZED BY ALL

6 Point No. 3   27 A $1 00
IF WE FORGET TO MENTION ALL THE JOBS FOR WHICH THIS TYPE IS AVAILABLE DO NOT CENSURE US. ORDER A SERIES WITH THE CONFIDENCE THAT YOUR OWN GOOD TASTE WILL SUGGEST WAYS AND MEANS

6 Point No. 1   34 A $1 00
MANY BITTER DISAPPOINTMENTS MIGHT BE AVERTED IF WE COULD SCAN THE FUTURE. WHATEVER OF JOY AND PLEASURE WHICH IN THE COURSE OF HUMAN EVENTS IT IS OUR LOT TO ENJOY MAY WE NEVER LOSE SIGHT FOR A MOMENT THAT THERE ARE GREATER JOYS AND MORE

On this page will be found a beautiful series of reading type of the latest casting. The sizes indicated will be of service for exact specification of the size desired in any circular or book work.

Lining Roman No. 510

6 Point

WHEN, in the course of human events, it becomes necessary for people to dissolve the political band that has connected them with another, and to assume, among the powers of the earth, the separate and equal station to which the laws of nature and of nature's God entitle them, decent respect to the opinions of mankind requires they should declare the causes which impel them to the separation. We hold these truths to be self-evident, that men are created equal and that they are endowed by their Creator with certain inalienable rights; among these are life, liberty and the pursuit of happiness. That, to secure these rights, governments are instituted among men, deriving their just powers from *the consent of the governed; that, whenever any form of government becomes destructive of these ends, it is then*

Lower case a to z, 15 3-4 ems

ABCDEFGHIJKLMNOPQRSTUVWXYZ
1234567890

8 Point

WHEN, in the course of human events, it becomes necessary for a people to dissolve the political bands which have connected them with another, and to assume, among the powers of the earth, the separate and equal station to which the laws of nature and of nature's God entitle them, a decent respect to opinions of mankind requires that they should declare the causes which *impel them to the separation. We hold these truths to be self-evident, that men are created*

Lower case a to z, 13 3-4 ems

ABCDEFGHIJKLMNOPQRSTUVWX
1234567890

9 Point

WHEN, in the course of human events, it becomes necessary for one people to dissolve the political bands which have connected them with another, and to assume, among the powers of the earth the separate and equal station to which the laws of nature and of nature's God entitle them, decent respect to opinions *of mankind require that they should declare the causes which impel them to separation.*

Lower case a to z, 13 ems

ABCDEFGHIJKLMNOPQRSTUVW
1234567890

10 Point

WHEN, in course of human events, it becomes necessary for one people to dissolve the political bands that have connected them with another, and to assume, among powers of the earth, separate and equal station to which *the laws of nature and of nature's God entitle them, a decent respect to opinions*

Lower case a to z, 12 3-5 ems

ABCDEFGHIJKLMNOPQRSTUV
1234567890

11 Point

WHEN, in the course of human events, it becomes necessary for people to dissolve the political bands which have connected them with another and to assume, among the powers of the earth, the separate and equal station to which the laws of nature and of nature's God entitle them, a decent respect to opinions of mankind requires that they should declare the causes which impel them to the separation. We hold these truths *to be self-evident, that all men are created equal; that they are endowed by their Creator with certain inalienable rights; that among these are liberty*

Lower case a to z, 12 1-3 ems

ABCDEFGHIJKLMNOPQRSTUVWXYZ
1234567890

12 Point

WHEN, in the course of human events, it becomes necessary for one people to dissolve the political bands which have connected them with another, and assume among the powers of the earth the separate and equal station to which the laws of nature and of nature's God entitle them, a decent respect to the opinions of *mankind requires that they should declare causes which impel them to the separation. We hold these truths to be self-evident, that all men*

Lower case a to z, 12 2-3 ems

ABCDEFGHIJKLMNOPQRSTUVWXYZ
1234567890